EL CLÁSICO

BARCELONA v REAL MADRID:
FOOTBALL'S GREATEST RIVALRY

Richard Fitzpatrick was born in Ireland. He has worked as a journalist in Dublin, San Francisco and Toronto. He currently lives in Barcelona, where he covers football for the *Irish Times*, *New York Times* and *El País* among others.

EL CLÁSICO

BARCELONA v REAL MADRID:
FOOTBALL'S GREATEST RIVALRY

RICHARD FITZPATRICK

BLOOMSBURY
LONDON · NEW DELHI · NEW YORK · SYDNEY

First published in Great Britain 2012
This paperback edition published 2013

Bloomsbury Publishing Plc
50 Bedford Square
London WC1B 3DP

www.bloomsbury.com

Bloomsbury Publishing, London, New Delhi, New York and Sydney

A CIP catalogue record for this book is available from the British Library

ISBN 9781408158807

10 9 8 7 6 5 4 3 2 1

Typeset by seagulls.net

Printed and bound in Great Britain by CPI Group (UK) Ltd, Croydon CR0 4YY

CONTENTS

Para Michelle

FOREWORD

FC Barcelona versus Real Madrid – *El Clásico* as it has become known to fans all over the world – is without doubt the biggest club game on the planet: the clash that stirs the strongest passions; polarises families, friends and nations; and enjoys the largest TV audience of any football rivalry. It has become a regular, essential event in the football fan's calendar and is as likely to spark debate among English-speaking fans as any domestic fixture. *El Clásico* may be more international than ever but, as this book explains, it's as partisan as at any point in the past, and in recent times the addition of José Mourinho into the mix is exactly the kind of theatrical confrontation that this symbolic clash thrives upon.

Throughout the previous century, *El Clásico* was frequently presented as a David and Goliath story, with Barcelona relishing its status as the underdog, while Real Madrid has been more than happy to play the role of the big guy. But how much do those roles reflect reality? Barcelona fans will tell you that their club spent half the twentieth century struggling against the odds to overcome a rival that enjoyed the backing of a brutal dictator; yet, while General Franco was known to have enjoyed a flutter on the pools, his actual engagement with club football was far more limited. In fact, most Barcelona fans forget to mention that in the immediate post-Spanish Civil War years, when the regime was at its most repressive, the Catalan club was considerably more successful than its rival in Madrid. Likewise, after Franco died, Barcelona fans waited a decade to see their side win a league title, while Madrid went on to win four of the first five during that period. On the other hand, those

Real Madrid 'ultras' who celebrate their club's Spanish identity in the extreme probably squirm at the realisation that it is FC Barcelona, not Real Madrid, who now provides more players for the national team.

But let's not let these facts get in the way of the entertainment. The Catalan writer and fanatical Barça fan Manuel Vázquez Montalbán once wrote that FC Barcelona is, for Catalan nationalists, 'the symbol of St George that periodically goes out and slays the metaphorical dragon of Real Madrid on our behalf – so we don't have to.' And as this book brings us up to date, we see how Mourinho has been more than happy to turn up in Barcelona playing the role of dragon, breathing fire, insults and witticisms in the direction of Pep Guardiola, a St George for the modern Catalans if ever there was one.

Of course, Barcelona versus Real Madrid remains essentially a Catalan and Spanish obsession. However, the fantastic level of research and broad spectrum of contributions from all sides of the great divide included in this book mean that you're holding an incredibly valuable, objective account of this sporting rivalry that is all the richer for being an attempt by a non-Spaniard to comprehend it. For anyone who wants to understand why Barcelona v Real Madrid means so much more than a straightforward match between an unparalleled array of footballing stars, this book should become essential reading.

Guillem Balague, March 2012

PROLOGUE

It was an extraordinary day. On 27 April 2011, the front page of *El País*, Spain's newspaper of record, led with a story about Barcelona's manager, Pep Guardiola. The Catalan is known as a calm person. The previous day he exploded on national television, cursing twice during a 45-minute tirade. He was provoked. José Mourinho, Real Madrid's manager, had been goading him all season. The sour relations between the two clubs had reached fever pitch during an unprecedented four-game series in 18 days. Later that day, the teams were set to play in their third instalment, the first leg of the Champions League semi-final at Madrid's Bernabéu stadium.

Spain was consumed by the conflict, which has long been a proxy war in a divided land. Distracted by the match later that day, Spanish national radio's flagship current affairs programme shelved talk about the country's collapsing economy so its leading political analysts could hold a 30-minute discussion on a football rivalry. The rest of the world looked on agog. When the teams took to the field at 8.45 p.m., the bones of half a billion people watched on television. The teams were stocked with the men who won Spain its first World Cup and the planet's two greatest players – Cristiano Ronaldo and Lionel Messi.

The aesthetes among those viewing, however, were disappointed. The match was a grim, tense encounter, the football dreary. There were several flashpoints. Just before half-time, Sergio Busquets and Real Madrid's Marcelo clashed in the middle of the pitch. As they dusted themselves down from their jostle, Busquets was caught on camera twice calling the Brazilian a monkey, or so it appeared, although he was later cleared of racist abuse charges by a UEFA tribunal. When the teams stopped for the half-time interval, a mass scuffle erupted as they made their way to the dressing rooms. Barcelona's reserve goalkeeper José Manuel Pinto got a red card for a set-to with Chendo, Real Madrid's suited match-day delegate.

Barcelona continued to hog the ball in the second half; Real Madrid were content to hunker down in their half of the pitch. In the 61st minute, the game's defining play happened. Pepe, Real Madrid's midfield enforcer, was sent off for seeming to clobber Dani Alves in a reckless, studs-up tackle. Replay footage showed he mightn't even have made contact with the Brazilian defender. While the Barcelona full back was being stretchered off dramatically – only to return in rude health two minutes later – Mourinho also got his marching orders for sardonically applauding the referee's decision. He walked a few steps along the touchline and took up a seat in the stands beside his team's dugout. He spent the remaining half-hour of play passing written instructions to a lieutenant. Conspicuously, he had to pass the notes through bars in front of his seat. The screeching, whistling and bollocking around the Bernabéu stadium, which had accompanied Barcelona's keep-ball play throughout, was raised a notch. It was grating, like the shrill sound effects from a bad horror movie.

In the last quarter, some football broke out. Messi got on the end of a low cross on the edge of the six-yard box to open the scoring for Barcelona. With three minutes left on the clock, he did something divine. He gathered the ball by the centre circle in Real Madrid's half. He found his way blocked by Lassana Diarra. He moved the ball gently forward to Busquets who had his back to goal. His teammate trapped it and swivelled 90 degrees. Then, like a second handing a duelling pistol to a nobleman, he casually presented the ball for Messi who bore down on goal. The Argentinian flashed his way past five defenders before clipping the ball low into the corner of the net. Iker Casillas, Real Madrid's goalkeeper and captain, who had fallen onto his backside, sprung reflexively back to his feet. His hands were still spread wide in saving mode, as he asked no one in particular what on earth had transpired.

When the final whistle blew, fist fights broke out in the stands. Some irate fans invaded the pitch. Missiles rained down onto it. Police made a shield for the match officials as they fled for sanctuary. Later in the night, Andy Townsend, the ITV commentator who is unfortunate enough to bear an uncanny resemblance to match referee Wolfgang Stark, was set upon in a restaurant by an angry mob. In the clubs' backrooms, both their legal teams scurried around, hatching cases to be presented to UEFA about each other's deceit.

The teams' two generals – and their soldiers – were confined to barracks for a cooling-off period before emerging for the post-match press conference. Whatever the theatrics of Barcelona's players earlier, they were nothing to the pathos served up by Mourinho. The press room is his domain. He sat back in his throne. He wasn't angry. He was confused, lurching between indignation and disbelief. '¿Por qué?' he kept asking. Why? He wanted our understanding, our sympathy. He cast about wearily, flicking imaginary fluff from his trousers. He longed to return to the bosom of his family. He was disgusted with this world, he said. He generously gave us insight into his tactical approach, into the 'organisational moments' that he seeks to manipulate, like a deity, the fate of a match. But he had just been foiled by the ref, a patsy, like three others he named from the refereeing trade who did the dirty work of larger, mysterious forces. Why was Barcelona spoiled? Was it because of their affiliation with UNICEF, he wondered? Oh, they were a brilliant team, he conceded, toying with our feelings, but when the digs came, amidst his train of conspiracy theories, they were vicious.

Guardiola, his nemesis, had profited from 'the scandal of Stamford Bridge' two years earlier when Barcelona benefited from favourable referring decisions in a semi-final against Chelsea. 'I would have been embarrassed to win that title,' he said. Now, after 'the scandal of Bernabéu', his counterpart at Barcelona was on course for another defiled crown. 'I hope that one day he can win a proper Champions League.

Deep down, if they are good people, it cannot taste right for them,' he said, twirling his moral compass. 'I hope one day that Guardiola has the chance of winning a brilliant, clean championship with no scandal.'

The battle lines of *El Clásico* had just frosted over.

INTRODUCTION

National anthems are curious things. The Netherlands played Spain in the final of the 2010 World Cup at Soccer City, Johannesburg. When the Dutch team stood to attention for its national anthem, with the exception of midfielder Nigel de Jong, each team member mouthed the song's lyrics with gusto.

Then the cameras panned to the Spaniards for their number, a shortened version, as is the norm for a sporting team, of *La Marcha Real* – the Royal March. As the tune played out, they looked like a bunch of blokes at an airport waiting to find out which gate they were leaving from. They were impassive, stony-faced. Yet unemotional is not a trait you associate with the Spanish, nor bloodlessness, from the land of bullfighting, flamenco and *Guernica*, a feature of their national culture. Isn't Spain's football team, after all, supposed to be the self-styled *Furia Roja* – the Red Fury?

True, Carles Puyol jigged from side to side a little on his feet, but purely because he was straining at the bit to get on with the action. Xavi, the team's field marshal, with those hooded eyes of his, was in his own little world. Only Real Madrid's Sergio Ramos, standing beside him, with his head tilting backwards and eyes skyward, looked moved. It was strange. Two compatriots arm in arm – one absent, with a blank expression, the other on the verge of tears. But then national anthems are adept at casting a light on the fissures of a country's identity.

La Marcha Real is one of the world's oldest national anthems. It is also one of the few without lyrics. It has been without words since

1

those approved by General Franco were retired in 1978, three years after his death. A competition was held to come up with new lyrics a few years ago. The words of the winning entry, which was announced in January 2008, didn't sing enough towards Spain's regional differences, while its opening line '*Viva España*' brought back distressing memories of Franco's rallying cry during his fascist dictatorship. And so, following acrimonious national debate, it was withdrawn. Its four verses lasted five days.

Of the Spanish team that idled its way through the national anthem on the night of the World Cup final, seven were from Barcelona's ranks. People called the team *Barceloña*, a play on the words Barcelona and *España*. Previously, West Germany started the 1974 final against the Netherlands with six players who were on the books at Bayern Munich, including Franz Beckenbauer. When Italy played the 1982 final, their winning captain Dino Zoff was one of half a dozen Juventus players on the team. Now Barcelona was going one better and creating a record for the most players provided by a club side for a team in a World Cup final. But their fans were conflicted. A friend of mine from Barcelona, María José, a 57-year-old retired school principal, was secretly rooting for the Netherlands. Many Barça fans dreaded a win for Spain because of the triumphalism and the waving of Spanish flags it would unleash. A chunk of them in their city, including María José's son, wore Dutch jerseys, a treasonable act in all but the most divided of football nations.

Walking around Barcelona on the night after Spain's last-gasp semi-final win over Germany was an eye-opener. You might think they'd be going barmy about it all. But they weren't. The celebrations were a lot more subdued than, for example, if Barcelona had just won another Champions League title. Sure, there was a *fiesta* atmosphere. In the narrow side streets off Las Ramblas, the city's main thoroughfare, you had to watch out for people tossing pails of water out of apartment windows onto the revellers below. The city was sprinkled with people wearing Spanish jerseys and draped with Spanish flags over their shoulders. A lot of them, however, were what Catalans would derogatively call *guiris*, or Northern European tourists. The old part of Barcelona, the downtown, is very multicultural these days, full of either ex-pats living in the city or their tourist brethren visiting for a few days. Most Catalan natives live on the outskirts or along the northern part of the city.

At the famous Canaletes fountain, where Barça fans cavort to celebrate their club victories, fans assembled in Barcelona and Spanish team jerseys and bantered good-naturedly, chanting 'Barcelona is Spanish'. There was no animosity. A good thing, obviously, but if you wanted a barometer of the Catalan's emotion about the Spanish team's progression to the final maybe the best place to look was the police records. On that Wednesday night, there were five arrests. In comparison, when Barcelona captured its La Liga title the previous May, there were 105 arrests. Riot police flocked the city, leading to bloody collisions in which 120 people were injured. It was as though the Indians were coming – the place was alive with the sound of drums. Blazing firecrackers littered the streets. Cars were tipped over. A giant poster of some of the Barcelona players, which draped one shopping block, was pulled down. For the real Spanish World Cup celebrations, you had to be in Madrid where 300,000 fans flooded the Paseo de Recoletos boulevard to watch the final on giant screens. Catalans just didn't fully dig the Spanish team. They were ambivalent. One of *La Vanguardia*'s columnists, writing for the Catalan newspaper before the semi-final with Germany, said that the average Barcelona fan had been watching the Spanish matches in the World Cup 'out of the corner of his eye'.

For all the hoopla in Madrid and around the villages of Spain for the few days before and after the World Cup final, it masked a lack of conviction behind the team's fortunes. According to Pegazus Sport Tours España, FIFA's official Spanish tour operator, only 2,500 to 3,000 football folk, including press, travelled from Spain to support the team over the duration of the tournament. In comparison, Thomas Cook calculates that 10,000 England fans trekked to South Africa for England's first game alone. Almost ten times as many England fans travelled to see their team's matches in the tournament compared to their Spanish counterparts. And Spain, as reigning European Championship holders, set off for South Africa as favourites to win the tournament. Why is the country with possibly the world's most popular football league so blasé in support of its national team?

While rambling around the country, particularly in the south, one of the first things you'll notice if you wander into a pub is the presence of a Real Madrid team poster or scarf draped on a wall. A report by the *Centro de Investigaciones Sociológicas* calculated that 33 per cent of the Spanish population supports Real Madrid, with 26 per cent supporting Barcelona and 5 per cent following Valencia, lagging behind in third place. In fact, an internal study conducted by Real Madrid a few years ago found that there are more Real Madrid supporters in Seville than there are for the two cities' fierce rivals, Sevilla and Real Betis, combined. Can you imagine if Chelsea had more supporters in Manchester than United and City put together?

The pair has a stranglehold over affections globally, too. Added together, they've about as many supporters as the population of North America. Barcelona has over 1,400 *peñas* (supporters' clubs) around the world, from Al Hoceima to Zutphen. Real Madrid has an even greater number. Whichever way you dice it, they are arguably the world's greatest clubs. The pair has won the Champions League – the benchmark for club football – six times over the last 15 years. In the annual Deloitte Football Money League, they top the accountants' tally; Real Madrid has won its title for eight consecutive years, with Barcelona in second place for four years running.

The Madrid–Barça derby, as it's referred to in Spain, is a unique pairing in world football. Madrid and Greater Barcelona are cities of a similar size. They are the capital cities of two nations, one being a nation in waiting, maintain Catalan separatists, of whom one million marched through Barcelona on the day before Spain played in its first World Cup final agitating for greater political freedom. Perhaps it is this issue of contested nationhood, allied to the presence of the world's finest players corralled on either side, which makes their rivalry so intense, so compelling. Every year, at least twice a season, it throws the representatives of two ostensible countries into the ring together.

The half-time brawl during the 2011 Champions League semi-final at the Bernabéu stadium wasn't an aberration in the history of football rivalry. Where do you start in cataloguing the violence over the years at the world's infamous derbies, of Celtic v. Rangers or Boca Juniors v. River Plate? A Tehran derby between Pirouzi and Estegahl in 2000 was so ill tempered that three players from either side were arrested, not to mention the fleet of police wagons needed to ferry warring fans on the terraces away to custody. Confrontations have occasionally transcended petty turf battles and moved into the realm of international relations. Who could forget June 1969 when neighbouring countries Honduras and El Salvador met each other in the play-offs to qualify for the World Cup? Rioting at the matches triggered a 100-hour war in which thousands were killed, following incursions by both sides' national armies across their borders.

What's different about the unsavoury incidents at the Bernabéu is that they involved the two biggest clubs on the globe. We watched agape. When their players lined up, there was over £1 billion worth of talent on display. Spanish football sits on top of the world. Never before has so much talent resided in the clubs' squads. Ten of the 11 players who started the 2012 European Championships final for Spain are drawn from their number, not to mention their international stars, most notably the most recent FIFA World Player of the Year award winners – Cristiano Ronaldo of Real Madrid and Barcelona's Lionel Messi. In fact, every FIFA World Player of the Year since 1996 has played for either Barcelona or Real Madrid during their careers. Football is the sporting world's biggest stage, and these are its biggest actors. The clash between Barça and Real Madrid is, therefore, the defining feud in sporting history. It shines a light on us all. The antics on their terraces and playing fields tell us much about ourselves – about our delight and obsession for rare, perfect moments of sporting skill, of our need for distraction from a messy world by Messi et al; of our clannishness, our bloodlust; and, at times, of our misbehaviour.

The Barcelona v. Real Madrid rivalry, though it feels like it sometimes, is not eternal. Both clubs were founded at the turn of the twentieth century. It took another half century, notwithstanding the occasional skirmish, before their rivalry properly took root, sometime in the 1950s. During the 1930s, for instance, players from Barcelona and Real Madrid used to go for dinner together after matches. This was an arrangement, points out Carles Santacana, a historian at the University of Barcelona, which would be inconceivable today. Geography had a role to play in the late blooming of their animosity. For a long time, both teams were preoccupied with local rivalries. The Spanish League didn't kick off until 1928. Initially, Spanish football wasn't the duopoly it is today. There were other teams, most notably Athletic de Bilbao, who dominated in the early days of organised Spanish football.

However, the origins of Barça–Madrid rivalry stretch back centuries. The environment – or *entorno*, to borrow a Spanish football phrase – of *El Clásico* springs from complex political and cultural factors. This book attempts to unravel some of them. Many of the ingredients of their rivalry are like those of any tribal conflict. Others are unique to Spain. Both clubs are owned by their members; they act as mutual organisations. They are not meat for the talons of obscure market investors. Their democratic make-up, however, renders them politically unstable. Unpopular presidents and their boards come and go at the whim of the voters.

Both clubs have fascinating institutional histories, full of the shenanigans – and personality clashes – of a medieval court. Since democracy came to Spain in the mid-1970s, rival factions have continuously jostled for power within Barcelona's club. Real Madrid has its own distinct way of doing things. It has a regal air. Was it really General Franco's team? Were referees in hock to the club during his dictatorship? What of

Barcelona? Was it a pariah during his reign? I've tried to debunk a few of the myths at the centre of their stories, and to examine the differences between the clubs' philosophies, their approach to football and its sideshows.

I've also looked at other questions. What effect does the rivalry have on the cultural life of Spain? Why does it consume the country? The great club rivalries of other European countries remain within the ramparts of their city walls. Why, in Spain, do its tentacles reach across the land? Why does the rivalry take precedence over support for the national team? What does the obsession of Spanish people with the rivalry say about the politics of the country? For the last decade, Spain has been scratching its soil. Bereaved families have been unearthing bodies of 'the disappeared' from unmarked graves, the physical remains of 113,000 people executed during its civil war. In one village recently, there were newspaper reports of a trio of elderly women crowing old pro-Franco songs as the bones of some hated Republican neighbours were re-interred. To what extent, in a country enthralled with its ghosts, is the Spanish Civil War still being played out on the football fields of Barcelona and Madrid?

1

THE DIFFERENTIATING FACT

'The problem with Catalonia,' said a friend of mine, a supporter of Real Madrid, 'is that it keeps losing its wars.' The region embraces its blighted history. The Catalan national anthem, *Els Segadors*, harps back to its unsuccessful part in the War of the Reapers in the seventeenth century, wailing about the role those 'conceited and arrogant' Castilians played in their misfortune.

Catalonia was a dominant, independent force in Europe – with a democratic parliament older than Westminster – until the fifteenth century. It gradually ceded sovereignty to a Madrid-based court, a fate that was copper-fastened when it backed a loser, the Archduke Charles of Austria, in a succession race for the crown at the start of the eighteenth century. A bloody siege of Barcelona ensued, an invasion that culminated in defeat on 11 September 1714, significantly the day that Catalonia celebrates as its national day, its *Diada*, its very own 9/11. Repression followed. Barcelona's university was closed. Catalan books were burned and its language was banned. For the next few centuries it remained under the heel of Madrid rule, with a notable interlude coming when the anarchists ran the city for a year at the start of the Spanish Civil War. In keeping to the letter of their thinking, among other innovations, the anarchists removed the rules of the road, deeming one-way systems to be a hangover of the old regime.

All roads led to Madrid, however, once General Franco took control of Spain at the end of the Civil War in April 1939, as he began an oppressive national centralising project. His ascent to power came after three years of conflict, with Barcelona being the last fortress to fall. In one week alone in the last year of combat, 10,000 members of the anti-Franco brigade were executed in Barcelona. A further 25,000 were shot after the ceasefire in the city. Executions continued into the 1940s and 1950s, casualties of what Nigel Townson, a Madrid-based historian, claims was the harshest peacetime repression in any country in Europe, bar the Soviet Union.

'Barcelona is like a haunted house,' says Carlos Ruiz Zafón, the Barcelona-born writer who spends most of his time living in Los Angeles. He talks like he's in a hurry. His novel *The Shadow of the Wind* is second only to Miguel de Cervantes's *Don Quixote* in Spanish-language book sales and features, incidentally, a character called Pep Guardiola, although the author assures me he's not a reference to the famous manager of FC Barcelona. 'The Spanish Civil War is still hanging there. It's like a smell that's fading away but when I was a kid, even in the 1970s, even if you didn't know anything about it, there was a feeling: "What the hell happened here?" It's something in the air,' he says, inhaling deeply. 'It's like going to Berlin.'

Two months after Franco took power, Barcelona, which had been founded in 1899, played its first home match of the new regime. It was preceded by a bizarre shamanic political exorcism. Giménez Caballero, one of Franco's chief propagandists, who helped draft *El Caudillo*'s 'decree of unity' at the end of the Civil War, made a grandstand speech to commemorate the match. Taking a whiff of the air, he rejoiced at the smell of 'flowers and empire' in the stadium and the fact that Catalonia had just been 'redeemed' by a glorious army. The daughter of José Solchaga, one of the generals who led Franco's military raid on Barcelona, took the game's inaugural kick.

There were no such purging exercises with the other clubs around Spain, points out Carles Santacana, not even with Athletic de Bilbao in the Basque Country. With his glasses, beard and reddish-brown hair, Santacana looks a ringer for a younger version of Bill Bryson. He's the author of a well-regarded, literary-type history of the club's most political period, *El Barça i el Franquisme*. A lackey, the Marquis of the Mesa de Asta, who had never seen a football match before but had served as an officer in Franco's army, was installed as president of Barcelona. The club's crest was altered. Its Catalan flourish, the *senyera*, was removed – four bars of red on a yellow background being reduced to two bars. The name of the club was changed to the Spanish-sounding Barcelona Club de Fútbol. The club's membership files were pored over. Security police compiled a lengthy file on its members' subversive activities. Recent indiscretions included the laying of floral wreaths by Barça's directors and players at the statue of Rafael Casanova, commander in chief of the city during the siege of 1714, and, during the war, Franco's troops had captured from the 'reds' a Catalan flag with the inscription, 'To our heroic comrades in the Ebro from the members of FC Barcelona' in reference to the Civil War's bloodiest battle.

For Catalans in the 1940s, to become a *socio* (member) of the club was a political act. 'My father was born 2 January 1945,' Joan Maria Pou, the radio presenter, said to me in a meeting room at RAC1, the Catalan station where he works. 'The first thing my grandfather did when his child was born was to bring him to Les Corts, Barcelona's stadium at the time. He was told, "Your son doesn't exist officially yet. You have to go to the register first and then you can make him a member." My grandfather did this and came back to Les Corts on the same day.

'Behind this there is a message. It wasn't that my grandfather was crazy about Barça – he was – but he was Catalan and he was against Franco. He was against official institutions. Barça was the only institution that represented his feelings. His thinking was: "I go to Barça first and then to the government." Today, you don't need Barça to explain yourself. Politics is in the corner. But at that time you did.'

The whole city knew where the allegiances of the club's members lay. 'My daddy told me that when the war finished if you went to Les Corts, you could see all these people in the doorways begging for money,' said Guillem Martínez, a journalist with *El País* and the author of several books on the city of Barcelona and its history. 'They were without hands or legs. They were all invalided Republicans from the war. But at the stadium of Espanyol, the other premier league team in the city, there were none of these people.'

Franco also banned the speaking of Catalan in public. Martínez was born in 1965, a decade before the dictator died. 'I only lived the last moments of the dictatorship,' he said, 'but I remember when I was a child, my parents telling me, "Don't say this in the street."' At Barça's stadium, fans could talk more freely. Les Corts – and later the Camp Nou when it opened in 1957 – became a haven for Catalan separatists, at a time when Catalans refrained from joining the Spanish army or police force. From the 1950s onwards, dissidents handed out leaflets at the ground and painted slogans on its walls. The '*subversivos*', says Santacana, did this at Barça's ground, where they felt safer, but not at other stadiums. Yet for all the insubordination, Franco didn't suppress the activities of the club. He never shut the stadium, as Primo de Rivera, a previous dictator, did for six months in 1925 after Barça fans insolently whistled while the Spanish national anthem was played before an exhibition match. Franco understood the usefulness of sport as a distraction, and was content to let the disaffected masses in Barcelona take their opiates through football.

'I remember when I was a child, here at Canaletes,' said Martínez, turning to point towards the little fountain below us. 'It was the first day of May, Labour Day. It was a Monday morning. There were a lot of people, old people speaking with a special voice that I never again heard in my life, talking about football. On days like that there would be a thousand people, two thousand people going, "Did you see the penalty? Rah, rah, rah." They were talking about football instead of talking about society. I remember being with my daddy and asking him, "What are these people doing?" "Bastards," he replied. "They're talking about football. They should be talking about politics."'

The poor bastards had a lot to moan about during the 1960s and early 1970s. Barça went through its worst stretch in history on the field during that period, failing to win a league title in 14 years. Off the pitch, though, the club's symbolism and identity grew stronger. Increasingly, people invested their identity in the club. There had been a gradual loosening of the reins of the club from the Falange Party, the state's ruling fascist party machine, in the late 1960s.

The sea change was reflected in the *catalanista* politics of Barça's presidents and directors who until then were largely *Franquistas*, and was prefigured by the choice of a Catalan hymn for the Camp Nou's inauguration in 1957. Barça never had a club hymn in Spanish; in the 1940s it operated without one. Barça's motto – '*mes que un club*' (more than a club) – was coined in 1968, and is credited to its president Narcís de Carreras, who only served in office for a year. He was succeeded by Agustín Montal, who began, during the dying days of the Franco regime, to more aggressively colour in the club's official pro-Catalan politics. Many of Barcelona's leading left-wing thinkers who were opposed to Franco embraced football – and the club in particular – for philosophical reasons. This was contrary to the disregard the European intelligentsia tended to have towards sport at the time, argues Santacana. In 1968, Catalonia's star left-wing intellectual Manuel Vázquez Montalbán penned an essay entitled 'Barça! Barça! Barça!' Its publication in *Triunfo*, a radical journal for the chattering classes, was also seen as a key moment.

'It was the first time that an intellectual from the left, who was a member of the Communist Party in Catalonia, confessed to being a supporter of Barça,' says Santacana. 'He argued that the club was about more than sport; that it was about social policy. Vázquez Montalbán was a pioneer.' Vázquez Montalbán died in Bangkok in 2003, but his influence on the cultural life of Catalonia still lingers. He had a particular skill in capturing the essence of things, through his journalism or by allegorical allusion in his novels. He recognised the diversionary role football played in the lives of disenchanted Catalans, as a character from his 1980s novel *Off Side* suggests with a dollop of hyperbole: 'In our present mediocre and so-called civilised world, in which wars are almost unthinkable between civilised countries, you find that the sporting hero has taken the place of the previous local Napoleons, and the club manager takes the place of those gods whose role was once to make order out of chaos. Then you transfer that schema to Spain, to Catalonia, and to our club. Our club represents Sant Jordi, and the dragon is the enemy without: in other words, Spain, for those who have high symbolic aspirations, and Real Madrid for those who are more down to earth.'

Sant Jordi is the patron saint of Catalonia. During Franco's time, Catalans were also forbidden to christen their sons with Catalan names, of which Jordi is one – Jorge being the accepted Spanish version of George. Johan Cruyff joined Barcelona in the summer of 1973, two years before Franco died, maintaining to the European press corps en route that he chose Barcelona over Real Madrid because he could never join a club 'associated with Franco'. Six months later, in February 1974, he nearly caused an international incident when he named his only son, Jordi. (Jordi, in turn, rewarded the Catalan moniker by playing for a stint with Barça and later with Manchester United.)

A few days before his son's birth, Johan Cruyff, with a goal and a couple of assists, helped Barcelona beat Real Madrid 5–0 at the Bernabéu, a significant victory on the path to the club's first league title since 1960. The stadium fell quiet as the goals went in. Charly Rexach, Cruyff's teammate and later his sidekick when the Dutchman went into management at the club, said that you could hear the flies buzzing in the stadium. Cruyff had been coveted by Barcelona for years before he joined the club. The attraction was mutual. On one of several forays to the Catalan capital while still an Ajax player, he was photographed wearing a Barça jersey in the magazine *Revista Barcelonista*. In 1970, the year the picture was published, Spanish league clubs were not allowed to sign foreign players. They were restricted to signing '*oriundos*' – players of South American extraction with Spanish roots. The system, Barcelona felt, was corrupt, and often discriminated against their club. Barça administrators looked on hopelessly, for example, as their efforts to sign South American players Irala and Heredia stalled. For 18 months, the players' paperwork floated aimlessly around the bureaucratic corridors of the Spanish Football Federation. Real Madrid, as well as other clubs, faced no such logjams, says Santacana.

Barcelona commissioned a lawyer, Miquel Roca i Junyent, to look into the world of *oriundos*. Roca found corruption. Of the 60 *oriundo* players in the Spanish league, he revealed that 46 were operating with illegal paperwork, most of which could be traced to a pliable Spanish consul in Paraguay with limited imaginative powers. One player's family originated, it was discovered, in Celta, Galicia. Celta is the name of the football team in Vigo, a port city in Galicia. A chastened Spanish Football Federation met with Agustín Montal, Barcelona's president, and agreed to allow each Spanish team to sign two foreign players if Montal put a stop to his club's genealogical enquiries. And so Cruyff, who fell out with Ajax in the summer of 1973, could finally sign for Barcelona.

Barcelona draws much of its identity from *antimadridista* sentiment. Since its foundation, there has been a strain of *victimismo* running through the club's history. The roots of its persecution complex can be found in the story of Spain. The country is a veritable federation, an assortment of autonomous regions, 17 in total, with Catalonia being one of its most distinctive constituents, while Madrid sits at its centre, both geographically and politically. Each region in Spain is unique, different to the next in terms of weather, architecture, food and preoccupations.

Extreme national sentiment in the Basque Country, another one of the ill-fitting pieces of Spain's jigsaw, was often vented through the terrorist organisation ETA. Catalonia, in contrast, has eschewed violent nationalism since the Civil War with the exception of a lunatic fringe called Terra Lliure. During a 15-year campaign which came to an end in 1995, its only casualties were a knee-capped journalist; an innocent woman in the Catalan town of Les Borges Blanques crushed by a wall that collapsed in a bomb blast; and three of its own members blown up by mistake. Instead, Barcelona's identity has found its greatest expression through its football club. 'In times of political difficulty it took on all the force of a political party, an unarmed army,' as Colm Tóibín writes in his paean to the city, *Homage to Barcelona*. 'Its victories were political victories, its games mass meetings.'

Catalonia has always cherished its distinct identity. 'They are neither French nor Spanish but *sui generis* in language, costume and habits,' argued the English travel writer Richard Ford as far back as the early nineteenth century, following four years wandering around Spain. 'No province of the unamalgamating bundle which forms the conventional monarchy of Spain hangs more loosely to the crown than Catalonia, this classical country of revolt, which is ever ready to fly off.'

The pervasiveness of the Catalan language in Barcelona is the most striking feature of life in the city for an outsider. It's more than just a dialect of Spanish; it is more similar to French than it is to *castellano*, Castilian Spanish. Dismissive *madrileños* call Catalans *polacos*, or Poles, because of the alien, slurping sound of their language. Seven million people speak Catalan, more than the populations of New Zealand or Norway. Barcelona's street names are in Catalan only. It's a language whose tentacles reach beyond Catalonia into southern France, Valencia, the Balearic Islands and Sardinia, and one that is enshrined in Barça's philosophy. Eidur Gudjohnsen, who played for the club from 2006 to 2009, told me that there was a clause in his contract that stated that the player must embrace the Catalan language.

'"Why do you speak Catalan?" I have to answer this question all the time,' says Joan Maria Pou in exasperation. 'I travel with Barça to stadiums for all its matches around Europe to commentate for the radio station. A lot of people ask me: "Why do you speak in Catalan?" "Well, Chinese speak in Chinese. It is my language," I say. There are a lot of Catalan people who speak Catalan and they feel Spanish. It's not a political thing. When I was one year old, my father said to me, "*Bona nit*" not "*Buenas noches*". Good night for me is "*Bona nit*". If I was afraid, my father sung for me a song in Catalan, not in Spanish, not because he was a separatist or a radical but because he was using our language. Catalan is a tool to communicate. It's not a flag.

'My name is Joan Maria Pou, a Catalan name. My second name is Camino, which means "way" in Spanish. All my mother's family speak in Spanish. I speak in Spanish with my uncles, with my grandmother, the mother of my mother. And with the mother of my father and with my father, I speak Catalan. I can be in the same room, at the same table, and look one way and speak Catalan to my uncle and look the other way and speak Spanish to another uncle. It's comfortable. There is no one shouting, "What are you doing? It's not polite to speak in Catalan at the table." Everybody understands. Last night, I interviewed the Barcelona player Andrés Iniesta who is from Castile-La Mancha in the centre of Spain, but is a product of La Masia, Barça's youth academy. He came here. I questioned him in Catalan and he answered in *castellano*. My audience understood perfectly. He understands and speaks Catalan but prefers to speak in Spanish. For him, it was no problem. It makes life interesting and rich.

'All these things are mixed in the rivalry between Madrid and Barça because Madrid is the symbol of centrality, of Spain. It is the capital. It thinks it is the best. For them, Catalonia is a strange place – they want more money, they want more autonomy, they have a club that all the time speaks in Catalan. Now the coach, Pep Guardiola speaks in Catalan with journalists in Coruña, in Sevilla. What is happening? They have the Catalan flag on their jerseys. All this is very strange because we are a little bit different. They don't understand that we are different but we don't pretend to be better than a Castilian or a person from Andalucía.'

Catalans even have an expression for what makes them different to other Spaniards, *el hecho diferencial* – the differentiating fact. They prize sobriety, enterprise and hard work. They reckon that they have their own yin and yang; that they're a mix between *seny i rauxa*, common sense and madness. Barça fans maintain that Pep Guardiola, the club's precociously successful manager, who won six titles in his first year in charge of the club in 2009, is the quintessence of *seny*.

'In a way, Johan Cruyff's way of thinking is the embodiment of *rauxa*,' says Justin Webster, the English documentary-maker. Webster has lived in Barcelona for the last 20 years. His films include *The Madrid Connection* on the 2004 terrorist bombings; and a fly-on-the-wall documentary about Barça's turbulent 2003–04 season called *FC Barcelona Confidential*. 'Cruyff when he was a player and manager at Barça was always doing revolutionary things because he came, rather like the Catalan chef Ferran Adrià, from a working-class background. Nobody's taught them to do anything. They start with a blank slate and they invent themselves. That appeals very much to a certain kind of Catalan idea – they're absorbed with reinventing the nation.'

While Spain – and Madrid – is known for its Catholicism; Catalonia has a history of anti-clericalism, most colourfully captured in the clarion call of Alejandro Lerroux, a Radical Party leader at the turn of the last century and hero to Barcelona's proletariat: 'Enter and sack the decadent civilisation of this unhappy country! Destroy its temples, finish off its gods, raise the skirts of the novices and elevate them to the status of mothers!' The region has an independent streak and a tradition of progress and freedom, enshrined in artists it has nurtured like Pablo Picasso, Joan Miró – who painted the poster to commemorate FC Barcelona's 75th anniversary – and Salvador Dalí. Madrid, in comparison, has historically been more insular, parochial though paradoxically at the centre of things. Right-leaning *madrileños* believe themselves to be *castizo*, of high caste, unsullied by mixing with the Moorish invaders of the Middle Ages, and hardened by their environment.

'Castilians are the Spaniards with the biggest and most rounded *cojones*,' claimed Santiago Bernabéu, Real Madrid's iconic former president. 'Those who live on the Castilian *meseta*, moulded by the cold and the heat, have been sufficiently tough to prevail in every sense over those of other regions. Castile imposed its language on the whole world and gave fruition to all the enterprises and ideas that in their days made Spain great. I am sorry for the Catalans, the Galicians, and the Basques, but the Castilians were always cleverer than they were, and on the battleground, in hand-to-hand fighting, they gave them a right ear-bashing through every stage in history. Me a separatist? No. What I hear is a lot of stupid things said which no one stands up to.'

Perched in the north-east corner of Spain, Catalonia thinks of itself being closer culturally to its Mediterranean neighbours France and Italy than it does to Madrid, off to the west. This came to light when Catalonia banned bullfighting, *la fiesta nacional*, a couple of weeks after Spain's World Cup victory. Carles Puyol, Barça's captain, among other celebrities, came out in support of the ban in the run up to the parliamentary vote on the matter. In a country that cherishes bullfighting as a cultural form – it's covered in the culture pages of Spain's daily newspaper, *El País* – the 2010 debate was illustrative. While Catalonian lawmakers were banning it, Madrid legislators were elevating it to the status of protected art form, alongside its buildings and monuments. Observers saw a subtext here. Catalonians weren't talking as much about animal rights as they were proclaiming their national rights.

'There are a lot of people in Catalonia who like bullfights,' says Ruiz Zafón. 'There are a lot of people who hate it, and there are a lot of people don't really give a shit, who say: "If you like bullfighting, go." Bullfighting in many ways is a very strong symbol of what traditional Spain, especially the south of Spain, is about. It's not a Catalan thing so it's very easy to target, and it's very easy to get stuck on both sides: "Hey, these people want to ban bullfighting because they hate Spain," and the other side say, "No, it's because it's a barbaric practice," and what they are doing is calling the other people barbaric because they do it.'

Catalans are frugal, according to stereotype, yet wealthy; their taxes subsidise much of the rest of the country. They gripe about this. They complain that Madrid fails to recognise Catalan identity as a part of Spain. TV3 is the Catalan language television station. Real Madrid fans living in Catalonia call it '*Culé* TV'. *Culé* means ass in Catalan. A *culé* is a nickname for a committed Barça fan. It stems from the days, almost a century ago, when the team's working-class supporters used to sit on the wall surrounding their old stadium, with their backsides, their *culés*, flapping in the wind. Culé TV is blocked from airing in neighbouring Valencia. This makes Catalans paranoid. They see Madrid as domineering, which finds expression in the way Real Madrid play.

'The essence of Real Madrid, the good side of it, is their incredible vitality, exuberance and directness,' says Justin Webster. 'They never give up. They're so secure in being Real Madrid. They have pride, pride, pride, *el orgullo*, which has its sinful side. Pride can be a sin when it turns into arrogance, which is how it's seen from over here, in Catalonia.

'I joke with my friends in Britain, we text when there's a match on. When Barça win, I say, "Good is prevailing" basically because these days it's a battle between good and – in the personification of Real Madrid plus Mourinho – evil. Of course Real Madrid isn't the equivalent of evil, but from a Catalan's perspective, it is quite easy to see Cristiano Ronaldo as the embodiment of the worst kind of Real Madrid player because of what is called his *chulería*. The Spanish word for arrogance is *chulería*. It's having a sort of offensive swagger, a scorn for others.

'Unfortunately, if you start to follow it for a while you can detect it all over the place. There's a relationship between authoritarianism and submissiveness, which is all to do with hierarchy and Catholic faith – and that's where it starts to feel a bit like Francoism. Real Madrid doesn't get any critical coverage from Televisión Española, the national broadcaster, for example. It's all puff, smiling coverage, basically because there are so many Real Madrid supporters scattered around Spain. Real Madrid is like a power. It's treated as a power.'

Catalans resent the fact that the heir to the throne never makes an effort to pepper his speeches with Catalan or indeed Basque or Galician. Of course, while the flourishing of the Catalan language is the product of a commendable project, there is an unpleasant side effect. It is all but impossible, for instance, to get a civil service job in the region without fluency in the language. Education is also through Catalan. Catalonia's political parties exploit their voters' insecurity mercilessly, happily cooking up grievances to help muster extra votes. It's an age-old ruse. The Catalan parliament, which was reinstated in 1980, is awash with small, nationalist parties who squeeze Madrid for favours.

'In both right- and left-wing parties, there are people who are stoking the fires,' says Ruiz Zafón. 'For both, it's mutually convenient, although it's detrimental for Catalonia and Spain. It plays into specific interests. It turns out that Madrid is to blame for all that is wrong. This has been heating up, heating up to the point that nowadays it's ridiculous. There are many small towns in Catalonia that are organising referendums on whether to separate from Spain. Legally, they cannot, but it's a symbolic gesture. It's a slap in the face for the rest of Spain – we don't want to be here.'

For *madrileños* and many Spaniards around the country, the Catalans' push for autonomy is an affront to their own notion of a unified Spain. Yet there is an inexorable drift away from Madrid. There's a sense that the tension between Catalonia and Madrid can never be resolved, which feeds into the eternal nature of the Madrid–Barça rivalry. 'Catalanism is a car with no reverse gear,' writes Giles Tremlett in *Ghosts of Spain*. 'It may go slow, it may go fast, but it only goes in one direction. At what stage, I wondered, would nationalists say: "That's enough. We have achieved our aims. We don't want any more power here. You can keep what is left in Madrid?" The answer to that question is almost certainly "never". A nationalist needs, by definition, to keep demanding more – and to claim always that they are the victim of injustice.'

General Franco died in his bed on 20 November 1975. He was the longest-ruling fascist dictator of the twentieth century. He was a divisive figure in Spain, even in Catalonia. Carlos Arias Navarro, Spain's prime minister, went on television the morning of his death to break the news. He was in tears, his sinuses clogging with phlegm, as he told the nation: '*Españoles, Franco ha muerto.*' A Catalan friend of mine watched this broadcast with her family. When her kid brother started giggling and pointed out that the prime minister had big ears, her father took a swipe at him. It was the only time he ever hit one of his children. Authoritarian leadership is strangely alluring for many people. The Italian Fabio Capello, who twice managed Real Madrid, once remarked that he admired 'the order Franco left behind' in Spain.

News of *El Caudillo*'s death filtered through to the Camp Nou where Agustín Montal, the club's president, was having a meeting with senior officials, among them Jaume Rosell, the club secretary and father of Sandro Rosell, the current president. 'There were two reactions,' Jaume Rosell later recalled, 'those who said, "Let's open a bottle of cava," and others who stayed silent and were scared shitless. Among the latter was a director who said he didn't feel well and went home. Poor guy, it seems the news gave him a stomach upset. Among the happier reactions was that of his brother – he was a Communist.'

After the meeting broke up, Rosell and Joan Granados, the chief secretary of the club, stayed behind. Granados picked up a bust of Franco and threw it at Rosell in exhilaration. Rosell ducked, allowing it to break into smithereens. A few weeks later, Granados convened a meeting to discuss the upcoming fixture against Real Madrid. A plan was hatched to discreetly sew 700 Catalan flags, the band of yellow-and-red stripes seen on Carles Puyol's captain's armband today. They were smuggled into the stadium on the night of the match, 28 December 1975. The few discovered by police were let through, something that would never have happened under *El Caudillo*'s watch. The flags were unfurled before kick-off and again for Barça's two goals, the second scored by Charly Rexach in the dying seconds of the match for a 2–1 victory.

Granados surpassed himself with the spectacle he organised to celebrate the first visit of Josep Tarradellas to the Camp Nou. Tarradellas, who was a *culé*, a Barça fan, as far back as the First World War, was installed as president of the Generalitat, the Catalan parliament, in October 1977. He had spent almost 40 years in exile. As he entered the stadium, a giant Catalan flag spread out over the entire pitch in celebration. 'In those days we were few in number,' he said, recalling his youth as a Barça fan, 'but we had the same faith as you have today. That is the Barça you have inherited, the Barça rooted in its Catalanism.'

Catalonia regained its autonomy in 1980. Politically, Spain is similar to Britain – it is devolved in parts, but ostensibly loyal to a monarch. Government is decentralised in spending but centralised in political philosophy, although there are differences in degrees to the make-up of each region's autonomy. Catalonia, for example, is not allowed to hold onto its tax revenue, while the Basque Country is. Catalan separatists would also like to control, for instance, important social policy such as immigration legislation.

'You'd expect with democracy that the Barça–Madrid rivalry would be finished, but without *Franquismo*, it's different,' says Santacana. From the 1980s, it has symbolised the struggle between Catalonia and the rest of Spain, of which Josep Lluís Núñez made hay. Núñez became president of Barcelona in May 1978, a few weeks before the death of Santiago Bernabéu. Núñez stayed in office for 22 years, becoming Barça's longest-serving president. He never met Bernabéu, Real Madrid's longest-serving president, but there is a picture of him at the side of his coffin. Although Núñez was from the Basque Country, he used his hatred of Real Madrid as a tool to prop up his own wavering popularity. He had several rows with Real Madrid's presidents. During presidential elections in 1989, he baited his opponent, Sixte Cambra, for having a wife from Madrid. Núñez was also remarkable for the ease with which he broke into tears. For someone brought up on British football, who is only used to seeing players cry if they're booked (Paul Gascoigne) or if they miss a penalty (John Terry), it's always a surprise to see how freely Spanish football people cry. Núñez, though, was excessive. Cruyff, when he was manager of Barça, made him cry a lot. In one of his first acts, Cruyff banned Núñez from the dressing room, a marker in how autocratic his management of football matters would be. Núñez eventually fired the Dutchman in May 1996, a termination that Cruyff first heard about in the press.

Johan Cruyff is an enigmatic character. When he talks about himself in Dutch, he refers to himself as 'you'. He's full of nonsensical sayings like, 'If I wanted you to understand it, I would have explained it better' and 'Before I make a mistake, I don't make that mistake.' As a player, he was one of the all-time greats, helping the side win the league title in 1974. He is also arguably Barcelona's most successful manager, given the transformation in fortunes he inspired, and revered by a number of former players and current club coaches I've spoken to, having led the team to four straight league titles and its first European Cup win in 1992.

Cruyff is very anti-Madrid and he identifies with the Catalan cause. He ought to be Barça's *éminence grise*, like Alfredo di Stéfano at Real Madrid; instead he is surprisingly distrusted by many of the hierarchy at the club. In a hasty measure before leaving office as president in June 2010, Joan Laporta appointed Cruyff as honorary president of the club without conferring with either the board or the members. Sandro Rosell, Laporta's successor, rolled back on the appointment, announcing that it had to be properly ratified first. The dithering irked Cruyff and he returned his honorary president's badge. Cruyff has lost the faith of the club – its directors and a swathe of its *socios* – that he helped stop losing. His Dream Team, it is widely acknowledged, obliterated the club's loser mentality and its inferiority complex towards Real Madrid.

'Children of 10 or 12 have only known a triumphant Barça,' says Carles Santacana. 'They don't know that for many years Barça didn't win anything. Young people take it for granted that Barça wins. They are optimistic. Only older people foresee the possibility of having bad luck. The editor of a sports newspaper in Barcelona said to me that he dare not write about the possibility of the club "not winning".'

I went to watch Barcelona play on 11 September, Catalonia's National Day. It was the club's first league match of the 2010–11 season at the Camp Nou. It was a sunny Saturday evening. Kick-off was set for 6 p.m. As well as the contemporary stars of the team, people wore old replica jerseys, which celebrated some of the club's dinosaurs like Stoichkov and Ronaldinho. There were also fans with an even longer memory, ones who had '1714' stitched into their shirts, a nod to Catalonia's landmark military battle.

I took up my seat. I was reminded of something Guillem Martínez said to me: 'All the businesses in Barcelona are not so old. Maybe the oldest business in Barcelona is the club. We have *El Palau de la Música; Estrella Damm*, the brewery; *La Caixa*, the bank; *La España Industrial*, the textile factory, although that doesn't even exist anymore. Barça is the only shit that we have. It's not a football ground. It's a Spanish institution. We feel that we have constructed something important for our families, for our friends. We feel the same thing that our parents felt. I don't know what exactly Catalonia is, but at Barça there is a look that we share amongst each other. It's a good look because it's not a football look.'

This day was certainly about more than football. It was like sitting down to the Military Tattoo at Edinburgh Castle. Before the match started, army types launched a volley of rifle shots into the sky. A giant Catalan flag was spread out over the pitch while a 58-person choir sang the Catalan national anthem. The flag wasn't as big as the one that greeted Josep Tarradellas on his return from exile at the stadium in 1977, but it was easily the size of an 18-yard box.

Hércules provided the opposition. The Alicante side had just been promoted. The club's owner, Enrique Ortiz, sat in the directors' box smoking a cigar. He was recently caught on tape saying he paid Córdoba's goalkeeper €100,000 to help nudge Hércules's promotion along. The evidence surfaced as part of an ongoing corruption case involving a trash-collection contract, but was inadmissible for a separate, match-fixing charge. Ortiz has been unable to comment publicly on the case because the court investigating him imposed a gag order, and Raúl Navas, Córdoba's keeper, has been quoted in local media denying taking a bribe. Hércules was playing in the premier division for the first time since 1997. The budget the club had to spend on the team for the year was less than the fee Barça forked out off-season for its striker David Villa, who was starting up front alongside Leo Messi. On its march towards the league title the previous season, Barcelona won 18 of its home games and drew the other one. After the summer break, normal service resumed with its first game of the season when it eased past Racing de Santander 3–0, away. This should have been one-way traffic but, as the next day's newspaper headlines gushed, in a Herculean effort, on the day of Catalonia's ghastliest military defeat, Hércules won 2–0.

2

HE PREFERRED TO SIGN DEATH SENTENCES

In 1943, Real Madrid met Barcelona in the semi-final of the *Copa del Generalísimo*, Spain's version of the FA Cup. The cup was renamed at the time in honour of Franco. It was a decade since either team had won a league title so there was a lot at stake. In the first leg, Barcelona, playing at home, won 3–0. Before they took to the field in the second leg, the director of state security, José Finat y Escrivá de Romaní, dropped into the visiting team's dressing room. 'Do not forget,' he cautioned, 'that some of you are only playing because of the generosity of the regime that has forgiven you for your lack of patriotism.' Three of the team in particular – José Raich, Josep Escolà and Domingo Balmanya – weren't keen on having their files 'reconsidered'. They had left Spain during the Civil War and so, possibly, avoided the fate of Josep Sunyol. A month after the war started, in August 1936, Sunyol, president of Barça and a member of parliament for Esquerra Republicana de Catalunya, the left-wing Catalan nationalist party, was driving in the Guadarrama mountain range outside Madrid when he was captured and shot dead by Franco's forces. His body was never found.

Eight goals to the good at half-time, Real Madrid won the match 11–1. In Real Madrid's official centenary book the match is remembered as '*El baño del siglo*' – the 'bath', the drowning of the century. Juan Antonio Samaranch, the future president of the International Olympic Committee, covered the match as a journalist. 'It was not a question of playing badly or well,' he wrote. 'Barça simply ended up by not playing at all. Individual players were fearful of making even the most innocent of tackles.' Samaranch's account is interesting because, although Catalan, he was a lifelong, stiff-arm saluting supporter of Franco. Real Madrid and strangely Barcelona too were fined by the Spanish Football Federation for the unruly behaviour of fans at the match. Both their presidents resigned in disgrace. At Real Madrid, Santiago Bernabéu was installed as the club's new president.

Bernabéu was born in 1895. He joined Real Madrid as a 14-year-old and played for the club, whom he captained, as a striker, and later served as a manager. He was a lawyer by profession and had the large, corpulent frame of a well-fed judge. As president of the club, he shook things up. He was a canny operator. 'He was on the train to Barcelona in 1946,' said Julián García Candau, his biographer. 'The train used to make a lot of stops along the way. You could go to the bar for a drink or you could eat a *bocadillo* in the cafeteria of the station. He arrived in Reus and went out and bought a newspaper. He read that Barça had sent their technical secretary by boat to the Canaries to sign Luis Molowny. He phoned Madrid and told his technical secretary, Jacinto Quincoces, to go to Las Palmas by plane. He said bring a suitcase full of money and sign Luis Molowny. When the technical secretary of Barcelona arrived in the Canaries, Molowny was already in Madrid.'

Bernabéu had lots of what Spaniards describe as *enchufe* – connections. He was 'plugged in' – he cultivated and used his contacts tellingly, none more so than in his ambitious building project for Real Madrid's new stadium, Chamartín, which would later bear his name. There is circumstantial evidence to suggest that the ground was built with the same consignment of strictly rationed cement that Franco used to construct the Valley of the Fallen, the sequestered fascist theme park in the Guadarrama Mountains where *El Caudillo* is buried.

In a prescient piece of planning, Real Madrid's new stadium was built on five hectares of land in an underdeveloped, northern part of the city, which today is one of Madrid's plushest avenues, home to several mansions, ministries and museums. It was opened just before Christmas

1947. Hitherto, the venue for the final of the *Copa del Generalísimo* rotated around the country, skipping between Barcelona, the Basque Country and Madrid, and to a lesser extent Andalucía in the south, as it still does today. From 1948, Real Madrid's stadium was chosen to host the final every year for 25 seasons except three – 1957, 1963 and 1970 – when it was played in Barcelona, finals which coincided with Franco's visits to Catalonia.

Estadio Santiago Bernabéu's default position as the 'neutral' venue for cup finals was symptomatic of the workings of football during Franco's reign. Francoism drew its authority from the Falange Party, the only legal political party in Spain. One of the Falange Party's offshoots was the National Delegation of Sport. It appointed the president of the Spanish Football Federation. In turn, the Spanish Football Federation nominated presidents of the football clubs and also of the National Referees' Committee. 'They were very controlled,' says Carles Santacana. 'It was an arbitrary exercise of power. Appointments were made '*a dedo*', by pointing a finger. It was a power system from top to bottom because Franco was boss of the Falange Party.'

This was the milieu in which Bernabéu did his business. He was a pragmatist who worked in conditions which, given his political persuasion, suited him. 'Bernabéu had good friends in the Spanish Football Federation,' says Fernando Carreño, a *Marca* journalist and author of *La Historia Negra del Real Madrid*. 'He manipulated things. He obtained favours. In public, Bernabéu said that, "Real Madrid didn't oblige people to do anything. They just convinced the rest." He was anti-democratic.'

He was, in Spanish parlance, *cacique*, the important person of his village, who operated in the shadows. He was the local, clued-in rich guy who, when democracy arrived, the peasants turned to for guidance on how to vote. Everything was directed by him. He was chief of a football club that towered over the other ones in Spain. After its famous quintet of European Cups from 1956 to 1960, Real Madrid went on to win eight Spanish league titles during the 1960s, a domestic hegemony that is unrivalled in the great leagues of European football.

'Yes, Bernabéu was a supporter of the regime,' says Santiago Segurola, Spain's foremost football writer, 'but during the Franco dictatorship it was unusual for an institution not to be controlled by *Franquistas*. Dictatorships are so named because they transmit power from all walks of life, from a municipality to a club. I cannot imagine that Colonel Gaddafi allowed clubs in Libya to be chaired by anti-Gaddafi elements.'

But to paint Bernabéu as a card-carrying Francoist is wrong, stresses Carreño. He was right wing and conservative. He was a monarchist, with an independent streak, and certainly wasn't an apparatchik of the Falange Party. Bernabéu quarrelled, for example, with José Millán-Astray, the founder and first commander of the Spanish Foreign Legion. Before he died in 1954, Millán-Astray was one of Franco's most vocal propagandists, famed for his idiotic rallying cry, 'Long live death!' Millán-Astray married a general's daughter in 1906 who failed to tell him, until after their wedding, about her decision to live a chaste life. Their marriage was, in Millán-Astray's words, like a 'fraternal relationship'. For brothers in arms on the right wing of Spain's political spectrum, Millán-Astray's relations with Bernabéu were fratricidal. The pair jousted publicly on political matters. Bernabéu also criticised Franco in 1944 over the National Delegation of Sport's refusal to subsidise Real Madrid by more than four per cent of the costs to build the club's new stadium.

He is, nonetheless, vilified in Barcelona for his army record. 'For people who are not from Spain,' suggests Joan Maria Pou, 'it should be weird to hear that Real Madrid's ground is named after a big Franquista. Could you imagine if one of Berlin's stadiums was called after a Nazi soldier?' Bernabéu was a corporal in General Franco's army during the Spanish Civil War. There's nothing sinister about this, points out Sid Lowe, the *Guardian*'s football correspondent in Spain. In civil wars, people take sides. Lowe earned a doctorate for his book about the Juventud de Acción Popular, a Hitler Youth-type organisation which helped foster fascism in Spain during the 1930s. Bernabéu was the organisation's sports secretary, and was serving as Real Madrid club secretary when civil war broke out. Real Madrid was seized by anti-Franco forces during the war, which spelt trouble for Bernabéu as they carried out a purge of officials of opposing politics. A fellow board member denounced him as a fascist, but he managed to escape certain death by taking refuge in the French embassy thanks to the intercession of Álvaro de Albornoz, the Spanish ambassador in Paris who happened to be a Real Madrid supporter. Bernabéu later slipped away into exile, before re-emerging as part of Franco's nationalist army that overran Catalonia, a formative experience which, contentiously, he harped on about during his 35 years as president of Real Madrid.

It's not unusual, of course, for a club's patriarch to goad rivals in the press. Bill Shankly used to say he would draw the curtains if Everton were playing in his back garden. Alex Ferguson vowed not to rest until he knocked Liverpool off its 'fucking perch'. Bernabéu, however, made a practice of firing politically loaded insults at Barça during a fascist dictatorship under the guise of football banter. He used to publicly refer to his role in the 'reconquest' of Catalonia; and mocked Catalans at a time when the country was still reeling from the horrors of its civil war, most notoriously when he said in 1968, 'I like Catalonia very much except for Catalan people.'

'The problem was that he never apologised for this statement, which could have been helpful,' says Carles Santacana. 'I found some police reports saying that, "Bernabéu is making life difficult for us." The comment had political connotations. It was not about Barça or the city of Barcelona, but against Catalan people. He was proving the identification of Barça with Catalonia. He was promoting it. He ridiculed Catalan people, not Barça supporters. There were also Catalans who supported Barcelona city's other team Espanyol.'

At Real Madrid, Bernabéu is, of course, an inviolable figure. He was uncorrupted by power himself. He wasn't venal, which adds to his lustre for the club's fans. During highlight reels at the Bernabéu stadium before matches, over 30 years after his death, he is still remembered in images alongside Real Madrid's famous players. He is renowned internationally for the mark he made in football and for his role in kick-starting the European Cup. When he died in June 1978, there was a minute's silence for him during the World Cup, a rare honour. Vicente del Bosque, who managed Spain when they won the tournament 32 years later, was a Real Madrid player at the time. He helped carry his coffin at the funeral.

Ignacio Zoco was Bernabéu's favourite player. Zoco married María Ostiz, a fresh-faced singer who was famous on the Spanish folk music scene. Their wedding was a family affair with only 22 guests. She met Bernabéu for the first time after they got married. The newlyweds were walking through Real Madrid's training ground when Zoco spotted Bernabéu approaching. 'I told her, "Sorry, we're going to have to say hello." So I went to him and presented my wife. The first thing Don Santiago Bernabéu said to my wife, whom he had never spoken to before, was: "Maria, the day Ignacio retires you'll have to leave him with me as a breeding bull." Maria was speechless.'

I interviewed Zoco one morning at stud – in the Veterans' Association bar at the Bernabéu stadium. He has a shock of fine, brown hair and is tall, angular and slightly hunched over. Rafa Arias, a TV commentator with Televisión Española from 1970 to 2006, told me Zoco was muscular and lithe as a player, reminiscent of the French international player Patrick Vieira. He played for Real Madrid from 1962 to 1974 and reckons he must have played against Barcelona 25 or 26 times. In fact, he signed a pre-contract with Barça but while in Morocco with the Spanish national team a Real Madrid director approached him to sign for the club so he plumped for Los Blancos instead. 'Paco Gento made a *madridista* out of me,' he says. He used to watch Gento, the Real Madrid player, on TV as a teenager in his native Navarre. They say in Spain that Gento was so fast the ball used to run behind him.

Zoco played with and against a lot of football's greatest players. He reels off some of their names at one stage like a Gregorian chant: 'Pelé, Eusébio, Cruyff, Yashin, Beckenbauer, Muller, Bobby Charlton, Matthews.' None were the match of di Stéfano: 'He was better than Pelé. He was the only player I didn't want to play against. The poor players he faced were going around with their tongues hanging out,' he says, gesturing to his midriff. 'He was so anxious to win. He wouldn't tolerate guys who didn't give a hundred per cent.' Apparently, di Stéfano had a specific wake-up call for reckless, underperforming teammates: 'You're messing with my money!'

Zoco used to order his boots from a store in Barcelona. He would get an apprentice to wear them for a week in order to break them in. European Cup away ties often involved five-day round trips. There were no meals on planes so after disembarking players would scramble to a bar for sandwiches or sausages. They were warned off pasta – it made you fat, they were told. They were fêted on arrival around the cities of Europe. Thousands would step out to greet them. Before matches, Don Santiago said little to them. 'The only thing that Bernabéu asked before we went out onto the pitch – and he spoke very rarely – was that we leave our balls out there. "There are millions of Spanish people that are going to watch us," he used to say. "Let's give them happiness."'

Zoco's last game for Real Madrid was against Barça in the final of the *Copa del Generalísimo* in 1974. A couple of months beforehand, Barça, with Cruyff in their ranks, had beaten them 5–0 at the Bernabéu. 'It was the most beautiful thing that happened to me. I had said I was going to retire. I was the captain of Real Madrid for my last three years and captain that night. We wanted to get revenge. We won 4–0. I received the cup from the hands of Franco. The poor man was very sick.'

I asked him if he ever met Franco in person. 'Yes,' he said. 'The day after Spain won the European Championships in 1964. We had a dinner after the match and stayed up all night celebrating, as you can imagine. The following day he received us one by one at his residence at 11 a.m. When he saw me he said, "You are number 4, the blond from Navarre." "Yes, Your Excellency," I replied.'

I also asked him if Real Madrid was Franco's favourite team. He refuted the insinuation, pointing out that Barça also won a lot of cups under Franco. 'Franco got more benefits from Real Madrid than Real Madrid from Franco,' he said. 'None of his ministers had the importance that Real Madrid had.'

'Did Franco say this?' I asked. 'He knew it. He was many things but he wasn't a fool. He knew everything.'

'So Real Madrid wasn't the team of Franco? Was Real Madrid favoured by the regime?'

'Ostia,' he said, getting irritated. 'No way – are you going to tell me that all the cups that I won, Franco won them for me? The people who have no idea always say this, but they don't know anything.'

Real Madrid drew Barcelona in the quarter-final of the *Copa del Generalísimo* in 1970. Real Madrid won the first leg at home 2–0. In the second leg at the Camp Nou, Charly Rexach put Barcelona in front just before half-time. Zoco was playing.

'We were losing 1–0 and Guruceta, the ref, blew the whistle, awarding us a penalty. It wasn't a penalty. It was outside the area. It wasn't even on the edge of the box. It was out here,' he says, gesturing to a point a couple yards away from where he's sitting. 'Anyway, we should have won. We would have eliminated them anyway.'

What did you think when Guruceta awarded the penalty? I asked. 'What did I think? With all the penalties that were awarded against me? Some referees blow the whistle when it's not a penalty so I thought, *Olé*.'

Rexach and several Barça players left the pitch in protest, but were persuaded to return by their English manager Vic Buckingham. When Real Madrid scored the penalty, Eladio Silvestre, a Barça player, applauded sarcastically and said to Guruceta, 'You're a Madrid stooge. Haven't you got any shame?' He was sent off for his impudence.

Joan Golobart, an Espanyol player in the 1980s who writes for *La Vanguardia*, was at the match. 'I was with my father,' he said. 'He is a *socio* [member] of Barça, number 400. It's his only defect. My father is *muy tranquilo*. He's quiet, a serious man; he's very polite. He never utters a *palabrota*, a curse. I suddenly saw another man that night. He shouted abuse at Guruceta. I didn't recognise him. I couldn't see anything else on the field because everyone got up, complaining, shouting and throwing things onto the pitch.'

Golobart, incidentally, went along to the Camp Nou 30 years later for another ethnographical exercise – to see Luís Figo's first *clásico* match with Real Madrid in November 2000. The Portuguese star had moved from Barça a few months beforehand. 'I took my wife to observe the human behaviour,' he said. 'I told her not to bother looking at the pitch, but to watch the spectators instead because it was the biggest show in the world. It was terrible, terrible. I've never seen a crowd as indignant, as angry as that day. I've never heard people shouting in that way. It was anguishing. My wife said they were *locos*, mad. The people who were screaming abuse looked like normal people, but they were possessed. They were transformed, as my father was that night with Guruceta.'

To this day, at Spanish football matches, fans bring – or rent – cushions to sit on. Infuriated by Guruceta's actions in 1970, Barça fans rained thousands of cushions down onto the pitch. At several stages, Guruceta had to stop play to clear them off the playing surface. When the ball went into the stands at one stage, it never returned.

Rafa Arias was also at the Guruceta match, sitting beside his elderly uncle. 'The seats at the Camp Nou were made from wood,' he says. 'My uncle broke the wood off his seat. "Please, what are you going to do?" I said. He started hurling pieces of wood – as other people were doing also – onto the pitch. It was a moment that I will always remember. To do what Guruceta did – in a Madrid-Barça match – was too much.'

With a few minutes remaining in the game, thousands of Barça fans invaded the pitch, causing Guruceta and his linesmen to flee to the dressing room, later spending the night in a police station for their own safety. The fans paraded around the pitch chanting, 'Barça! Barça! Barça!' When the floodlights were turned off, straw from discarded cushions was set alight, as were advertising hoardings. Having dispersed from the stadium, clashes with riot police in the avenues surrounding the ground continued into the night. For decades afterwards, whenever there was a dodgy refereeing decision made against Barça in a match, frustrated fans chanted, 'Guruceta! Guruceta!'

Emilio Guruceta died in a car crash in 1987. Three years beforehand, he was paid a bribe of approximately £15,000, according to a Belgian intermediary involved in the pay-off, to ensure Anderlecht turned around a 2–0 deficit against Nottingham Forest in a UEFA Cup semi-final. Anderlecht won the second leg 3–0, with the help of a penalty decision in their favour.

I asked Zoco if he was scared leaving the Camp Nou pitch that night under such a cloud. 'We weren't frightened because it was normal to have problems when we got out of a place that ended in a fight,' he says, clapping his hands and dusting them off. 'When I hear a lot of noise I think they are cheering for me.'

Were referees biased towards Real Madrid during the Franco era? There are other controversial refereeing incidents involving Madrid–Barça matches – although not all of them were in favour of Real Madrid. Real Madrid played against Barcelona, for instance, in the second round of the European Cup, late in 1960. Leading 2–1 in the first leg at the Bernabéu with three minutes to go, English ref Arthur Ellis ignored a linesman's flag for offside when Barça's Sándor Kocsis broke through, but whistled for a penalty when he was fouled. The spot kick was converted. It was the first time Real Madrid had not won a home tie in six years of European Cup competition. In the second leg, another English ref, Reg Leafe, disallowed four Real Madrid goals, which, from archive footage, seem to have been valid. After the game, Bernabéu sulked: 'Leafe was Barcelona's best player.'

When the two sides met in a league match in November 1966 at the Bernabéu, the referee José María Ortiz de Mendíbil played 11 minutes of extra time. He blew for full-time after Real Madrid scored the game's only goal, which meant they overtook Barça at the top of the table. He said afterwards that his stopwatch was broken. Gallego, a centre back with Barcelona, was suspended for three matches for abusing him. 'I saw this match when I was young,' says Rafa Arias. 'The referees' system is different today compared to then. Long ago, everything was directed from Madrid. The referees from that time weren't the same as now.' In the early 1970s,

Antonio Camacho, a former referee in the Spanish league, claimed that Barcelona would never win a league title while José Plaza, a committed *madridista*, was president of the National Referees' Committee.

'I haven't studied it,' says Justin Webster, one of whose films is a football study called *The Ref*, 'but I would tend to believe [most referees were biased against Barcelona] because of the mentality of that sort of system – under Franco – which is hierarchical, quite corrupt. Principle is a fairly flimsy thing here. You could imagine that a lot of referees under that sort of regime would have been self-influenced.'

Simon Kuper, the author of *Football Against the Enemy*, has an interesting theory about the hand of Franco – and dictators in general – in the affairs of football. It is silly to think that Real Madrid was a fascist team, he argues, or that Franco rigged games and paid off refs. He didn't need to, but he created the environment in which Real Madrid, the team of the capital, could thrive. Dictators tend to concentrate their resources – generals, secret police and bureaucrats – in their capital cities. *Todo se cuece allí* – everything is cooked there, to borrow a culinary expression. Kuper points out that it is no surprise each team that has won the European Cup from a dictatorship comes from a capital city, as Real Madrid did six times during the Franco era. Its *palco*, its VIP box, was always full of people who gave orders, *corta el bacalao*, as the country's decision-makers in policy and economics. In contrast, nearly every team from a democracy to have won it comes from provincial cities. Barça won its first European Cup in 1992, 17 years after *El Caudillo* died. If the Royal Palace of El Pardo, where Franco lived, was in Barcelona, Barça would have enjoyed the fruits of his patronage, claim the club's supporters. But (unfortunately for them) their city, as one Barça *socio* said to me, wasn't 'where the apple fell down'.

I asked Julián García Candau, a former sports editor of *El País* and the author of a book on the history of Madrid-Barça, about impartial Spanish league referees. García Candau went to his first Madrid–Barça match in 1959 at the Bernabéu stadium. I interviewed him in his apartment in Madrid, which is spilling over with books. He was born in Vila-real in the community of Valencia in 1939, and played a few friendly games for Villarreal, but had to pack in the game at 19 owing to injury. He was categorical: 'Yes, of course.' He cites an incident from 7 May 1972. There were two league games left in the season. Barcelona trailed Real Madrid by two points. Real Madrid faced a sticky tie against Atlético de Madrid at the Vicente Calderón. Barça was playing down in Andalucía against Córdoba, who had two Real Madrid players on loan – Vicente del Bosque, the future World Cup-winning manager, and a young *madrileño* called José Fermín Gutiérrez Martín. Someone had a word in Fermín's ear before the match, says García Candau. 'Fermín was told to fall in the penalty box. "Just fall," he was told, "the ref will give you a penalty." He fell. Córdoba was awarded a penalty. He scored. Córdoba won 1–0.'

Real Madrid lost 4–1 in their derby match, but won their final league match against Sevilla at the Bernabéu to secure the title.

In March 1952, the Colombian side Millonarios visited Spain to take part in a tournament to celebrate Real Madrid's 50th anniversary. On the eve of the tournament, one of their players, the Argentine-born forward Alfredo di Stéfano, unknown in Spain, took part in a radio debate with the presidents of Millonarios and Real Madrid, a chat which prompted Bernabéu's famous premonition: 'This guy smells of good football.' After impressing in the tournament, he returned to Bogotá. Both Real Madrid and Barcelona – who had an agent scouting at the tournament, the famous Pepe Samitier, a star player before the Civil War – pursued him. Barça stole a march, managing to lure him to Barcelona, setting him up with an apartment and getting him involved in a few friendly matches.

Di Stéfano's contractual standing was complicated, however, by the fact that he was on loan to Millonarios from River Plate, the Buenos Aires team, until October 1954. Barça signed a deal with River Plate. Real Madrid got their oar in by signing a counter deal with Millonarios. Negotiations deadlocked. Barça got nervy. Di Stéfano got bothered by the Viennese fog that enveloped their thinking. 'I went to the senior management,' he wrote in his memoirs, 'who told me that they couldn't fix things, that they needed a third man, like in the Orson Welles film. "You need a third man? But I am the third man. What is going on here? I'm going to buy myself a ticket and I'm heading back to Argentina. What am I doing here?"'

With negotiations at an impasse, the Spanish Football Federation stepped in to mediate. Confounded, they referred it to their masters at the National Delegation of Sport, headed up by General Moscardó. The general, a notably religious man, found a very Christian solution to the stalemate, decreeing that di Stéfano should be shared, alternating between both clubs over the next four seasons, after which a definitive arrangement could be hit on. Both Bernabéu and Barcelona's president, Martí Carreto, agreed to the deal, signing up for it on 15 September 1954.

Within a week, Carreto resigned. Barça's directors and members were furious that he had been outwitted by Real Madrid. In a fit of pique, Barça surrendered their interest in di Stéfano, agreeing to forfeit their share in him for a compensation payment of 4.4 million pesetas, which was about what they had originally paid River Plate for a stake in him. Trias Fargas, a Catalan lawyer who had been tasked with brokering a deal for Barça with Millonarios, denounced Carreto for his incompetence and also claimed that Barça were the victims of a conspiracy between Real Madrid and Franco's government. A Catalan TV documentary, broadcast in 2000 to celebrate Barça's centenary, maintained that Carreto was blackmailed by the government who had him over a barrel for tax evasion. It is an unsubstantiated claim. A few weeks after signing for Real Madrid, di Stéfano scored two goals against Barça in a 5–0 drubbing at the Bernabéu. The win set Real Madrid on a march towards its first league title in 21 years. They retained the title in 1955 and the following season won the first of five European Cups in a row. Their *época dorada*, a golden era which has defined the club ever since, had begun.

Over half a century later, the transfer saga still sizzles. Author Fernando Carreño told me he gets '300 comments' on his blog whenever a conversation thread is opened about the affair. Yet Barça's conspiracy theories are uncorroborated. If anything, argues Jimmy Burns, a writer who has chronicled both clubs' histories, the kerfuffle reflects poorly on Barça. Consumed by wounded pride, it willingly coughed up the player. And besides, in 1950 Franco's government stood by while Barça swiped star Hungarian player Ladislao Kubala – who is celebrated in the club's museum for 'introducing new football techniques that had not been seen before, such as curling the ball' – from Real Madrid's grasp.

Di Stéfano was a phenomenon. He scored 216 goals in 282 appearances for Real Madrid even though he wasn't a striker *per se*, preferring to forage for the ball as an attacking midfielder. He scored in each of Real Madrid's five-in-a-row European Cup finals, including a hat-trick in the 1960 final against Eintracht Frankfurt in Glasgow, a ten-goal classic and probably the most famous match in the competition's history. Alex Ferguson, a young striker making his way in the game with Queen's Park, looked on from the terraces, enchanted, along with 127,000 other spectators who crammed into Hampden Park to see *Los Blancos*.

When I mentioned that Real Madrid team to Brian Glanville, the football writer, who was also at the game in Hampden, he said they were 'a one-man show' during those years. Di Stéfano was pre-eminent, 'inexhaustible' in Glanville's estimation, and a finer player than Maradona, given his greater versatility. The world had never seen a team like Real Madrid before. 'I thought, these people aren't human,' said a baffled Bobby Charlton after his Manchester United teammates had just lost to them in the semi-final of the 1957 European Cup. 'It's not the sort of game I've been taught.' The team was an assortment of attacking talents, with di Stéfano and the Hungarian hotshot Ferenc Puskas wreaking havoc alongside, among others, Raymond Kopa, who had spent his youth down the coalmines in the Nord-Pas-de-Calais region of France beside his Polish father, and Gento, the speedy Spanish outside left, the only man to have won six European Cup medals and, it is said, Franco's favourite player.

El Caudillo basked in their glory, his favouritism evident in the manner in which he bestowed the Imperial Order of the Yoke and

Arrows on the club's players in 1955. It was part of the regime's honours' list, awarded for their success in that year's Copa Latino, a precursor of the European Cup. Barcelona, who had won the trophy twice before – the only other Spanish team to win it – remained undecorated.

At the time, Spain was knackered economically, more impoverished in the 1950s than Iraq. 'Spain in this moment was so dirty,' says Guillem Martínez. 'I remember Manuel Vázquez Montalbán once wrote that "Spain and its stadiums smelt of *anís*," of cheap liquor. People used to walk around wearing *calcetines a cuadros*, ugly, square-patterned socks. We didn't have blue jeans until 1978. It was a poor country, but spiritually poor, too.'

Real Madrid's European triumphs gave *madrileños* and the club's fans in the *pueblos* around the country something to cheer about. If Barcelona represented the spirit of Catalonia to the world, Real Madrid was the standard-bearer of Spain's essence overseas. Their successes were exhilarating, their natural aristocratic ascendency a throwback to the halcyon days of Philip II's empire in the sixteenth century, a time when he plundered vast tracts of the world with an army of mercenaries for Spain just like Real Madrid, with its roster of glamorous foreign talents, conquered all before them in club football. The club, as Ignacio Zoco suggested to me, was an invaluable tool for diplomacy. After the Spanish Civil War, Spain had been ostracised in the international community, unwelcome at the doors of the United Nations and the Vatican until well into the 1950s. Because of Real Madrid's panache they were no longer pariahs. 'Real Madrid is a style of sportsmanship,' maintained Fernando María Castiella, Franco's Foreign Minister at the time. 'It is the best embassy we ever had.'

Did Franco like football? Although born in Galicia, in the northwest of the country, Spanish folklore has it that he could recite Real Madrid teams going back through the ages. According to Paul Preston, his biographer, he twice won Spain's football pools, which he signed for a while under a pseudonym, Francisco Cofran. 'It is somehow difficult to imagine Hitler or Mussolini doing the pools,' wrote Preston. Guillem Martínez challenges this claim, pointing out that Franco listened to a programme on Sundays that listed the pools but the show wasn't exclusively about football. 'Franco was very dour and boring,' concludes Santiago Segurola. 'He was bloodthirsty. He liked to watch movies at the El Pardo palace, but had no special interest in football. He preferred to sign death sentences to playing football or watching a game.'

How much of a *madridista* was Franco? According to Raimundo Saporta, Real Madrid's press secretary during the Franco years, *El Caudillo* never betrayed any emotion during Real Madrid matches. Maybe he was bored. Did he ever try to influence the outcome of their matches? Real Madrid failed to win a league title in the first 15 years of his reign. 'There is a contradiction there,' says Segurola. If anything, in the 1940s Atlético de Madrid – who were called Atlético Aviación at the time because of their merger with the Spanish Air Force – were more closely aligned to Franco's regime; several of the club's players were from the air corps. From the 1950s though, Atléti – as the club is referred to – has been eclipsed by its city rivals.

For Real Madrid, *el derbi*, its clashes with Atléti, often took precedence over its rivalry with Barça until the arrival of Cruyff's Dream Team in the 1990s definitively established Barcelona as the other great force in the land. What is remarkable is that football fans around the country – not just Real Madrid supporters – refer to the club as Madrid. When Real Madrid play Atléti at the Bernabéu stadium, Real Madrid's *Ultras Sur*, their hardcore fans, block out half the south end of the stadium with a giant *tifo*, an illustrated banner rendered in comic book artform. In it, an *Ultras Sur* fan, his face half-hidden under the shadow of his hoodie, wags an index finger in warning mode. He is stationed in front of the Bernabéu stadium, with the Madrid city skyline in the background. In huge letters under the banner is written: 'This is Madrid.' Atléti fans accept this appropriation, it seems. If you go to watch *el derbi* at Atléti's ground, street vendors outside hawk *antimadridista* flags and jerseys embossed with cartoon images of an Indian's head. Atléti fans are called Indians. Scarves proudly announce: 'My mother made me beautiful, smart and *antimadridista*.' It is strange, and perhaps instructive, that a club named Atlético de Madrid, in a sport renowned for the territorial nature of its fans, so willingly relinquishes its own city name.

Historically, there has always been a degree of whoring when it comes to Real Madrid's political affiliations. The club is resented around Spain for its political expediency. It always, argues Julián García Candau, aspires to be where the power lies. The club was founded in 1902 by two Catalan brothers, ironically, Juan and Carlos Padrós. It remained the plaything of Madrid's liberal, upper-class elites in its early years. Rowing in behind Spain's King Alfonso XIII, it was conferred with the title of Real, or Royal, in 1920. After Spain's second republic took root in 1931, the club was content to drop the royal appendage to its name and it removed the crown emblem from its jersey. It went by the name of Madrid FC until it reverted to its existing name and royal-crowned crest in 1941.

When civil war struck in 1936, the club's membership and hierarchy split into opposing factions, as did the rest of the country. One of the plotters behind Franco's uprising in Madrid, for example, was General Adolfo Meléndez, a former president of the club; while the club's serving president in 1936, Rafael Sánchez-Guerra, was a moderate Republican. Sánchez-Guerra fled into exile shortly after the outbreak of hostilities, and returned to Spain after the war. When his wife died he became a Dominican monk. Lieutenant Colonel Antonio Ortega, who was one of his successors as acting president of Real Madrid during the conflict, had no truck with religion. A former head of security at the club, he was a communist army officer who actually took his orders from the Soviet secret police. Once Franco's forces got the upper hand in Madrid, Ortega took flight, trying to get to England by boat. He got as far as Alicante where he was apprehended and executed. Ortega has been airbrushed from Real Madrid's official history and is not listed in the club's records of past presidents. While Barça wallows in its civil war experiences, Real Madrid sidesteps the memory of its own traumas. For example, in Real Madrid's official commemorative history, *One Hundred Years of Legend*, three years of civil war merits one paragraph of insipid analysis.

Real Madrid's politically promiscuous days ended when Bernabéu took over the club's presidency in 1943. For over 30 years, his chiefdom overlapped with Franco's rule. Given the closeness of their political persuasions, there was natural symbiosis, reinforced by the mutually beneficial nature of the relationship. 'Real Madrid took advantage of the regime's influence,' says García Candau. 'Franco's government benefited from Real Madrid because Real Madrid was a good propaganda tool outside Spain. It was its Trojan horse. That's why I've asked several times who benefited the most – Real Madrid from the regime or vice versa? Don't underestimate the *potencia*, the grandiosity, of Real Madrid. It can never be in doubt.'

Miguel Aguilar, an editor with Random House and a *socio* of Real Madrid, disputes the charge, believing it to be disingenuous. 'I think it's much more a matter of the dictatorship tagging on to Real Madrid than the other way around,' he says, 'in the same way that Cuba has done with athletics or the Soviet Union with chess. You can't really say that all chess players in the Soviet Union were communists. It just so happened that the Soviet Union supported its chess players because it gave it outside credibility.'

When Real Madrid travelled abroad for European Cup matches, Bernabéu used to pack a recording of the Franco national anthem, the one with lyrics approved by *El Caudillo* in use at the time, as well as the Francoist Spanish flag. He used them to counter, as sometimes happened, the singing of the Republican anthem by the host country or the waving of Spain's Republican flag by Spanish emigrants. Is it any wonder the 'regime team' label has stuck, however unwitting the collusion by players and vast tracts of the club's pluralist membership? It is an association that still lingers today, embodied in the club's superiority complex; and, indeed, isn't resented in all quarters. 'I don't think they mind being called Franco's team as much as we would think,' says Justin Webster.

What is unquestionable is that the incomparable glories of di Stéfano's team cast a spell on Madrid's youth from the 1950s and their children, that has yet, over a half century later, to dissipate. It created a monster – an army of supporters with an insatiable hunger. It begat a stadium of spectators more than fans, famously expectant of thrilling, attacking football by the heirs of FIFA's Team of the Twentieth Century, and crabby when it isn't served up, as critical of their own players as they are of the opposition. They wait, to use the most popular analogy, like Caesar in the Roman Colosseum, to pass their verdict on a performance – thumbs up, thumbs down. Or, to put it in the players' perspective, the Bernabéu crowd, according to Ronaldo, Real Madrid's Brazilian star from the middle of the last decade, is like a woman – you have to find a new way of pleasing her every day.

3

DREAMS FROM MY FATHER

One of Santiago Bernabéu's legacies was to elevate the status of his job. At Real Madrid, the president is the club's *faro*, the fans' lighthouse. The culture at the club is to look to their president unlike Barça who, historically, are identified by their manager. Practically everyone in Spain knows that Florentino Pérez, or Florentino as he is referred to, is Real Madrid's current president. During televised matches, the camera will pan intermittently to take in his emotions. People ask him for his autograph. He is lampooned on satirical shows like *Crackòvia* and scrutinised endlessly in the media. Apparently, he likes to know what people say about him. A journalist at *Marca* told me Pérez employs staff to log press statements about him. Since Bernabéu's death, no president at Real Madrid has so evidently tried to emulate his presidency than Pérez. His *galáctico* policy, where the world's most sought-after player is added to the team's roster every year, is a re-imagining of the audacious recruitment drive of the 1950s. According to Santiago Segurola there are Freudian roots to it.

Pérez was born in 1947, the year that the Bernabéu stadium was inaugurated. He was first brought along to watch Real Madrid as a four-year-old by his father, a *socio*. 'He is fascinated with the team of di Stéfano, the one which won five European Cups,' says Segurola. 'It's one of those infantile fixations that affect the personality of a person. In his childhood his team is king of the world. Then he becomes a successful entrepreneur, cold, calculating, with great influence, great links with Spanish politicians, and he tries to reproduce Bernabéu's model from the 1950s. If you look at the signings Bernabéu made: di Stéfano, Kopa, Didi, Puskás. Florentino Pérez practically plays the same cards year after year by buying renowned figures like Figo, Zidane, Ronaldo and Beckham. He's copying the model as a gift to his father.'

During his first tenure in office, from 2000 to 2006, he turned the club's team into the Harlem Globetrotters of football by signing a string of galactic superstars, all attack-minded. He started with Luís Figo, who he nicked from Barcelona's ranks. It was an outrageous strategy; the football was thrilling, most of the time, as could be expected with Figo, Zinedine Zidane and the Brazilian Ronaldo leading the line. At the time, the three men were passing the FIFA World Player of the Year trophy between themselves like a hookah at a hashish party. Successful initially, as the club's ninth, record-breaking Champions League title was added to the trophy cabinet in 2002, it quickly imploded when essential water-carriers like Claude Makélélé were offloaded in favour of midfield extravagances like the Asian favourite, David Beckham, who, in a marketing ploy, was given the number 23 jersey, the same as Michael Jordan's at the Chicago Bulls. Mystics who thought otherwise saw a numerological explanation in the runes: there are 23 letters in David and Victoria Beckham.

Pérez, unlike the Beckhams, is unspectacular in his social life. He wears glasses, parts his hair to the side and has a wan smile. He tends to dress in nondescript suits, of bland hues, is teetotal and claims that his favourite dish is egg and chips. There's nothing simple, mind, about his bank account. Pérez's personal wealth, accrued from the building trade, isn't far off the £2 billion mark, which means he can easily afford as president of Real Madrid, a not-for-profit organisation, to do his job without getting paid a salary. He's one of the top five most power-ful men in Spain, on a similar footing with the chairman of Santander bank and the prime minister of the country, which obviously guarantees enormous power for Real Madrid.

In 2001, he wiped away the club's debt of over £200 million at a stroke. With both the city hall and the regional government in the hands of his friends from the *Partido Popular*, the country's conservative party, he succeeded in re-zoning Real Madrid's old training ground on the outskirts of the city. Four skyscrapers, the tallest in the city and soon dubbed 'the *Galácticos*' by the Madrid-based English journalist Giles Tremlett, shot up on the Madrid skyline, 'They have just let Pérez have whatever he wanted,' complained Madrid's Socialist Party leader. Environmentalists were enraged. A Barça-supporting MEP got the European Commission to investigate. It reported nothing untoward had happened, but the deal reeked of cosy cartels. 'Let's just say it was a very comfortable agreement for everyone – Real Madrid, the People's Party, and for several real-estate developers who were the kings of Spain,' says Tremlett.

John Carlin, *El País* journalist and author of the book on which the movie *Invictus* is based, has got to know Pérez. Carlin has an enviable Rolodex of contacts. Nelson Mandela wrote the foreword to one of his books. He's been living in Sitges – the chic seaside village on the outskirts of Barcelona where José Mourinho used to live while working for Barça – since 1998. He spent a year sallying around Europe and Asia with Real Madrid chronicling the turbulent first year of Beckham's sojourn in Spain, which commenced in the summer of 2003, for his book, *White Angels*. He had unrivalled access to the club's inner sanctum, the kind that the Watergate journalist Bob Woodward enjoys at another White House.

'Florentino Pérez has a dry sense of humour,' says Carlin. 'He's got extraordinary attention to detail. He's the one person in the Real Madrid hierarchy that when I send him a text message he will reply to me on average within five minutes. I'm sure he does that with everybody. Real Madrid is but a tiny element of the empire that he runs. He's known for Real Madrid, but he's got a hell of a day job. He has very few personal indulgences. He's kind of the anti-Berlusconi. His one extravagance is this yacht he sails around Mallorca. He's extraordinarily ambitious. He thinks big – in business and in football, and he almost always gets what he wants. He's extremely cool under pressure. The hotter the atmosphere in the room, the cooler he will be.'

Pérez was brought back for a second spell as president in June 2009, announcing at his election that his Second Coming would be a 'spectacular project'. True to his election promise, he picked up where he left off. He coughed up £212 million to bolster the team's squad that summer, which included the signatures of the latest pair of FIFA World Player of the Year award winners, the Brazilian Kaká, and via Manchester United, Cristiano Ronaldo. The 2009–10 league race went down to the last weekend of fixtures. Real Madrid set a points' record; that is until their Catalan rivals' tally was added up. Barcelona amassed 99 points, three more than Real Madrid, in a race that Barça manager Pep Guardiola called 'fucking barbaric'. To seek redress, Pérez announced that his next major off-season trade would be José Mourinho. The Portuguese man was wheeled in, lured from Inter Milan who he'd just led to the Champions League crown, the final of which was played at the Bernabéu stadium. He cost Real Madrid more than his compatriot Ronaldo's transfer fee – over £80 million, between salary for himself and his entourage and the pay-off to his predecessor.

At one stage during Carlin's year inside Real Madrid's court, he was invited to take a look at Pérez's bedchamber. Hanging on one of the walls was a framed photograph, half the size of the bed, of his first four *galáctico* purchases. Pérez stood in the middle of them, with his hands cupped out front like a boy at his First Communion. Where Mourinho, 'the *galáctico* on the bench', fits amongst the fantasies of Pérez who can tell?

José Mário dos Santos Félix Mourinho puts great store in getting into his players' heads. 'I must be a psychologist. I go inside their minds,' he once posited, promising, 'after a few months I will control them blindfolded.' Nothing, seemingly, must come in the way of the communion he shares with his players on match day. Once, while serving a pitchside ban as manager of Porto and unable to get into his team's dressing room at half-time when pitted against local rivals, Boavista, he delivered his team talk on the speaker phone of one of his assistant's mobiles.

A couple of years later, while banished from the dugout for a Champions League quarter-final clash with Chelsea against Bayern Munich, he sent a text message to one of his pitch-side lieutenants with the dreamy instruction: 'Tell the players where I am. I want them to look at me before the game.'

In this regard – his attraction for offbeat motivational techniques – he resembles Helenio Herrera. Both men managed Inter Milan. Mourinho emulated Herrera in bringing football's greatest club prize, what we now know as the Champions League title, to Inter after a 45-year gap. Herrera used to hang signs around the dressing room, prodding his players into self-reflection: 'Why not be the best?' During team talks, he'd throw a ball at each player in turn, while yelling, 'What do you think of the match? Why are we going to win?' The players had to shout back answers like, 'We'll win because we have to win.' The ploy, if it seems quaint at this remove, is nothing to his final exhortation. Holding a ball in front of the team, he'd get them to reach towards it and shout: 'It is the European Cup! We must have it! We shall have it! Ah ah ah!'

Mourinho shares several other similarities with Herrera, who, among other triumphs with various powerhouses from European club football, steered Barcelona to back-to-back league titles half a century ago. After his death, Herrera's widow published his notebooks, which are awash with his aphorisms and illustrations. Mourinho, too, is famed for his notebooks, which he has been keeping throughout his coaching career since taking charge of the youth team at Portuguese outfit, Vitória de Setúbal, in the early 1990s; in their compilation form, he refers to them as his 'Bible'. He's also a neat illustrator. During Porto's Champions League final against Monaco in 2004, before substitute Dmitri Alenitchev took the field he briefed him with an illustrated tutorial.

Herrera was enamoured with niggardly defence – his effective deployment of *catenaccio*, the stifling, 'door-bolt' system he used to grind out victories, has bewitched Italian coaches since before Mourinho was born. On arriving at Real Madrid, Mourinho's teams, remarkably, had not lost a home league match since February 2002. Mourinho, like

Herrera, has an itinerant streak. He's international in outlook. He is, of course, a polyglot; he's articulate and engaging in several languages, a rarity in a game where managers can usually only trade in the clichés and platitudes of a single tongue.

Before managing Real Madrid, Mourinho won league titles in three countries – Portugal, England and Italy. He's established himself as, arguably, the greatest manager operating in football today. He's certainly the most interesting. There's no one quite like him in the modern game. He's contrary, outlandish. He brings to mind Brian Clough, the man who led unfashionable Nottingham Forest to back-to-back European Cup glory, Derby County to a league title and Leeds United to player mutiny. Old Big 'Ead could certainly see the likeness. 'I like the look of Mourinho,' said Clough, sizing him up, shortly before he died in September 2004. 'There's a bit of the young Clough about him. For a start, he's good-looking.'

Mourinho has a raffish air, an Iberian swagger, and the smouldering looks that endear him to female fans and high-end clothing brands, most notably their lines in grey, cashmere coats. On settling into the job at Real Madrid, *Marca*, a Madrid-based newspaper, dedicated a half page to analysing the studiously casual 'Mou Knot' he uses for his ties. Celebrity sits easily with him even though, perhaps paradoxically, he's a family man. Apart from an interest in playing tennis and his eclectic collection of cars, he's consumed by his work in football.

Like Clough, too, Mourinho exudes unshakeable self-belief. He's eccentric and unpredictable in his media exchanges. He can never, it seems, resist an impish comment. There was that jibe thrown at Arsène Wenger, his rival as manager of Arsenal: 'I think he is one of these people who is a voyeur,' he said, sending the Frenchman into a spiral of apoplexy. 'There are some guys who, when they are at home, have a big telescope to see what happens in other families. He speaks, speaks, speaks about Chelsea.'

Some suggest he's a master of mind games; that his facility for winding up opponents and the grandees from football's ruling elite is some kind of premeditated plan to distract attention – and pressure – from his players.

Indeed, he cultivates the conceit himself. 'I prefer,' he remarked in an interview with the *New York Times*, 'to be, before the game and after the game, the man where all the rifles are pointed.' Nonsense. Like Clough and Herrera, he just loves the sound of his own voice. He's a rogue. In Spain, they say he's *bocazas*, big-mouthed.

But Mourinho keeps winning. He's only the third manager, alongside Ernst Happel and Ottmar Hitzfeld, to win Champions League titles with two different clubs. However, Real Madrid is no ordinary employer. The expectation of success for the manager at the club is perhaps unrivalled. When Mourinho arrived, it had just discarded ten managers in seven seasons. It's not, needless to say, unusual for football clubs these days to get rid of their coaches after a short stint. Inter Milan, for instance, ploughed through 14 managers in as many seasons before settling for Mourinho, and he only stayed around for two seasons, departing of his own accord after he'd become the first manager to win an Italian Treble.

What distinguishes Real Madrid is the petulance with which they guillotine their successful managers. Fabio Capello managed the club twice. Both times he won La Liga. Both times he got the sack, denunciations of his defensive tactical approach ringing in his ears as he departed the Spanish capital. Jupp Heynckes had to walk the plank after bringing the club the Champions League crown in 1998, its first in 32 years. His face is prone to reddening when under stress or agitated. The kink has earned him the nickname 'Osram', a reference to a lighting manufacturer from his native Germany. God knows what physical reaction the dismissal prompted in him.

Even sentiment doesn't get in the way with the kingmakers at the Bernabéu. Vicente del Bosque, who steered the club to two further Champions League titles and, of course, led Spain to World Cup glory, was sacked the day after guiding the club to a domestic league title. The news was broken to him in a Spanish TV studio by a journalist just as he was about to go on air for an interview. It was a grotty end to his 35-year association with the club as player and coach. 'Coaches,' quipped Juande Ramos, another man who briefly held the tiller at Real Madrid, 'are useful to have around – as someone to burn'.

'I see Real Madrid as a very good example of turbo capitalism,' says Miguel Aguilar. 'Companies need to have an ever-increasing rate of profit; if one year they get 25 per cent of profit, the next year they need to have 30 per cent. Real Madrid is a little bit the same. Unless it wins every single trophy every year, it's a failure. It has generated this notion partly by itself, partly through the media and partly through the supporters. You want your team to win every single game, which is not possible. Nothing is ever enough. The amount of coaches sacked after winning first-rate trophies is unparalleled. To look on as a fan, it's quite tragic.'

This is the beast that Mourinho sought to tame, a raging bull, to allude to one of the clichés peddled about Real Madrid. It's not good to win there, it's said, as it's not enough to merely kill the bull. You have to do so in style, with grace, with artistry. The performance must be *espectáculo*, a show. Mourinho is certainly a show-off, but his teams ain't necessarily so. His success is built on rigorous defence, organisation and counter-attacking, or, in the words of Jorge Valdano – a World Cupwinner with Argentina in 1986 and Real Madrid's director general and resident intellectual under Pérez – football that's like 'shit hanging from a stick' to watch. How would Mourinho reconcile his style of football with Real Madrid's *joie de vivre* tradition, which, under the Pérez regime, had become even more pronounced?

True, he arrived in a position of strength. Real Madrid hadn't won a trophy in a couple of years; they hadn't won a knockout tie in the Champions League since 2004, a period in which Barça secured two European crowns. Mourinho, shrewdly, pointed out that results would be 'the best argument to defend' himself. His appointment, surely, suggested that Pérez was allowing pragmatism to overrule romanticism, but for how long? Pérez and the Real Madrid board were fickle creatures. The club is, after all, the most confounding one in the world of football, something hinted at by Sir Alex Ferguson as his old sparring partner got down to work that summer: 'The Real Madrid job is the hardest challenge in José's career. I've spoken to José a couple of times and he's not managing a normal football club. Sometimes he's managing a circus, sometimes a fantastic outfit in terms of the quality of the football they can produce and the kind of players they always want. But it's a very difficult club to manage.'

Meanwhile, Mourinho was throwing a hostage to fortune, boldly pronouncing: 'The construction of your team must be carried out in accordance with the culture of that place. I will respect the cultural aspect at Madrid. I have an obsession to play attacking and attractive football at Madrid.' Was this hubris? He'd been prone to a bit of it lately. When the referee blew the whistle at the end of Inter's 2010 Champions League semi-final defeat of Barcelona, Mourinho was giddy. He took off on a celebratory run, wheeling around the Camp Nou's pitch, finger in the air, as if he was Achilles dragging Hector's corpse behind his chariot. Barça's infuriated goalkeeper, Víctor Valdés, tried to stop him, but was led away by a match official. Barcelona's club anthem, a screeching, triumphal number which sounds like it was taken from the same songbook as the Champions League anthem, played incongruously over the tannoy as he came to rest in front of Inter's travelling band of supporters. There was a crazed look in his eyes as he stood before them. Chagrined, the officials at the Camp Nou turned on the pitch's sprinklers to cut short the Italian club's celebrations.

Mourinho had history with Barcelona. He arrived at the club in 1996 under Sir Bobby Robson's wing, initially as his interpreter. Robson departed after a year, but Mourinho stayed on to work for his successor, Louis van Gaal, where his coaching skills began to flower, although the club's hierarchy insisted he kept his original job description. Van Gaal said that at the time even the president, the long-serving Josep Lluís Núñez, used to call Mourinho *El Traductor*, the Translator, a disparaging nickname that has stuck to him, if you're chatting to Barcelona football people.

When Frank Rijkaard left the Camp Nou in 2008, Barcelona's board chose to appoint Guardiola as manager instead of Mourinho, staying in-house, claimed Joan Laporta, the club president at the time, because it preferred 'a philosophy, not a brand'. Mourinho had been needling them over the years. Back in 2005, when he landed in Barcelona as manager of Chelsea for a Champions League tie, he let off one of his typical stink-bombs before the match, pointing out that he'd won as many European Cups – i.e. one with Porto – as Barcelona had in their entire history. It drew ire. *AS*, a Madrid-based newspaper not normally prone to defending the honour of Barça, felt compelled to address the quip in an editorial, its tone akin to the po-faced manner in which the Barcelona club often carries itself: 'Although he won many trophies in Portugal, there were too many bad manners shown to opponents and too many dirty tricks. He has continued that at Chelsea.'

Do we overestimate the commitment or bond that players or coaches have for clubs? Very few remain with one club for their entire career. Their attachment is nothing to the love experienced by lifelong, committed fans on the terraces, the hardcore Fever Pitch ones. Mourinho, for example, cantered through six clubs in his first decade of management. How much does he love his clubs? We don't know. We have an idea how much he likes to be hated by their rivals, though. He welcomes it.

'I made a point of walking on alone, before the team,' he told Luís Lourenço, his authorised biographer, about his return with Porto to Benfica, the first club he managed. 'It was fantastic, an amazing feeling. I had never been a first-class player who could feel, for example, what Figo had felt upon returning to Barcelona [with Real Madrid], and so I had no idea what it would be like to have 80,000 people whistling and jeering at me. I believe that, when we are mentally strong, those people who seek to intimidate and disturb us have exactly the opposite effect. Upon hearing the whistles and jeers... I felt as if I were the most important person in the world.'

4

MANITA

José Mourinho must have felt important on 28 November 2010. The coach he was travelling in got a good stoning from Barça hooligans. Real Madrid led Barcelona by a point at the top of the league table. The teams were set to clash the next day at the Camp Nou. Real Madrid's squad was making its way from Barcelona's international airport – where, in contrast, it had been mobbed by 2,000 besotted fans – to the Hotel Rey Juan Carlos I when it was set upon by a group of Barça thugs. Some of the Madrid press maintained that poor security facilitated the attack. A window where defensive pair Raúl Albiol and Álvaro Arbeloa was sitting was smashed, as stones and bottles hammered off the bus. A member of Real Madrid's security staff was hit in the neck. On disembarking from the bus the players had to run from the coach to the sanctuary of the hotel foyer for cover.

It was alleged that the *Boixos Nois*, Barcelona's most notorious hooligan brigade, carried out the ambush. While it's not the defining feature of their rivalry, both Barça and Real Madrid have sprouted hooligan offshoots. If you're a Real Madrid hooligan you'll most likely run with the *Ultras Sur*. Not many of them travelled to Barcelona for the match, which was controversially taking up the graveyard slot of the league's *jornada* – on Monday night of Match Day 13 – because of security fears over it being on the same day as the previous day's Catalan elections. It was the first time the tie had been on a Monday since April 1972 when Barcelona won 1–0 but still ceded the title to Real Madrid.

Of the 98,700 fans that would be in the stadium for the game perhaps only 150 or 200 would be from *Ultras Sur*, whose moves were shepherded by a large section of the 500 Barcelona police detailed for the match. It's nothing like the 1980s when the *Ultras Sur* would have wandered around without a police presence, which led to riots. Now there are police football violence units and each La Liga club has a coordinator of security that liaises with hooligan groups. It is one of the conspicuous features of La Liga matches – the minuscule number of fans who travel to support their team, owing to the vastness of Spain, regular kick-off times of 10 p.m., even midnight sometimes, and, most confounding, the fact that league fixture dates, spread from Saturday to Monday, are usually only finalised eight days beforehand.

'In Spain, they're crazy about their football,' says John Carlin. 'You've got dedicated daily football newspapers and it's the great subject of conversation. But there isn't quite that degree of fanaticism that you'd find, say, in England or Argentina. The way to illustrate that is very simple. In England, every weekend, you get these mass migrations of fans up and down the land, going to watch their teams play away. Here in Spain, it doesn't happen. You might get the odd trickle of people, but very, very few away fans at any game. Indeed, because you've got a lot of Real Madrid and Barcelona fans sprinkled around the country, you'll go to a game in Sevilla, and you'll see a pocket of Barcelona fans but they'll almost certainly be local people who happen to be Barcelona fans.

'I remember asking a friend of mine about it, a Barcelona fan. It was several years ago. He was nuts about Barcelona. It was all he ever spoke about. I said, "Do you ever go to an away game? Do you ever go to see them play against Zaragoza?" It's not very far. It's about a two-and-a-half- or three-hour drive away. He said, "No, of course not." I said, "Why?" And he said, "I've got other things to do on a Sunday." That's the thing. In England, people have really only got their football. Here, they've got namby-pamby stuff like going to lunch with their grandmothers or going for a walk by the sea. They've got other things in their lives. There isn't that same degree of rabid, all-absorbing football fanaticism here as there is in England.'

*

Michael Robinson has had an interesting second act. I met up with him in a hotel bar in Barcelona, just across the street from the Camp Nou, a few hours before the match. As a footballer in the 1980s, Robinson drifted through several clubs. His goals, including the winner in the semi-final at Highbury, helped drag Brighton, more renowned for funfairs than football, within a whisker of FA Cup glory in 1983, only to go down in a replay to Manchester United. A year later, having moved to Liverpool, he was part of the club's historic Treble-winning season. After a sojourn at QPR, he fetched up at Osasuna, the Spanish side from Pamplona, where injury forced him to retire prematurely at the age of 29. He's still in Spain, a quarter of a century after arriving.

Robinson is full of bonhomie. He sprinkles his English with Spanish phrases and has a habit of ending statements with a rhetorical 'yeah?', which is a curious inversion of many Spaniard's tendency, like Rafa Nadal, to put a 'no?' at the end of their sentences when they're speaking English. Maybe it's a sign of the innate optimism that has served Robinson so well. Through his irreverent, matey style of broadcasting he's become a national icon in Spain. He's known as Robín. He's done voiceovers in the dubbed Spanish version of the *Shrek* movies. For years, his rubber double adorned the front of the country's *Spitting Image* show. And as the presenter for 14 years of the weekly review show *El Día Después* (The Day After) his journalistic eye for a good, offbeat story delighted the football-mad Spanish public, even though he initially secured the gig despite only having, he says, 100 words in Spanish, 90 of which were expletives. These days, he fronts a show called Informe Robinson, an award-winning sports magazine programme, where his guest for a half-hour interview at the start of the season was José Mourinho.

'He's very chameleonic,' said Robinson. 'I know José quite well and I find him to be a very charming man, a very warm man, a kind man; then all of a sudden you see this public figure. The game starts for him when he does his press conference before the game and finishes after the post-match press conference. He tries to distract attention from the players and irritate the others.

'For example, in society, normally, we all want to have a go at some-body, *todos quieren cagarse en los demás* – everyone wants to shit on somebody. When Mourinho was manager at Chelsea, nobody would want to have a go at Frankie Lampard or John Terry, they'd want to have a go at Mourinho. The players are almost free of sin. Strangely enough, the players win for him, but he loses, to make sure that the players are always insulated.

'In that interview, I said to him: "Your wife fell in love with José Mourinho about 20-odd years ago. Is she also in love with The Special One?" He said, "No, no, no. She detests The Special One and so do my kids and so do I sometimes when I see myself on the television, silencing Liverpool's supporters in a League Cup final, falling down on my knees at the Camp Nou when we scored a goal with Chelsea. There are things I shouldn't do and I don't like watching myself on television, but it's my work, and my work is to create the best atmosphere that serves my football teams."'

Nobody seems to be able to fathom Mourinho. The Spanish public is desperate to get to the nub of his contrary ways. Four weeks earlier, Real Madrid travelled to Alicante to play Hércules, who were hovering over the relegation zone, at the Rico Pérez stadium. It was Halloween weekend. After the match, four pieces of scrunched-up paper were salvaged by the away team's dugout. They were from Mourinho's notebook. There were notes scrawled like 'depth, dead balls, switch wings'. There were initials. Maybe they corresponded to players – DM (Ángel di María); XA (Xabi Alonso); K (Sami Khedira). One note mentioned ten months, which corresponds to the length of a football season. Another listed numbers like 38. Real Madrid plays 38 league games a year. The papers were spirited to the studios of *El Día Después*, Michael Robinson's old show on Canal Plus television. They were pored over by a psychologist and a handwriting expert. What could they tell us? Mourinho is 'a strong, decisive character'; he has an 'astonishing capacity for leadership,' the experts told us. He is a 'good man', a 'noble' man.

Not everyone agrees. Two weeks later, Real Madrid travelled up to the Cantabrian coast in the north-west of Spain to play Sporting de Gijón, the home team of Asturias. Mourinho was not welcome in the Molinón, home to one of Spain's most feared set of fans. He'd raised their hackles by having a go at Manolo Preciado, their manager. The tête-à-tête went back to September when Sporting de Gijón took the field without eight normal starters against Barcelona at the Camp Nou and lost 1–0. 'Look,' said Preciado in despair at the time, 'you need to understand algebra to beat this Barcelona side.' Mourinho fumed, claiming Sporting de Gijón should be punished for rolling over. Preciado, a man comfortable fondling a microphone, let it go.

But when Mourinho raised the subject again on a radio interview on the Thursday before their encounter, Preciado opened up. 'In September I thought he'd just got it wrong but then I hear him again and not only does he not take it back, he goes and extends it. If no one at Real Madrid is going to tell this bloke how to behave, I will. Who the fuck does he think he is to say things like that? Who does he think he is to say that about a team like us: a humble side that fights to the very last to stay in the top flight? Well, we might be poor but we're not idiots. He is a bad colleague, egotistical. He is a *canalla*.'

A *canalla* is a swine, a creep. As it happened, Mourinho was serving a two-match ban for abusing a referee in a *Copa del Rey* match, so he had to take up his seat in a VIP box for the match against Sporting de Gijón. He was abused by hometown fans outside its glass windows: '*¡Ese portugués, hijo puta es!*' – That Portuguese, he's a son of a bitch – they chanted. He mightn't have been able to hear them, but if he could read Asturian, polyglot that he is, one of the banners in the stands was telling him: 'Mourinho, don't you come here and wind people up.' Real Madrid stole a late goal to win 1–0. Mourinho made his way to his coach flanked by three security staff. He took up his seat in one of the front rows, casually flipping two fingers to screaming Sporting de Gijón fans as the bus pulled away.

*

It wasn't always this way for Real Madrid's managers when they toured the Spanish backwaters. Born in Perafita, Catalonia in 1958, Ramón Besa is a doyen of Spanish football writing. In the past, he says, Real Madrid would be fêted by smaller, regional teams in Spain when they visited their stadiums, from Almeria to Zaragoza. It was like the circus coming to town. The locals would be entertained by Real Madrid's sumptuous, attacking style of play served up by some of the world's greatest football stars. Now, with Mourinho at the helm, busy needling people wherever he went, they're maligned. In fact, in October 2011, an *AS/* Ikerfel study found that there was less aversion to Real Madrid at Barça than at several of Spain's other clubs, with higher rates of hate coming from, among others, Osasuna, Athletic de Bilbao and Real Sociedad.

Historically, Barcelona has always been identified by its manager. One thinks of Helenio Herrera in the 1950s, the man who preached *catenaccio*, the dour, defensive system; Dutchman Rinus Michels, the godfather of its free-flowing antithesis of Total Football in the early 1970s; César Luis Menotti, Argentina's 1978 World Cup-winning coach and bon vivant who used to schedule training sessions for 3 o'clock in the afternoon, the better to allow him time to recover from the rigours of Barcelona's nightlife; and, of course, Johan Cruyff, who still pontificates about club affairs from the wings.

Unlike Barça, Real Madrid's managers have always lived in the shadows. In *Casa Madrid*, they've occupied a little backroom, illustrated for me in a comical pencil drawing by Besa, sandwiched between larger presences like the president, his directors and the club's *galáctico* footballers. 'What is the name of the Real Madrid manager?' asks Besa in mock confusion. 'Nobody knows.' Now everybody knows. Mourinho is the face of the club, to the extent that some call it Real Moudrid.

Tonight in the latest edition of *El Clásico*, he returns to the club that nurtured his fledgling coaching career in the late 1990s, a fact recalled to us in the TV run-up to the game by the continually looped film of his oratorical flourish to Barcelona fans at the Plaça de Sant Jaume in 1997 after a *Copa del Rey* victory. It was the first of four years Mourinho spent at the club as a translator-cum-assistant coach. Clutching the microphone on a balcony, his breast aflutter, he gasped: 'Today, tomorrow and always I have Barcelona in my heart.'

As for his reception, Charly Rexach, a former Barça coach and player, reckoned it would be worse than Figo's in 2002. Mourinho, nonetheless, arrived in imperious mood. Real Madrid were unbeaten to date; Mourinho having recorded the best start by a new coach in La Liga's history. Mourinho reckoned Barcelona was 'obsessed' with him; chief among their grievances, he mentioned, was that he foiled their chances to lift the Champions League crown at the Bernabéu the previous season. If they were preoccupied with him, Pep Guardiola, Barcelona's manager, wasn't showing the signs, having refused to be drawn by any of the controversies orbiting his Portuguese counterpart since the season's start.

Besides, there was so much to conjure with on the pitch. Had an early season league match ever attracted so much excitement? The international press were swooning at the thought of it. In France, *L'Equipe*, not normally given to hyperbole, had christened it, 'The Match of the Year.' It was, after all, lending a stage to 13 World Cup winners. Also on view would be Lionel Messi and Cristiano Ronaldo, who after 12 league games had scored 13 and 14 goals respectively, both having bagged hat-tricks in their latest league outings.

As to the pair's competing merits, Michael Robinson made a distinction. 'I think Messi's a far better player,' he said. 'Nobody can deny Ronaldo's absolute brilliance, but I think there are moments where he becomes an exhibitionist. Sometimes he's not sure who he's playing for – himself or Real Madrid. If you're to look at his qualities, there isn't anything that he hasn't got, but sometimes he doesn't apply them in the right manner.

'I think anything that Messi does has got a collective reason behind it. For example, tonight will be one of those typical nights, I think, whereby we know how Messi's going to play, but we're not too sure how Ronaldo's gonna play. Will he get the ball and try and dribble past the linesman in front of the stand, saying, "Look at me. Look at me?" He plays with a great conflict of interest: "Fuck, have I got to play for the team? Can I just do it all on my own?"'

Later that evening, across the street from the hotel where Michael Robinson was staying, a cadre of Barcelona's most vociferous fans gathered outside a street corner pub, drinking cans of Estrella Damm, the local Pilsener brew. It was cold, maybe 6 or 7°C with a light drizzle of rain. A police wagon was stationed nearby. Draped on a railing across from them, there was a banner, made up in white cloth with a cartoon image of a Casper-type ghost squeezing between a do-not-pass road sign, under which was written '*FantasMOU fora del Camp Nou*', Ghost get out of Camp Nou, with a play on Mourinho's name to, er, spook him.

Many of the fans were draped in flags, either St George's flags or Catalan national flags, tossed over their shoulders like an old woman's shawl. Sant Jordi, St George, is Catalonia's patron saint; the St George's cross adorns the club's crest. At matches in the Camp Nou, it's always a feature to see a St George's flag with its striking red cross on a white field billowing in the stands. Many of the Catalan national flags have black donkeys superimposed on the yellow-and-red stripes. A breed of Catalan donkey was co-opted decades ago as the region's emblem, in marked contrast, obviously, to the bull that is synonymous with Madrid. During the summer when bullfighting was banned in Catalonia, *El País* ran an editorial cartoon with a Spanish bull saying to a Catalan donkey, '*Muchas gracias*', to which the donkey replied '*De res*,' Catalan for 'Not at all'.

The fans let off loud bangers every few minutes. Flares, too, seemed to be screeching into life constantly. Fans are no longer allowed to release flares in stadiums in Spain. They belted out their favourite chant, coordinated by a ringleader who wielded a loudspeaker. One, '*Madrid se quema, se quema Madrid*,' wanted Madrid to burn, baby, burn. For theatrics, at one stage, a poster of Mourinho was torched ceremoniously, while fans circled the embers, dancing manically. Another song, '*Mourinho y Ronaldo se enculen en Montjuïc*,' suggested that Real Madrid's most prominent Portuguese staff members were in *flagrante delicto* on the hill overlooking Barcelona.

It wasn't long to kick-off. The Camp Nou was only a few hundred yards away. Over 50 years old at this stage, it's not a particularly imposing edifice. The structure is hewn from a brownish-grey stone. It's almost drab, nothing compared to the grandeur of the Santiago Bernabéu, Real Madrid's ground, as seen from the outside; nor does it have the breathless elegance of a more modern stadium like the Stade de France in Paris. Its underwhelming facade catches you off guard, though. I had been to the Camp Nou several times at this stage but still got a tingle as I emerged from the bowels of the stadium to take up my seat. It is such an impressive coliseum within, especially when lit up on a cold, dark night. There's something about the way its five tiers seem to reach so high, with a swirl, towards the sky.

The house was full, needless to say, one of only four or five times a year that the Camp Nou is at capacity. It can be a frigid place to watch football, where it is said people wait like at the opera for a high note, but not on a night like tonight. The players came onto the pitch for the first time about 30 minutes before kick-off, went through a few warm-up drills and then returned to the calm of the dressing rooms. They got ready to re-emerge five minutes before kick-off. I could see them in the tunnel across from me, some, like Xabi Alonso and Xavi, international teammates with Spain but rivals on the night, exchanged hugs with each other.

As they ran out onto the pitch, Barcelona's jingoist anthem played over the PA system, while fans, almost 100,000 people, reached for the glossy sheets of red, yellow or blue paper that had been left on their seats beforehand and pointed them skywards, transforming the stadium into a flowerbed for the gods. Cristiano Ronaldo, one of their representatives on earth, if you were to believe the Madrid tabloid press, received an awkward pass from Sergio Ramos in the game's first passage of play. He was right in front of me. With the rain spitting and a greasy playing surface, he failed to control the ball, which slipped out for a throw. Cue a barrage of abuse.

The last time I was at a comparable derby match was in Glasgow on a cold night in November 1996. Rangers, bastion of British Unionism, were coming across the city to play at Celtic Park. The atmosphere was visceral; what I imagined it to be like at a stoning. Paul Gascoigne, Rangers' star player at the time, had married that summer, but the marriage had already gone awry. Beside me, before the match had kicked-off, a father stood up and broke into song. His son, who couldn't have been much more than eight or nine years of age, stood beside him, aping him, swaying backwards and forwards on his hind legs, thrusting his arm forward in universal football chanting mode, belting out the words of the latest terrace ditty: 'He beats his wife. He beats his wife. Ga-zza beats his wife!'

Here again, in a different country many years later, were the same decibels of vitriol, if lacking a bit of the seething, primal edge in the air that night in Glasgow. There were no kids around me, so there was none of the parent role-modelling that was on display at Celtic Park. Instead the Barça fans in my orbit were men in their twenties and thirties, well-heeled by the looks of it. They launched into chants at Ronaldo's sloppy ball control: '*¡Ese portugués, hijo puta es!*' What a noise. I remember Justin Webster telling me from his experience of filming pitch-side that the volume of noise on the pitch is markedly higher than if you're sitting in the stands. For the players, he said, it's like playing in a wall of sound.

Five minutes later, Messi, with his second touch of the ball in the match, tried a sneaky lob from the edge of the box, which grazed a post. A few minutes later, Ronaldo received the ball on the wing and proceeded to goad Puyol with, from my count, six step-overs. Puyol lost his footing; Ronaldo crossed to Ángel di María on the edge of the box, but his long-range shot at goal was a lame one. On the ten-minute mark, Andrés Iniesta broke free down the left-hand flank, carried the ball forward, switched inside before steadying himself enough to carve open the Real Madrid defence with a cross-field ball to Xavi. The faintest of touches by Pepe, vainly trying to intercept it, meant that the ball arrived behind Xavi, bouncing off his heel and fortuitously flipping up into the air in front of him, allowing him to execute a cheeky little volley over Iker Casillas for the game's first goal.

It wasn't long until the second one came. For over a minute, Barcelona passed the ball this way and that among themselves, in their trademark possession-style of football. They were like a cat toying with a mouse, before Xavi switched play from the right side of the pitch to David Villa wide on the left. He skipped past Sergio Ramos, and crossed to Pedro, who tapped in from close range.

Some minutes later, Pedro was in the middle of a 21-man mêlée over by the dugouts, following a push by Ronaldo on Pep Guardiola for peevishly not giving him the ball when it slipped out of play and into Guardiola's arms. During the bout of handbags, it emerged later, Ronaldo challenged Pedro, 'And who are you?' the Portuguese man asked the World Cup-winner. On the cusp of half-time, Messi made a dart with the ball at his feet from his deep-lying position in midfield towards the Real Madrid goal, but his path was impeded by Ricardo Carvalho who upended him with a clatter. Messi got up, nestled his diminutive frame into the back of Carvalho in some kind of protest or challenge. Carvalho raised his arm to shoo him away, which prompted Messi to fall to the ground theatrically. The ref was wise to his antics and gave Messi a yellow card for play-acting. It was the fifth yellow card the ref doled out in a stormy first half. The game had been at full throttle; although, noticeably, it didn't have the mindless, unending slide-tackling you'd get in a Celtic v. Rangers or Liverpool v. Man United game. But maybe that's because Real Madrid didn't seem to be able to get near enough to land any studs on Barcelona.

In a three-minute flurry shortly after half-time, two more goals sailed in for Barcelona, both of them were facsimiles of each other – Messi delivering slide rule passes through the defence to an on-rushing Villa who finished coolly, the second one a delightful, single touch that slid between Casillas' legs.

Mourinho, normally so conspicuous, was nowhere to be seen. Instead of prowling the touchline, issuing sign-language instructions to the ref or playing ballboy, he remained bunkered in his trench. All around the stadium, the chant went up: '*Mourinho sal del banquillo*' – Mourinho, come out of the dugout. This pleased Ramón Besa, he told me later. He said that fans of football in Spain are normally quite earnest, that their chants tend to be dour and militant. Lately they've been getting a sense of humour, he said, like their British counterparts. The humour extends to childishness. At several intervals during the match, the whole stadium, which was, of course, made up nearly entirely of Barcelona supporters, started jumping up and down, as though on pogo sticks, as they sang a familiar terrace refrain: 'Bounce, bounce, bounce; a *madridista* doesn't bounce.'

There were no laughs, no silly bouncing for Mourinho, though. At one stage, he was caught on camera pleading it seemed with Mahamadou Diarra, the Malian defensive midfielder who he had rarely been used up to that point in the season, to go on as a substitute. Diarra, who clearly recognised a sinking ship when he saw it, was in no mood to pointlessly bail water, and told Mourinho as much, refusing to go on. After the game, Real Madrid officials disputed the claim of insubordination, maintaining the pair was 'debating' tactics. A look at the incident on YouTube would suggest otherwise.

A minute into injury time, the final ignominy was delivered. Bojan Krkić, on as a substitute, crossed from the left side straight into the path of Jeffrén Suárez, another sub, who popped it into the goal. It was 5–0, a *manita* – a little hand. Gerard Piqué's hand, with his fingers opened and spread apart, was raised. Víctor Valdés did likewise. Within seconds almost a hundred thousand hands are raised, fingers spread, in solidarity.

The last time Barcelona administered a *manita* in a Madrid–Barça game was in 1994, courtesy of a Romário hat-trick, the first of which was his famous 'cow's tail' goal, one that's endlessly played on television reels on Catalan TV. There were three others – in 1935, 1945 and 1974, the latter the famous raid on the Bernabéu led by Johan Cruyff, who was looking on from the stands for this one. Real Madrid also, memorably, came a cropper by 5–0 in the semi-final of the European Cup against Milan in 1989. After that match, Silvio Berlusconi, Milan's president and future Italian prime minister, visited the vanquished Real Madrid team's dressing room and got the players to hold hands while he delivered a consolation speech. What a guy – that Berlusconi fellow, eh? What words could Pep Guardiola, who has a *manita* of his own, having won the first five of his Madrid–Barça matches as manager, possibly have to sooth them?

There was a grubby epilogue to proceedings. In the third minute of injury time, Sergio Ramos hacked down Messi as he broke from midfield. It was a particularly ugly scythe from the side, a wild boot aimed just below Messi's knee, who toppled as if he'd been standing on a chair that was pulled from under him. Another mass quarrel ensued. Sergio Ramos was given his marching orders. He had just become the most sent-off player in Real Madrid's history, a noteworthy achievement given he was still only 24 years of age.

The plaudits rang out afterwards. Watching on TV in his living room, Manchester United star Wayne Rooney stood up and applauded. When the Barça players got to their dressing room, they also gave themselves a standing ovation. For Ramón Besa, writing for *El País*, goals fell at Camp Nou 'like autumn leaves: naturally, beautifully and serenely.' *Sport's* cartoonist, instead of a drawing, simply scanned his hand on the newspaper's back page. *Marca*, usually notoriously pro-Madrid, conceded that Barcelona 'were too MOUch' for the opposition.

Barcelona's play was transcendent. We were spellbound. Had we seen anything like it before? They were, after all, playing against the most expensively assembled team in history, a team that were unbeaten in 20 games. Barcelona seemed to be playing a different game. Their passing was so smooth, so simple, so assured, their possession football wired by telepathic cables. 'They could have played with two balls,' reckoned Roberto Palomar, another famous Spanish footballing scribe, 'and

Barcelona would have controlled both.' Barça, remarkably, completed 636 passes, compared to Real Madrid's 279.

Mourinho, who had just recorded his biggest ever defeat as a manager, passed through his press conference quickly, although, incorrigibly, he had time for one dig before disappearing into the night, alluding to a heavy defeat he had suffered in the Champions League at the Camp Nou 12 months previously with his former club. 'Last season,' he said, 'I lost here with Inter before returning for the semi-final. We were the ones who reached the final – they watched it on television.'

His employers weren't as sanguine. Florentino Pérez, Real Madrid's president, felt it was 'the worst defeat in the history of the club,' troubling words for Mourinho, given Pérez once fired six coaches in three years. Jorge Valdano, the club's director general, was more specific. 'He couldn't bring a major correction to the game,' he said, railing against Mourinho's tactical inertia, before taking a swipe at his lack of courage: 'Today he didn't even leave the bench.'

Valdano was recalled in 2009 to the club by Pérez as his presidential aide, and was leant on for his greater football acumen. He was a World Cup-winner with Argentina in 1986. He finished up his playing career with Real Madrid and served as the club's manager in the mid-1990s. Known for his intellectualism – some call Valdano *El Filósofo*, The Philosopher – he writes and talks lyrically about football. Back in his playing days with Real Madrid in the 1980s, he once penned a column for *El País* that was critical of US policy in Central America. Footballers aren't known for ruminating on affairs of foreign policy. There is another side to Valdano though. While in charge of player transfers during his first stretch working as a director for Pérez, the players used to call him 'Dr Death' for his merciless streak. Mourinho would have taken note of his salvo, especially as it wasn't the first time he'd been critical of The Special One's management style.

5

IS THAT ALL THERE IS?

Lluís is in his mid-thirties. He's from Barcelona. He first went to see Barça play when he was five or six years of age. His dad, who has been a *socio* for over 50 years, took him. Lluís has been to many of Europe's great stadiums on the trail of Barça. He's hardly missed a home game in 20 years. He pays less than £270 for his season ticket. The reason it's such a good deal is because his seat is crap. It's behind the goal at the south end. Photographers and security personnel obscure his view of the play. Unless the ball is airborne, he can't see it. Often he'll only know if a goal has been scored when the belly of the monster erupts. But he loves it. He spends the 90 minutes of a match on his hooves trying to sing above the drumbeats of his mate beside him. The only downer is the other Barça fans.

'I can understand that people from Madrid hate us,' he says. 'Or that the police – who are supposed to protect us – hate us, but what I can't understand is that I don't feel good cheering on my own team because I'm worried that I will be attacked by [other] Barcelona fans. Even talking to you now is very dangerous for me.'

Barça is unique in football circles for the balkanisation of its core support. Barcelona's hooligan element differs from Real Madrid's – and other Spanish clubs – in that it is splintered. It's rare on the international hooligan scene, too, to have the level of intra-group conflict that you have in Barcelona's ranks. Its old-guard band of hooligans from the 1980s fragmented and declined, allowing new subgroups to rise up to fill the vacuum it left behind. These include *Supporters Puyol*, named after Carles Puyol, Barcelona's shaggy-haired centre-half. It's hard not to like Puyol. It takes a certain self-possession and a sense of humour to go about your day with a mullet like his. Apparently, he still didn't know the name of David Beckham's wife, Victoria, or Vicky as the Spanish tabloid magazines call her, a year into Beckham's Spanish adventure with Real Madrid. He's been captain of Barça since 2004. There are others such as *Grup Fidel*, founded in 2004, and the *ICC*, or *Inter City Culés*, who are styled after the Inter City Firm, West Ham's feared hooligan outfit from the 1970s. Spanish hooligans revere the longer, more violent history of their British counterparts. Initially, *ICC* travelled to away matches by train, in keeping with the Inter City Firm's mandated mode of transport, but they've lapsed in this practice.

The *Boixos Nois* are the most notorious of the lot. The group was founded in 1981. Their logo is a snarling English bulldog. At their inaugural assembly, 'Crazy Boys' was agreed as a name for their gang, but whoever recorded the meeting's minutes misspelt *bojos* (Catalan for 'crazy') as *boixos*, which means 'boxwood' – the close-grained wood of the box tree that is used to make tool handles. At an emergency session to discuss the mistake it was agreed to hold onto the misspelt name for its craziness.

Ideologically, the *Boixos Nois* is an unlikely alliance of Catalan separatists and Spanish 'Casuals', who are particularly neo-fascist and racist. Individual members' ideologies swing wildly across the political spectrum. They're often constructed on threadbare beliefs, as much the result of fashion as rigorous thinking and conviction. Bedroom posters of Che Guevara are replaced by those of Adolf Hitler on a whim. 'There have been some remarkable transformations,' said a former *Boixos Nois* member to Ramón Spaaij, a Dutch sociologist who spent several years embedded with football hooligans in Europe. 'Left-wing fans have transformed into right-wing skinheads overnight. I have photographs of people with swastikas who were left-wing separatists before.' The political incoherence of the *Boixos Nois* contrasts with the *Ultras Sur*, Real Madrid's main hooligan group, whose members all dwell happily on the right wing of the asylum.

The *Boixos Nois* put aside their superficial political differences whenever they're on the road for Barça matches. 'When they go to other stadiums, they stay together,' says Carles Viñas, a historian at the University of Barcelona who has written several books on skinheads and is a go-to guy for the press whenever there's a flare-up in the hooligan world. 'They say, "Don't worry – now we are all from Barça. No politics. You are safe."' Their sense of Barça solidarity doesn't extend, however, to fellow Barça fan groups. They terrorise the few hundred Barcelona supporters that occasionally travel for matches, as much as rival clubs' fans.

Until 2003, Barcelona's management condoned the dire behaviour of the *Boixos Nois*. Barça's president at the time, Joan Gaspart, was fond of saying he would join the *Boixos Nois* once he stepped down. The club doled out money and free tickets as well as subsidising their travel in exchange for the promise of good behaviour and their vociferous support. However, Joan Laporta, a young, politically ambitious lawyer who became Barça president that year, banned them from the stadium, a move that incurred their wrath. He received death threats. They painted graffiti outside his house – gun sights on the wall, with the words 'located' and 'we'll kill you' written on the pavement. He was also manhandled by seven of them in a car park in February 2004 when they attempted to engage him for a summit meeting. In the middle of being called a son of a bitch, among other insults, their leader asked Laporta why he wouldn't talk to the *Boixos Nois*. Laporta, who managed to escape in his car, later said that he was perplexed by the question. 'I didn't know this guy was their president,' said Laporta. 'I just thought he was mad.'

A number of the *Boixos Nois* were jailed in 2010 for extortion and drug trafficking. Ramón Spaaij spent six years studying football hooligan groups in England, the Netherlands and Spain. These days he lives in Melbourne, Australia. His latest project has been on the use of sport to help give kids from disadvantaged areas a leg-up socially. After several years as an anthropologist in football's swamplands, he says he's content again to be out on sunnier terrain. He travelled to matches with Barcelona fans at the time the *Boixos Nois* were thrown out of their temple.

Because of the clampdown, the infighting amongst Barça fans esca-lated, especially at away games within driving distance of Barcelona, at grounds such as Zaragoza, Valencia, Levante and, of course, Espanyol. Barcelona's fans, about 400 or 500 of them, would be corralled into the away section of these grounds, at the mercy of the *Boixos Nois*. He describes a typical experience from Barcelona's league match at Zaragoza in 2004: 'A small group of the *Boixos Nois*' Casuals pushed their way into the ground without having tickets. They basically trespassed. They pushed through just when the game was about to start; when there was low security – one steward, one policeman at the gate. They beat up the steward. Then they ran up to the terrace. What were the police going to do? Go into the terrace? They just let it go. Because it was late, the away section was full. In that really macho way, they pushed their way through and bashed a few people, fans of Barça. They stole their flags and banners. Basically saying: "We're here. We're the boss."

'There was very little regard for other Barcelona fans. It typified how polarised the Barcelona fan group had become. You'd expect that a fan group is quite unified and if violence does erupt it might be between, say, fans of Barcelona and Real Madrid, but what I saw in reality is that any fighting was amongst factions of the same club, who might be polit-ically aligned with either right-wing or left-wing extremism or might be heavily involved in crime. For many young fans, it was a reason not to go to away matches anymore. For example, the Real Madrid away game, Barcelona fan groups wouldn't go to the same section as other Barcelona fans. Once I went to Real Madrid v. Barcelona and one of the Barcelona *peñas* had seats with the Real Madrid fans. They preferred to sit in the home section than in the away section.'

Like many European clubs, such as Sporting Lisbon, Partizan Belgrade and Olympiakos, Barcelona is a multi-sport organisation. It has teams in 13 disciplines in total, from athletics to volleyball. As well as football, the club has professional teams in four other sports: basketball, *futsal* (indoor football), handball and roller hockey. These other teams play in the Palau Blaugrana, which is located opposite the museum in the grounds of the Camp Nou stadium.

Disillusioned by the behaviour of the *Boixos Nois*, a number of prominent Barça supporters clubs, most notably *Dracs 1991* and *Sang Culé* who both began life following the club's football team, gravitated towards its smaller arenas for refuge. Now *Dracs 1991*, for example, follows Barcelona's basketball and *futsal* teams, although members still support the football team on an individual basis. They took with them their fantastic *tifo* culture, a feature of Spanish football matches that was borrowed in the 1980s from the terraces of Italy, which involves choreographed fireworks (now banned from stadiums), singing and flag- and scarf-waving. They spend their weekends at Palau Blaugrana whose stands they turn into a Mardi Gras during matches.

Basketball is Spain's second most popular sport and its two greatest rivals are... guess who? Barça and Real Madrid. The Madrid side has won a record 30 Spanish basketball league titles, including a ten-in-a-row, but Barça are matching them lately. Barcelona won, for example, the 2010 Euroleague final in Paris. The last of Real Madrid's record eight titles in basketball's equivalent of the Champions League came in 1995.

Basketball, however, is the only other sport that Real Madrid plays as well as football. Several of Spain's native sons operate in the NBA, including Pau Gasol, the LA Lakers All-Star power forward, and Marc, his younger brother by five years. The pair signed their first professional contracts at FC Barcelona, their hometown team. The Gasols are not the only famous set of basketball-playing brothers to emerge from Spain. Fernando Martín was the first Spanish player to play in the NBA. He was drafted in the mid-1980s, but returned to his old club Real Madrid after a single, injury-hampered season with the Portland Trail Blazers. He died in a car crash in December 1989. Real Madrid retired his No. 10 jersey out of respect. A few weeks after his death, his younger brother Antonio, who played for 12 seasons with Real Madrid, turned out for the club against Barcelona in a game at the Palau Blaugrana. Barcelona's arena was a tight, 6,000-seater at the time.

'Where is your brother?' went up the chant whenever he got time on the ball.

Toni Valle is chairman of *Dracs 1991*. He's 45 years of age. He's a big hulk of a man with an infectious, throaty laugh. I met him at *Dracs 1991*'s clubhouse, which is in the Les Corts barrio in the north west of Barcelona, not far from the Camp Nou. From the outside, the clubhouse looks like a derelict, boarded-up, street-level dwelling. Inside, it's full of life. Its walls are strewn with framed photographs and racks of old match programmes; and draped, of course, with big Barça and Catalan flags. The front room has a bar counter.

Toni was born in Barcelona but lives in a village about 20 kilometres from the city these days. He's an old gunslinger whose six-shooter is on a shelf somewhere gathering dust. In his youth, he trucked around the cities of Europe following Cruyff's Dream Team, taking in the club's European finals in Rotterdam, London and Athens in the early 1990s. A decade earlier, as a penniless teenager, he often used to blag free match tickets from older fans; while to get around Spain for Barça's away matches he'd avail himself of the free seating on the floor of whatever bus was chartered. During those days he reckons he visited the Bernabéu about ten times. Without security to separate fans, they were helter-skelter affairs.

'Fifty of us went to the Bernabéu by bus one time,' he says. 'We were in the middle of one terrace when Real Madrid's fans started to throw bottles and stones at us. To defend ourselves, we huddled together in a circle and took off our belts from our pants and started swinging them like lassoes. It was the only way that we could keep them away from us. We couldn't watch the match. We spent half it swinging our belts in the air or trying to kick them back when they charged at us until the police arrived.'

The tables were turned for return fixtures at the Camp Nou. Before matches, Toni and his mates used to wait in the long grass on the outskirts of the city. They'd station themselves on the ridges of the city's highways and, once a Real Madrid bus was spotted, they'd pelt it with missiles until it stopped. Their objective was to make it turn around and head back to Madrid. They picked their targets carefully. There were clear rules of engagement, he says. 'We met the leader of Real Madrid's hooligan group. We knew him. We used to phone each other before going to a match. We never went after fans that weren't from a rival hooligan group.'

The 1980s, he says, was when the fighting was hardest between rival fans. In Franco's days, it was unthinkable that there would be any group violence between fans. In the 1990s, there was a crackdown on hooliganism and fighting between opposing fan groups, with the ushering in of increased police surveillance and security measures. 'Now there's a calmer atmosphere at the Camp Nou so it's better,' he says. 'It's a family show.'

Almogàvers was founded in 1989; it takes its name from a thirteenth-century platoon of Catalan mercenaries, although they're a non-violent Barça supporters' club. They're in it for the singing. A group of its members travelled by bus to the Bernabéu stadium in May 2002 for Barcelona's Champions League semi-final second leg tie against their greatest rivals. The journey between the two cities took them about eight hours. But it seemed worth it, as it had been over 40 years since the two sides had met in European competition, and this one was in Real Madrid's centenary year. In the first leg at the Camp Nou, played on St George's Day, Real Madrid won 2-0. Both Zinedine Zidane and Steve McManaman lobbing Barça's keeper to score.

In the afternoon before the match, ETA, the Basque terrorist group, exploded a car bomb on Paseo de la Castellana, the avenue that leads up to the Bernabéu stadium. It went off at 4.55 p.m. Six people were injured. The bomb blast was so close to the stadium that, according to press reports, the Real Madrid trophy room was damaged. Real Madrid's *Ultras Sur*, the club's hooligan posse, were on an assortment of manoeuvres. They attacked a CNN TV crew and hospitalised a photographer from *El Periódico de Cataluña*. The match represented a unique security threat for the police as there were between 2,000 and 3,000 Barça fans travelling for the match, ten times the number of *culés* who would normally make the trek for a *clásico* encounter in Madrid.

It was the third – and final – time that Albert Yarza, Almogàvers' president, visited the Bernabéu stadium for a Barça match. He was 28 years of age at the time. 'I won't go back there again,' he says. 'It's like going into the wolf's mouth.' On arrival in Madrid, they met up with the rest of Barça's fans at Plaza de Castilla in the centre of the city. 'The police kept us there until they said that it was time to go to the stadium,' says Albert. 'They said they'll bring everybody in two buses because it was the best way to get there. When they said this, I thought: the police are intelligent people; they are avoiding problems. I suppose they have prepared a safe way to arrive. I couldn't believe it then when I saw we had one police van in front of us and another one behind. We only had six cops to shepherd us! So then I thought maybe they had prepared something like a security zone, but when we were nearer the stadium I saw a lot of people from Madrid. The police had the siren turned on, too, alerting our presence to all these fans.

'The *Ultras Sur* were waiting for us. They threw stones, bottles, batteries, chairs and tables from *terrazas*, potted plants. Inside the bus we found a stapler, paper cutters… It was a terrible moment. Can you imagine? We were sitting ducks. It was very stressful. We were lying on the floor. We had no windows left on the bus. I was angriest with the police – I couldn't understand how they got it so wrong. Finally we arrived to our gate. There were police there on horseback, but everything was a mess.'

Getting from the bus inside the ground was another ordeal. 'The door of the bus opened,' says Carles Viñas, who travelled to the match with *Almogàvers*. 'I could see a policeman about 10 or 20 metres away at the door of the stadium saying, "Come on. Come on." I made a dash for it, sheltering a child as I ran.'

Not that the ground was a safe haven – there was no separation between Barça's block of fans and the rest of Real Madrid's support. During the match, one of Barça's fans threw a flare at Real Madrid's fans.

The police responded by charging at Barça's fans with batons. Viñas remembers taking cover with two Barça hooligans, the three of them huddled briefly together. The game finished in a 1–1 draw, which meant that Real Madrid progressed to the final, 3–1 on aggregate. Barça's fans were kept in the stadium for two hours afterwards before it was deemed safe for them to leave. Sorting out the bus home was the next headache for the *Almogàvers* crew.

'I remember,' says Viñas, 'one of the people from the bus company said that there would be no problem – that he had talked with an official and that they had arranged a hotel for us and a replacement bus to take us back to Barcelona in the morning. But after the match the police felt it would be safer to just leave straight away rather than just wandering around the stadium. They said: "We finish our shift in two minutes, go to Barcelona." It was incredible. We arrived back in Barcelona with only two panes of glass intact from the windows on the bus.'

I spoke to Antonio Salas on the phone one morning. He sounded tinny, as if the line was mangled. He was using voice-scrambling software. Antonio Salas is a pseudonym. Apparently if you dig deep enough around the bowels of the internet you can find his real name. He's Spanish and in his mid-thirties. He's an investigative reporter of the extreme kind. He was circumcised for his last undercover gig. The procedure left him sorer than anticipated, rendering him 'pretty delicate' for his first few days post-op. He got trimmed as part of his cover for the five years he spent investigating radical Islamic terrorists. During this time he befriended Carlos the Jackal and got him to confess on tape to some of the 82 murders he's believed to have carried out.

As well as infiltrating international terrorist groups and prostitute rings, Salas spent a year as a would-be hooligan with the *Ultras Sur*. It was part of an investigation into Spain's Hammerskins, a branch of the international white supremacist group. He produced a TV documentary and best-selling book, *Diary of a Skin*, which was first published in 2003, about his experiences of this netherworld of skinheads and football hooligans. To establish credibility, he shaved his head, wised up on neo-Nazi literature and went by the nickname Tiger88, a reference to the heavy tank the Nazis used during World War Two. He identified links between the *Ultras Sur* and the local branch of Hammerskin Nation, establishing a lot of overlap in membership between the two groups. In 2010, he testified as a protected witness in a case brought by Spain's public prosecutor against the Hammerskins.

Barça is the *Ultras Sur*'s natural enemy. As a fascist and ultranationalist body, which hankers after a unified, Francoist version of Spain, the notion of Barça's separatist ideology is anathema. During matches they occasionally sing 'Facing the Sun', the blood sacrifice anthem of the Falange Party which dates back to the 1930s, with their right hands raised in fascist salute mode. 'When Barça plays in Madrid,' says Salas, 'the *Ultras Sur* organise hunts in the vicinity of the ground for Barça's supporters. They look for people who wear scarves, hats or anything with Barça's symbol on it and steal them as a scalp. They look for the route of Barça's buses as well and throw stones and bottles against them.'

The *Ultras Sur* and *Boixos Nois* have established footholds in each other's territory. The local office of the *Boixos Nois* in Madrid is called *Boixos Centre*; while the Barcelona branch of the *Ultras Sur* is called *Ultras Sur Condal*, a play on the old name for Barcelona – *Ciudad Condal*. In May 2009, the *Boixos Nois* trashed the clubhouse of a Real Madrid *peña* in Figueres, the Catalan town where Salvador Dalí was born. It was the night Barça won that year's *Copa del Rey*. Yet for all their animosity, it is rare that things get bloody between the two groups.

'Spanish football culture is quite different from others in Europe,' says Ramón Spaaij. 'There's not really a hardcore group of fans who go to all the away games, which creates a more relaxed atmosphere. Even though people might be Barcelona fans, in their daily lives they might live and work alongside Madrid fans, maybe in the family as well. It's very much a fluid spectator identity rather than fixed, aggressive masculine identity in terms of defending territories, with the exception of the small cores of hooligan fans. It's quite a different away culture than in

England, for example. I once had a season ticket for West Ham United. It was the same guys travelling – 2,000 or 3,000 of them – every week to every away game. There was very much a sense of solidarity and group identity, going to the match, and for some maybe having a fight.

'For example Ajax-Feyenoord – which is the derby that I grew up with because my dad is a mad Feyenoord fan and so is my brother – or Manchester v. Liverpool might have serious fighting between large groups of people. Also because they're quite close to each other so there are lots of away fans. There are large groups of young males who want to prove themselves and go out and have a fight as part of that experience. Whereas at Barcelona v. Real Madrid, the number of away fans would be small, so they're less inclined to try and start fights. It's generally quite a peaceful, easy-going affair in the sense of real violence nowadays. Also, if you're talking about anti-social behaviour, it's much more about verbal abuse, even racist abuse sometimes, although nowadays both sides have got so many foreign players even that is less likely. There are a lot of fireworks and missile throwing. There's a lot of gesturing. There's a lot of provocation. There's a lot of intimidation and shouting and yelling. When they lose, there's crying. It's all very emotional, but it's very ritualised in that it doesn't often spill over into physical violence. It's hard to say whether that's because there's not many opportunities because there are fewer away fans who are well policed or is it because that's all there is, that ritualised aggression is enough for them?'

Antonio Salas was struck by the way in which the Real Madrid club pandered to the *Ultras Sur*. The club provided the *Ultras Sur* with a room to store their megaphones, *tifos*, flags and match paraphernalia, much of which was of a neo-Nazi hue. In March 1998, José Luis Ochaíta, the *Ultras Sur* leader, was detained by German police at Cologne airport along with 70 *Ultras Sur* members for exhibiting neo-Nazi symbols en route for a Champions League match against Bayer Leverkusen. The previous May, Ocha, as he is known, was arrested after a Madrid-Barça basketball match in Madrid. It was the last game of the season. He tried to attack one of Barça's basketball players on court as he celebrated the club's title win. With a hidden camera, Salas filmed Ochaíta operating an illegal ticket sales office out of the El Refugio bar on Marceliano Santa María, the side street that runs perpendicular to the Bernabéu stadium. He was flogging complimentary not-for-sale tickets the club had given to the *Ultras Sur*. Ochaíta was caught on camera telling people who bought the tickets to destroy them if they were apprehended by police.

In Salas's book, there is a picture of Real Madrid's former president Ramón Mendoza with the handwritten inscription 'For my Ultras Sur, with the love of your president'. Mendoza, who some people believe to have been a KGB spy as well as serving as president of Real Madrid from 1985 to 1995, once joined in with the *Ultras Sur* in a sing-song at Barajas airport. They were welcoming back the Real Madrid team after they had just defeated Barça at the Camp Nou in a *Supercopa* final. Tomás Roncero, a TV pundit and an ardent Real Madrid fan re-enacted Mendoza's airport celebration for me during an interview, gesticulating with a broad grin: 'He jumped up and down with them, chanting, "Jump, jump, jump, a *polaco* doesn't jump!"'

Since Florentino Pérez became president in 2000, the *Ultras Sur* have reined in their anti-social behaviour, and retain an official and legal status as a supporter's club. They are therefore not as violent as before, being mindful of losing their access to the Bernabéu stadium. The club has banned the display of swastikas, of which many are sprayed on the shutters of Marceliano Santa María, the street where they meet up for war dances before matches. Barça's *Boixos Nois* are unofficial, are still banned from attending Barcelona's home games and have no such restraints.

Salas stresses that there are logical reasons why Real Madrid tolerate their intolerant behaviour. The *Ultras Sur* spend a lot of money on merchandising; as members, they vote in presidential elections; and, in a stadium of difficult-to-please patrons, they're often the only bloody ones who cheer the team on. 'I lost my voice several times shouting for 90 minutes with them when I was a "member" of their group,' he says. Their unyielding singing and the fact that they are often the only Real

Madrid fans who travel to support the team for away matches, especially in La Liga, explains why the team's players also embrace them. In Salas's book, there are photos of Luís Figo posing with an *Ultras Sur* scarf and Raúl holding up an *Ultras Sur* flag adorned with an axe, a well-known fascist symbol. 'It surprised me,' he says, 'the support of some footballers for the *Ultras Sur* like Guti, Iker Casillas, Figo and Raúl, nearly all of the club's white players, but none of the club's black players obviously.' For the Real Madrid hierarchy, the *Ultras Sur* is like the mad uncle in the attic who occasionally springs into public view. When José Mourinho applauded them for vocal support during Real Madrid's 7–1 win against Osasuna in November 2011, the reference was airbrushed from a transcript of his press conference on the club's website. Casillas & Co. give little thought, one imagines, to the politics of *Ultras Sur*. They just like their singing.

Although their ranks have been swollen by black players over the last decade, Real Madrid, Barcelona and Spanish football in general have all been slow to address racism in their stands. The biggest fine the Spanish Football Federation has levied at a club for racist behaviour was a paltry £8,000 in 2006. It dished out the fine to Real Zaragoza. During a game against Barcelona, Barça's Samuel Eto'o was subjected to a chorus of ape noises from Real Zaragoza's stands. '¡*No más!*' he shrieked to the ref and fellow players, forcing a halt in play in the middle of the match, as he staged an abortive walkout. The previous year he had been pelted with peanuts at the ground.

'I remember,' says Ramón Spaaij, 'talking to some fans and what they were saying was, "Look, when the black player is on our team, he's one of us. When he's with them, he's a black bastard." It's neighbourhood nationalism. You're on our team or you're on the other team, especially in a Barça–Madrid match. Someone like Samuel Eto'o in the past copped a lot of racial abuse from Real Madrid fans because not only is he black but particularly because he was a black Barcelona player. A lot of fans would say it wasn't meant in a racist way. It was just a "joke":

"Ah, look, if we hurl enough racist abuse at this player, we might knock him off his game." It's almost situational racism.'

Racist abuse is not unique to the Spanish game. In June 2011, for instance, the Brazilian World Cup-winner Roberto Carlos walked off the pitch in protest during stoppage time in a Russian league game after a banana was thrown at him. Three months earlier, Zenit St Petersburg was fined $10,000 because a fan offered him a banana before a match. In November 2010, a group of approximately 100 right-wing Italian fans racially abused their own player, 20-year-old Mario Balotelli, who was making his second appearance for his country in Austria. Balotelli was born in Italy to Ghanaian parents. While playing for his old club, Inter, rival fans from Juventus once wielded a banner for him that read: 'A negro cannot be Italian'. 'What I noticed is how widespread it is on the terraces in Spain. It's similar to Italy,' says Ramón Spaaij. 'In England and the Netherlands, in contrast, where it still occurs is usually concentrated in one section of the ground, or it involves a particular player or coach against another player or coach, like the John Terry–Anton Ferdinand case in England. In Spain, it can happen with a majority of the crowd, across age, gender and education. The serious racist abuse might start with the right-wing group, a team's *ultras*, but you will end up with monkey chants going all around the stadium. I've been at games where 80 per cent of the stadium was chanting, including old men and women.'

Both Barcelona and Real Madrid have long rap sheets of racist offences over the last 20 years. At Real Madrid, for example, shortly before the Argentinian Jorge Valdano was appointed manager in 1994, there was graffiti scrawled on the walls of the Bernabéu Stadium: 'Valdano, stay in Africa' and 'No to cross breeding, Valdano never'. In 2004, UEFA fined the club because its fans racially abused Bayer Leverkusen players Roque Junior and Juan. In 2005, four members of the *Ultras Sur* were arrested for attacking a group of black North American students after a match against Juventus.

Members of *Boixos Nois* allegedly play amateur football for a club called Bada Bing. In January 2009, a match between Bada Bing and

Atlético Rosario Central, a team composed mainly of immigrants from Argentina, erupted in violence following sustained racial slurs and death threats. Ten people from Atletico Rosario Central, including seven players, were hospitalised with injuries after being attacked by broom handles, mops and other blunt instruments. Six of the seven Bada Bing players and supporters arrested by police ended up with lengthy prison sentences, ranging from two to almost seven years. In handing down such severe sentencing, the judge concluded that the racist motive for the attack was 'more than justified'.

'There is racism in Spanish society at large, but it's unconscious,' says Giles Tremlett. 'People are convinced they're not racist, but they are really, probably no more, no less than in any other country. Public expressions of it in football grounds here are [deemed] perfectly acceptable. They will call a black player a *mono*, a monkey.' 'There is permissiveness in laws and social ways to racism in Spanish society. It's the same in football,' says José Peñín, a spokesperson for the non-governmental organisation, SOS Racisme, who suggests it may be because Spain has only recently become a multi-cultural country unlike, among others, neighbouring France with its longer history of assimilating immigrants. The country was a repressed, homogenous society for half of the twentieth century. 'Spain has a problem,' says Ramón Besa, 'because neither in the schools nor in other places has anti-racism been taught. Now we suffer the consequences with, for example, the xenophobic political party, *Plataforma per Catalunya*, which is racist and is on the increase here. Spain is a young country. Here, there was a *cabrón*, a bastard called Franco who organised a dictatorship so this country has grown up later than England, France or Germany. We have missed out on other revolutions. We haven't even had land reform in Spain like in other European countries!' The result of this catch-up is that racism is more pronounced than in, say, Britain's stadiums. 'They just haven't been through the process,' adds Tremlett. 'Also they turn a blind eye; the refs don't report it; the press doesn't report it. They're on a different part of the curve.' Significantly, for example, the furore in November 2011 over the FIFA chief Sepp Blatter's controversial comments about racism – that players should shake hands after an incident and continue playing – failed to get a mention in Spain's main sports newspapers, *AS* and *Marca*.

Barcelona and Real Madrid have engaged in ad hoc initiatives. They promote anti-racist awareness in their football school foundations. Barcelona's players Lionel Messi and Gerard Piqué recently appeared in a 30-second 'Put Racism Offside' film. When their teammate, David Villa signed for the club in May 2010, he set a precedent by including an anti-racism clause in his contract. SOS Racisme commends these efforts, but stresses they are not enough. 'Something more radical is needed,' says José Peñín. 'All the players need to be involved in the cause and more than anything the teams' owners, directors and trainers.'

The abdication of responsibility from the game's figureheads is noticeable. Barça played its Barcelona city derby at Espanyol's Cornellà-El Prat stadium in the last round of league games in December 2010. Barça won 5–1. During the press conference afterwards, an English journalist from the BBC asked Pep Guardiola about the racist chanting which was directed at his player, Dani Alves. It was ugly stuff, and relentless throughout the match, with lone men springing to their feet to make monkey sounds. There were pockets of offenders around the stadium. It wasn't just restricted to the hooligans' corner. 'Sometimes it happens, at home and away. It's a very tough game. Forget it and keep going,' said Guardiola, answering the question in English.

Another missed tackle?

6

ALL THE PRESIDENT'S MEN

The day after Barcelona beat Espanyol, Real Madrid played Sevilla at the Bernabéu stadium. Real Madrid won 1–0. The win kept them on Barcelona's tail going into the two-week league break over Christmas. This would annoy those who wished ill fortune on Mourinho's team. 'Tonight's victory will be very frustrating,' he said, 'for those who wanted us to fall four or five points behind Barcelona. This makes us stronger. Everything was set up for us to drop points, but we didn't.' As an aesthetic experience, however, the match displeased him. It was not the beautiful game. He wouldn't have paid money to see it, he said; if he'd been sitting at home, he would have turned over the channel to watch a game from the Vietnam league. The referee issued 12 yellow cards. Nine Real Madrid players were booked. Ricardo Carvalho, their centre half, and a player from Sevilla were sent off.

In the press conference afterwards, Mourinho brandished a list of '13 serious errors' the referee had committed. The charge sheet was carefully written up on Real Madrid-headed notepaper, but unfortunately he couldn't share the details of the offences. 'If I talk about them, I won't be at the next game,' he said. Instead, Mourinho made a public plea to the 17 men who sat on Real Madrid's board to intervene. Directors enjoy a kind of diplomatic immunity in football, which allows them, in Mourinho's rulebook, to lambast refs without fear of censure. 'This is a club,' he pointed out, 'with a structure, and I want them to defend my team, not only me.' He needed to talk to his president, he said. Someone asked him if it would help to talk to Jorge Valdano, the president's right-hand man. 'If I can talk to the number one, why would I talk to anyone else?' he replied. Did this imply a spilt in the club's management ranks? 'Why can't we have a division of opinion?' he said rhetorically.

Mourinho and Valdano had been on an uneasy footing from the off. Ten days before Mourinho was appointed to his post, Valdano said Mourinho wasn't the best coach in the world. He didn't think much of him as a player either. When he famously wrote in an article for *Marca* in 2007 criticising the style of football played by Mourinho's teams, he said the reason lay in Mourinho's frustrated youth. Mourinho failed to make it as a professional footballer. He'd been forced to channel his vanity into coaching. 'Those who do not have the talent to make it as players,' wrote Valdano, a goalscorer in the 1986 World Cup final, 'do not believe in the talent of players, they do not believe in the ability to improvise in order to win football matches.'

Valdano bothered Mourinho. He belittled Mourinho's tactics during the traumatic 5–0 loss to Barcelona. He congratulated Sergio Ramos for giving a press conference after the match to defend himself from accusations of foul play when Mourinho had told him not to. During pre-season, Mourinho pushed to sign a new striker. He said they'd be shanghaied if Gonzalo Higuaín or Karim Benzema got injured. His request was turned down. In mid-December it was confirmed that Higuaín, who missed the *clásico* through injury, would have to undergo surgery for a slipped disk. It would keep him out of action for four months at least. That only left Mourinho with Benzema. He was unconvinced about the young, languid Frenchman. He complained that training could not start until 10 a.m. because Benzema was 'still asleep'. He said that Benzema 'could learn a lot sitting on the bench'. When deputising for Higuaín up front against Barcelona, he didn't even get a shot on goal. Again, Mourinho pushed to sign another striker. Valdano, who had signed Benzema, vetoed the request. Instead, Mourinho was told to concentrate on the imminent return of Kaká, who was back in the fold after knee surgery the previous August.

Mourinho and Valdano also differed in style. Real Madrid likes to cultivate the image of *señorío*, that it is imbued with a gentlemanly,

Corinthian spirit. The Spanish word *señorío* comes from the French *savoir faire* – to do and to say things well or gracefully. In this regard, there is no smoother ambassador than the suave, finely dressed Valdano, a man of elegance and eloquence who has penned five books on the vagaries of football. 'He's a mightily articulate guy,' says John Carlin. 'He speaks in metaphors. He's quite brilliant, really.' Mourinho's brilliance lies elsewhere. 'Valdano transmits the image of a *señor*, a gentleman,' said Tomás Roncero. 'He always says the appropriate words. Valdano gives balance to the club. If Valdano was like Mourinho, then Real Madrid would be like a Mexican gang. They'd be like Pancho Villa's army.'

During the fractious match against Sevilla, there had been a brawl between the two benches at half-time. The Sevilla contingent had been taunting Real Madrid's staff by doing a *manita* – by raising their hands at them, fingers outstretched, one for each goal Barcelona had knocked past them a fortnight earlier. In his haste to get to the opposing dugout, Mourinho's goalkeeping coach, Silvino Louro knocked over Agustín Herrerín, a 75-year-old club delegate from Real Madrid. Due to restrictions on the number of staff allowed, Louro should not have been pitch-side. Mourinho got him in under the radar as one of his medical team.

At Real Madrid's next home game in the league, a thrilling 4–2 win over Villarreal, Mourinho responded to his side's fourth goal by parading past the Villarreal dugout. It was like a March Past. His strides were slow and deliberate. While facing their dugout he pumped his fist in celebration until Cani, one of Villarreal's substituted players, threw a water bottle at him. Mourinho claimed he was celebrating with his son who sits behind the away team's dugout.

Mourinho wasn't sold on the idea of *señorío*. Moments before delivering his rap sheet of refereeing errors from the Sevilla game, he upbraided a director in front of Real Madrid's players in the dressing room. 'You say this is a *señor* club. This is *una puta mierda* – a fucking shit – of a club! And now go and say that to the president! Now, I'm going on holiday and if you want to fire me, as far as I'm concerned I won't come back.'

The message was relayed to the president. He mulled over the idea of sacking him, but decided against it. Instead he used the club's Christmas lunch the following day to send his own communiqué. Addressing the assembled guests by microphone, he said: 'There are people here who think they are qualified for any enterprise and don't realise that Real Madrid is the biggest enterprise. Not all of them are qualified. The pressure suffered here is not for everybody. Some go mad.'

Mourinho was mad all right. At their next private meeting, he put Pérez on the back foot. 'Neither am I the manager you expected,' he said, 'nor are you the president I thought.'

In the middle of January, Real Madrid flew down to play Almería, the bottom-of-the-league team at the bottom of Spain. Mourinho left Karim Benzema out of the starting XI. When the team sheets were distributed in the directors' box, one of Real Madrid's heavyweights read between the lines for his colleagues: Mourinho was sending them a message. He wouldn't stop whining about the need for a new forward. Now he'd left out the Frenchman to make a point. The conspiracy theory was quoted anonymously in the following morning's newspapers. Mourinho was unmoved. 'I'm too old to be sent messages in the press,' he said. Everyone knew the rules, though, even if they are not stated publicly. The president likes to see his stars play. When Real Madrid's manager Mariano García Remón benched the Brazilian Ronaldo in December 2004, Pérez sent him packing within two weeks. Pérez, who marshals a construction business with over 135,000 employees in 41 countries, personally flew into Lyon and visited Benzema's house to cajole him into signing for the club.

Real Madrid drew 1–1 with Almería. Barcelona's relentless winning streak continued apace. The gap between them in the league stretched to four points. 'We have been distracted by all the talk of a new striker,' intoned Valdano after the costly draw with Almería. 'We had a No. 9 and he was on the bench.' Mourinho felt his advice about team selection was unnecessary. 'I pick the team,' he said, 'and if I need any assistance then I have my coaching staff to help me.' The media continued to cook the story. Mourinho was unperturbed by the hullabaloo. 'Normally the second season is better,' he said when quizzed on the Tuesday. 'The first is about analysing the people you are working with – those who are working seriously and those who are hypocrites.'

Mourinho was playing to form. 'I think this belongs to the drift of Mourinho,' said Santiago Segurola. 'He lives the life of a paranoid, thinking there are big conspiracies around him and he wants absolute power, without assuming any self-criticism. If you see what happened, Valdano never would declare anything against Mourinho in any meeting. But when Real Madrid lost 5–0, he felt disappointed because Real Madrid had signed him up to beat Guardiola and he failed, noisily. It was the biggest defeat of his life and an outrage for Real Madrid. Then Mourinho began an investigation to find out who was against him.'

On the Thursday, Real Madrid played Atlético de Madrid in the second leg of the quarter-final of the *Copa del Rey*. Benzema was an unused sub. For the first leg of the semi-final the following week, Real Madrid travelled to Sevilla. Mourinho refused to allow Valdano to travel with the team. Instead, Valdano flew to the match with Pérez in his boss's private plane. The majority of fans sided with Mourinho in the schism. Security guards at the Bernabéu stadium were instructed to stop people bringing anti-Valdano banners into the ground. The ones I spoke to said Valdano was a 'cancer' in the club. Still Mourinho felt he was not loved enough. He announced he had decided to return to manage a club in England. 'I just want to rediscover the joy,' he said.

Pérez yielded. He forked out money for a striker – the Togolese player Emmanuel Adebayor arrived on loan until the end of the season. I spoke to Alfredo Relaño on the day Adebayor signed for Real Madrid. Relaño is the editor of *AS*, one of Madrid's two daily sports newspapers, a TV pundit, a biographer of di Stéfano and one of Spain's most authoritative voices on football. Born in 1951, he's a short man with a beard who dresses conspicuously well – in a neat suit with a colourful tie – for work in a newspaper office full of dishevelled-looking hacks.

'Florentino Pérez is a very organised man,' he says. 'In Spain, we say *componedor*. He's a person that fixes things. He knows how to pull people together. He's a very good manager. He owns a huge construction company, but in Madrid, Florentino doesn't completely connect with football. He's an old football fan, a son of a *socio*, an admirer of Real Madrid's great years in the 1950s. He always wants to have more power than the coach. Finally, he decided to bring in a coach that has all the power. Now he regrets it. In general, he despises all coaches unconsciously.

'Once he told me that he sees *futbolistas*, football people, in this way: a football player is a man who lives from 20 until 34 making a lot of money for doing little work. When he retires from playing, the player becomes a trainer or a technical secretary at the club. He still wants to be the same – getting a lot of money but working very little. For Florentino, they're all useless. They're all part of a conspiracy to take all the money without working hard for it. They have to pay agents. He employs *futbolistas* purely because he has no choice. He has to make do with them. In the same way, he wears a *corbata*, a tie, to work because everybody has to wear a *corbata*, but Florentino doesn't like *corbatas*.'

Real Madrid headed north to play in a league match against Osasuna in Pamplona three days later. Adebayor came on as a substitute but failed to score. Real Madrid lost 1–0. They now trailed Barcelona by seven points. Meanwhile, Osasuna delighted in the three points they secured. Few were happier than their trainer, former Spanish national team coach José Antonio Camacho – the win was against his old club. (Nonetheless, he got the sack a few weeks later.) Camacho has round, chubby facial features. As a player, he was a hard case who spent 15 seasons patrolling the left flank of Real Madrid's defence. He also had a couple of shots at managing the club's first team. The last time was in 2004. Pérez hired him in the hope that his martinet style of management might whip the team's *galácticos* into shape. It didn't. He walked after three league games, later insinuating that the hierarchy at the club interfered with his team selection. He left out Raúl, Real Madrid's adored native son, and David

Beckham in his last game in charge. His other stint at the club in 1998 – under the presidency of Lorenzo Sanz – lasted 23 days. He took flight after a row with Sanz's right-hand man, Juan Onieva over an old chestnut – selection, this time over the composition of his backroom team.

Sanz sought out Dutchman Guus Hiddink to replace Camacho in 1998. Hiddink is good at his job. 'Lucky Guus,' they call him in the Netherlands, 'Goose' around Chelsea, where he parachuted in for a blistering, three-month fix-it job in 2009, which culminated in FA Cup glory. He has a thing for coaching national teams. He took South Korea to the semi-finals of the 2002 World Cup. It was an adventure the country can't forget. It made South Koreans curious to get to know him better, enough to churn out approximately 16 biographies and a 500,000 print run of his autobiography in Korean. When Real Madrid came calling in 1998, he had just steered the Netherlands to the semi-finals of the World Cup in France. He was jaded and wasn't keen on taking up another job immediately. He wanted to take a break, but decided to sound out Johan Cruyff, his friend and compatriot, about the overture. 'If they're offering the Madrid job, take it,' he was told. 'It's a logical move. It doesn't matter if you don't get much time off. Just work, take the money, and then get out of there.' A back-of-a-paper-napkin calculation told Goose that even if he lasted only two months at that club in Madrid, he stood to clear £2.5 million. He took the job.

'Getting sacked here is like a game,' he said midway through the season in an interview with a Dutch journalist. 'It's not really a disgrace... It goes like this. The president invites you to his office and says, "Mister, I think it is better that you don't continue." The atmosphere is good, very pleasant, very charming. The president gives you a hug and adds, "OK, drop by the treasurer's office tomorrow." So the next day you drop by the treasurer's office and you collect a cheque and you go to the nearest bank and they hand you a suitcase full of money, and boom it's all over. In Spain, they kill you romantically.'

Hiddink survived seven months before he was fired. He made a lot of money in Madrid.

7

CHANGE IS ALWAYS GOOD
– IF IT'S FOR THE BETTER

Real Madrid and Barcelona are owned by *socios*, or members, a structure that springs from Spain's love affair with cooperatives. *Socios* elect presidents to manage the club's affairs, men who are drawn to the job for power, social cachet or as a springboard for a career in politics. Some even look on it as a nice resting place after an arduous political life – José María Aznar, Spain's former prime minister, for example, would like to be president of Real Madrid one day.

Lorenzo Sanz stood for re-election as president of Real Madrid in July 2000. There were presidential elections at Barça in the same month. It looked as if Sanz was a shoo-in. There are portraits him, posing in a suit and chunky jewellery, in the clubhouses of Real Madrid's supporters' clubs. He looks smug, with black, bushy eyebrows under a head of oiled, grey hair. Florentino Pérez was his challenger. Pérez was one of Spain's wealthiest businessmen, but unknown in football circles. Sanz could reflect on the lifting of the club's great hex during his five-year watch. In 1998, 32 years after their previous triumph in the tournament, Real Madrid won the Champions League title in Amsterdam. It had been an interminable wait for the fans. Moreover, Real Madrid had just added another Champions League title on 24 May 2000 in regal fashion, dispatching Valencia 3–0 in Paris, the city where the club had won its first European Cup in 1956. It was heady stuff, immortalised after the final whistle in the image of Raúl aping a matador's passes with a large Spanish flag.

The balmy start to Sanz's summer was set to continue when he woke on the morning of 6 July, the day he was to give his daughter away in marriage to Real Madrid player Míchel Salgado. The family celebration was sullied, however, by a preposterous breaking news story. Pérez, it was reported, had signed a pre-contract with Luís Figo's agent José Veiga, which would bring Figo from Barcelona to Real Madrid if Pérez won the presidential election. Pérez was acting on a study he commissioned with Real Madrid supporters asking them to name the player they most desired. Their overwhelming answer was Figo. If Figo refused to come, Pérez promised to pay the subscription fees of Real Madrid's 70,000 or so *socios* for the year, amounting to several million pounds. In this eventuality, an indemnity clause would also kick in forcing Figo to pay a penalty of £18.6 million to Real Madrid, which effectively bound him to follow through on the deal. If Pérez did not win the election, Figo, it was claimed, would pocket a £1.6 million secret agreement fee, for *nada*.

Amidst the media storm that rolled in, Sanz and Figo denied there was any pre-contract, maintaining that Pérez was 'lying' and 'fantasising'. In Barcelona, Joan Gaspart, the front-runner in Barça's elections, insisted at several junctures that Figo would never be allowed to leave the club, especially – *¡Déu no ho vulgui!* (God forbid) – for Real Madrid. Meanwhile, Pérez deposited £37.2 million at the Spanish Football Federation, the sum put on Figo's *cláusula de recisión*, his buy-out clause.

I tramped up to José-Maria Minguella's house in Pedralbes, a posh neighbourhood overlooking Barcelona, to get his version of the story. The house is within walking distance of the Camp Nou, conveniently, as Minguella never misses a Barça match. He once ran for president of the club and served under Gaspart as a director, but is best known for his work as a football agent, having ferried Maradona and Messi, Rómario and Rivaldo, amongst others, to the club. He also co-brokered the deal with Veiga to bring Figo to Barça from Sporting Lisbon in 1995.

'Veiga, Figo's agent, came to Barcelona three times before the Pérez offer,' says Minguella. 'I went to the airport to collect him, and we tried to fix the contract with Barça. Barcelona at the time had no president because their old one had resigned. They were in the middle of elections. None of the presidential candidates were able to sign a new contract so Veiga said, "On this side, I have a very good offer from Florentino Pérez. On the other side, I have… I don't know. Not yet." Barça were undecided so Figo decided on their behalf – by signing for Madrid.'

On 16 July 2000 Pérez swept into office, having outflanked Sanz in the election race, who he blamed for the club's bad debts and ramshackle administration. The club had leaked losses of €50 million on a turnover of €120 million that year. Seven days later, Pérez unveiled Figo as a Real Madrid player in the trophy room at the Santiago Bernabéu stadium. Alfredo di Stéfano, in his maiden act as honorary life president, handed Figo his Real Madrid jersey for the cameras. For Barça fans, the image was galling. Di Stéfano, of course, in a murky episode involving Franco's government, had been wrestled from them by Real Madrid in 1953. Now, almost half a century later, they had more *madridista* treachery to contend with. It was an audacious swoop by Real Madrid who, having just won the Champions League title, had filched Barça's best player. Indeed, he was probably the finest player in the world at the time, and recipient of that year's *Ballon d'Or*.

I once asked Manolo Sanchís, who turned out over 700 times for Real Madrid at the heart of their defence, to name the most difficult opponent he'd played against. The old war dog said it was Figo, that he was even more of a handful than Maradona, Figo's boyhood hero, or the Brazilian Ronaldo. 'I remember before Figo arrived in Barcelona,' said Sanchís. 'I faced him in a match against Sporting Lisbon. He was very young, like 18 or 19, and nobody knew him. He came to the Bernabéu and he gave us a *baño*, a thrashing. I said, "Who is this guy?" All by himself, he drove us crazy, dribbling us. He was a tremendous player, a *crack*. First, his ability: he was capable of dribbling without touching the ball. He had a tremendous feint. Second, his ability to create goals: as soon as you gave him an inch, he was capable of putting through "a goal ball". Third, his capacity to score: every year, he ended up with 13, 14 goals, which for a winger is fantastic. And fourth, and most importantly, his character: you never saw him – not for a second of a match – scared or anxious. He came at you again and again. He was mesmerising. And he did it in every match.'

Installed as captain of Portugal at only 23 years of age, Figo was Barcelona's centrepiece, known as the Lion King for his commanding presence. He'd led them to several domestic and European titles, including two recent Spanish league wins. To lose him to Real Madrid was inconceivable, although from talking to Barça fans over a decade later, it was Figo's denials in the press, which hurt the most. 'At the time, Figo was an idol,' says Minguella. 'He saw the situation. He acted in a premeditated way. And Madrid benefited from the move. Until the last moment, Figo kept saying that it wasn't true that he wanted to go to Madrid so when he went to Madrid, the public here felt betrayed.'

Joan Gaspart won his presidential race in Barcelona on 23 July 2000. There was little time for a honeymoon. The following day, he berated Pérez and Real Madrid over the loss of his star player involving, in his words, an 'immoral' contract. 'I'll not forget this. Whoever is responsible for this will pay for it,' he said, before adding mysteriously, 'We'll see how and when.'

Figo's move made him the most expensive player in the world. He was, in Barça eyes, the worst kind of traitor – a *pesetero*, a money-grabber. Three months after leaving Barcelona, he made his way back to the Camp Nou with his new teammates for Real Madrid's annual league fixture in the Catalan capital. Armed police ran alongside their coach for protection. Still the bus was ambushed by demented Barça fans. Four or five windows were broken. The Real Madrid players cowered on the floor as stones and bottles whistled past them.

The Camp Nou was festooned with giant 5,000 peseta notes, Figo's face superimposed on them along with the statement: Figo, *pesetero*. Handmade banners announced his greed: '*No soy madridista; soy mercenario*' – I am not a *madridista*; I am a mercenary. Figo hadn't helped to placate matters by lending himself to a nationwide merchant bank-er's advertising campaign in which he tauntingly mouthed the words: 'Change is always good – if it's for the better.'

In the pantomime world of the Barcelona football fan, he was *un traidor*, a traitor. 'We hate you so much because we loved you so much,' exclaimed one banner melodramatically. Had he not, the Barça faithful asked themselves, dyed his hair blue and red, the colours of the *blaugrana*, and exhorted Real Madrid's 'cry-babies' to 'salute the champions' from a city centre balcony the last time Barcelona won La Liga? Where was his loyalty?

Fans yelled '*Die Figo*' as he took to the pitch, shattering previous records on the sound meter that Canal Plus television had installed for the match; noise levels were higher than at any nightclub in town. In vain, he tried to block out the din by plugging both ears with his fingers. Thousands of white handkerchiefs fluttered in the wind, a distortion of a practice borrowed from bullfighting, signalling that he should be sentenced to death. He had already taken 23 of Real Madrid's 29 corners that season. He took none that night, having been advised against it. Any time he ventured near one of the corners of the pitch, objects rained down on top of him. They included, recorded the referee in his notebook, coins, three mobile phones, several half-bricks and a bicycle chain.

Two years later, in late November 2002, in the same fixture, Figo felt emboldened to take Real Madrid's corners. He was playing on the right wing. Míchel Salgado, his teammate and right back, went up to support him for a short corner at one stage and claims he glimpsed a knife fly past him. He wanted none of it. 'No more short corners tonight,' he told Figo. 'Just put it in the box. You're on your own.'

After 75 minutes of play, the match was still scoreless; it was a dour, stultifying affair. Figo stepped up to take a corner amidst a shower of projectiles. Vicente del Bosque, his manager, looked on aghast. In the directors' box, Florentino Pérez, Real Madrid's president, pulled hard on a cigarette. Play stopped while Figo, his teammate Roberto Carlos and

Barcelona's Xavi brushed missiles off the pitch. Xavi's clubmate Carles Puyol remonstrated with Barça's fans to stop their assault, to no avail. A cordon of about a dozen riot police, kitted out in black gear and crash helmets, provided Figo with a human shield from his assailants. Finally, at his fourth attempt, he swung in his corner, a looping effort that was tipped over the bar by Barcelona's keeper, Roberto Bonano. Another corner, from the other side of the goal, beckoned. Figo trundled over to the other side of the pitch to take it, but the onslaught of detritus was too much. The referee was forced to abandon play for 16 minutes.

For its penance, the Camp Nou was supposed to be shut for two games, not that its people were repentant, angered as they were by Figo's nonchalance in taking the corners. Cheekily he'd back-heeled some of the junk in his way. 'Figo's provocation was out of place and totally unnecessary. I won't accept people coming to my house to provoke,' thundered Joan Gaspart, Barça's president. One of his directors rowed in. 'Figo lives off lies,' he spluttered. 'He's been provoking our fans for years.' Figo, for his part, was perplexed, wondering aloud: 'I don't know if Gaspart is taking the piss.'

Along with plastic bottles, lighters and beer cans, Figo had been assailed by a glass bottle of J&B Scotch whisky. Someone also tossed the head of a suckling pig at him, which was in keeping with the sight of him at the corner flag – helplessly prey to flying objects as if he were pilloried in an Elizabethan marketplace. 'Every corner a Vietnam,' declared *El Periódico de Catalunya*, while *Marca* christened it: '*El Derbi de la Vergüenza*' – The Derby of Shame. Such a ruckus.

When I asked Santiago Segurola about the reverberations of Figo's switch, he said it had a profound, immediate effect. 'His transfer generated a big trauma in Barcelona's team,' he said, 'and in some ways changed the club to the point where I think he created a distraction that lasted three seasons – three seasons of total frustration. There was more interest in hounding Figo rather than in solving their internal problems at Barcelona.'

In 2002, Inter Milan put the word out that they wanted to offload the Brazilian Ronaldo. Pérez and Real Madrid were interested. They were very interested after he scored eight goals in that summer's World Cup for Brazil. As the summer went on, the two clubs haggled over the star. The press called their little poker game Operation Ronaldo. On 30 August 2002, a day before the summer transfer window closed, Gaspart joined the table. The Barça president was in Monaco for a so-called 'G14' meeting of Europe's top clubs. He told Pérez that he was keen on his striker Fernando Morientes. Pérez said he could have him. It would free Real Madrid up to sign Ronaldo. The accountants stepped in and – for arcane reasons known only to them – packaged the Morientes deal in triangular fashion: he would be sold from Real Madrid to Inter, who would immediately sell him on to Barça.

The Morientes transfer was announced in the following morning's newspapers as a *fait accompli* even though the price had yet to be finalised. The horse-trading between Barça and Inter continued through to the following day. It proved a busy one. Inter signed Hernán Crespo, whom they had earmarked as a replacement for Ronaldo, from Lazio, even though nothing had been squared away about Ronaldo's sale. Still Gaspart and Barça dragged their heels on Morientes. They said they wanted him for €2 million less. At 5 p.m., Real Madrid stepped in, sensing something was up. They said they'd make up the difference – shelling out the €2 million to close the deal. At 6 p.m., Gaspart came back again – he wanted to shave another €2 million off. Real Madrid said OK – they'd stump up another €2 million. The lines went dead again. At 10 p.m., two hours before the transfer deadline kicked in, Gaspart sent a fax saying he was pulling out of the deal.

Valdano, who was in the middle of negotiations for Real Madrid, was in no doubt that Gaspart was trying 'to scupper the whole deal' by letting the clock run down on the transfer deadline. The oil tycoon Massimo Moratti, Inter's owner, was in a tizzy – he knew Ronaldo wanted to leave his club and that knowing this Inter's fans didn't want him to stay. He was so rattled he had to take five minutes to collect himself before going back on an open telephone line with Real Madrid. With a few minutes to spare before midnight, the clubs cobbled together an alternate arrangement. Ronaldo signed for Real Madrid.

Gaspart wasn't always so divisive. He had known carefree times at Barcelona, the club he served as vice president for over two decades. After Barça won its first European Cup in London in 1992, he jumped into the Thames to celebrate. As president, though, he was haunted by Figo's transfer. He resigned in February 2003, prematurely ending a trophyless term in office. The loss of Figo was exacerbated by his perceived poor judgement in the transfer market. Of the deals he did close, he splurged over £200 million on 16 players; the bulk of whom, like Emmanuel Petit and Marc Overmars, expired at the cash register.

· Veiga, Figo's agent, was also cursed by the Figo transfer. The deal marked the apogee of his power. He had a fist fight with Jorge Mendes, José Mourinho and Cristiano Ronaldo's agent, at Lisbon airport in March 2002. The scuffle signalled a kind of changing of the guard in the shifty world of football agents. Veiga's agency business, Superfute, founded in 1994, has recently been hauled through Portugal's bankruptcy courts. 'Figo's transfer to Real Madrid was a very hard case. I think it affected Veiga a lot, too,' says Minguella dolefully. 'After a while, he retired as an agent. He didn't want to know anything else about players.'

The legacy of Figo's transfer is evident today. It still ripples. Over a decade after successfully signing Figo as his first *galáctico*, Pérez is still paying homage to Bernabéu's team of the 1950s – he contunes to add galactic stars, like Cristiano Ronaldo and Kaká, to the club's roster. Barça, once known for luring football's greatest players to the club – such as Cruyff in the 1970s; Maradona in the 1980s and Rómario and Ronaldo in the 1990s – has adopted a philosophical approach antithetical to Real Madrid's. It has redoubled its youth academy efforts. La Masia, its football school, has become the most prestigious Spanish education institution since Salamanca university in medieval times.

*

Luís Figo has a reputation as a forbidding character. His unsmiling, Latin countenance adds to the impression. According to Steve McManaman, who played with him for a few years at Real Madrid, he was 'unteasable' in the dressing room; he was every inch the alpha male. Greenhorns on the Portugal squad felt he was aloof. Journalists on the Spanish football scene found him to be a difficult, disagreeable man. When Sir Bobby Robson hired José Mourinho as an interpreter at Sporting Lisbon in 1992, one of his duties was to find out what the squad's players were saying about him in the dressing room, especially, he stressed, 'Whatever Figo was muttering about me'.

During a 45-minute interview with him in a restaurant near his residence in Madrid, however, I found him relaxed and courteous, happy to laugh at himself. His mood only darkened on two occasions, both when prodded about Mourinho, a man who was around at the start of his career, at the end of it at Inter Milan, and also, of course, at Barcelona. The best thing he could mutter about his Portuguese compatriot, despite my exuberant exhortations, was a watery, 'He is smart. He has knowledge, and has gotten better with time.' It was clear he didn't think Mourinho is such a special one.

In contrast, he was effusive about his time working with Johan Cruyff at Barcelona and when I registered surprise that he included Pep Guardiola among the best players he played with – in company with the Brazilian Ronaldo, Zidane and Juan Sebastián Verón – he expanded at length about Guardiola's importance to the oiling of a team. He has no regrets, though, about leaving Guardiola – his captain at Barcelona and godfather to his daughter – in the lurch in 2000. 'At first I wasn't sure,' he says, 'but once I arrived at Real Madrid, I'm glad I did because I came to the club to gain more prestige and to get better financial conditions. I wanted to play better football and to win more titles.'

Which he did – in his first three seasons at Real Madrid, Figo won a league title (2001), a Champions League (2002) and a second league title (2003). His move precipitated a shift in the balance of power between the two giants of Spanish football, just as it had done when

Michael Laudrup, another traitorous character in the derby's morality play, departed Cruyff's Dream Team in 1994. Figo, however, fared better in weathering life at the Camp Nou as a Real Madrid player. Rattled by the hostile reception he received, Laudrup had to be substituted after 66 minutes of his first return visit to Barcelona in 1995, later claiming that it was 'the worst day of my life'. Figo, although part of a team that lost 2–0 in November 2000 at the Camp Nou, held his own. Carles Puyol was marking him that night. 'The thing about Figo,' he said after the game, 'is that he never, ever stops moving, pulling you this way and that. But the really amazing thing about tonight was that despite that brutal pressure he was under he kept asking for the ball all the time, as if nothing out of the ordinary were happening.'

'I didn't care much for the atmosphere,' says Figo, reflecting on the night. 'I knew it was going to be bad, partly because the media created it that way. In the end you never know what's going to happen. My main concern was that in sporting terms everything went well and that things didn't go any further, that they didn't transcend the boundaries of sport. There was always the risk that something odd could have happened. My idea was simply to go and play and to try and win.'

Perhaps the most telling incident of the night came straight after the final whistle. To a man, every one of Barcelona's players sought Figo out for an embrace. Having downed their tools on the factory floor, they recognised Figo for what he was – a comrade, a fellow worker. Barça's fans looked on through a different lens, a cartoonish, nationalist one. They fulminated at his defection from the tribe. They couldn't forgive him. 'I'm not bothered too much by the fans' reaction,' he says. 'What matters to me is that I lived there and had happy times there, and what I achieved there. My conscience is clear. I couldn't have done more, I think.'

Whenever Figo returned to the Camp Nou, bodyguards were detailed to safeguard him. He says he understands where the fans' animosity originated. 'Fans are people who don't have their own opinions,' he says. 'Many times, masses are moved by the opinion of others, in this case, the media. It's all about business. In the end, everything was generated by the press. I see it that way because the media always wants to take advantage of a situation. In this case, well, the press "heated" the ambience before the game. For me, despite the rivalry that there might be, football is a sport. Things shouldn't trespass the limits of sport because if in any situation something else happens – if something bad happened – then people, the vast majority, would feel guilty, remorseful. I see it as a game of football. There's rivalry, but this rivalry should not drift from the realm of sport into violence.'

Figo, of course, emerged unscathed from the encounters. He says he doesn't remember seeing the famous pig's head in 2002 until he saw some pictures of the match on the following day's newspapers. He avoided, for instance, a similar fate to Mo Johnston in Glasgow. Johnston joined Rangers in 1989 – via Nantes in France – from Celtic, becoming the first notable Catholic to play for the Protestant enclave. He once shipped a pie to the face from a fan after scoring against Celtic. It does take *cojones* to do what these men have done.

'In the moment one sees that it is a unique experience,' admits Figo, almost wistfully. 'I don't think there's another athlete that has played with a hundred-thousand-something crowd against him. It's good to remember that.'

8

FOOTBALL *IS* POLITICS

Joan Laporta is Barça's most successful club president. He took office four months after Joan Gaspart stepped down. At the time, by its standards, the club was in disarray. He served from 2003 until June 2010. His reign was decorated with two Champions League titles on the field and myriad controversies off it as a result of his decadent style of leadership. When I mention his name to Real Madrid fans, they usually just say one word: '*Cabrón*' – bastard.

I found him, as I'm sure most people do when given an hour of his anecdotes and conspiratorial laughter, to be very charming. He's full of enthusiasm and has that Mediterranean trait of clutching his fingers and thumb together and waving his hand to emphasise a point. Born in 1962, with black hair and the deep tan of old money, he has the boyish, puppy-fat looks of someone who enjoys life. The abiding image of his time in office came in November 2009. Barça had just beaten Real Madrid 1–0 at the Camp Nou. He was pictured dancing the night away in Luz de Gas, a nightclub in Barcelona. He was grinning. His suit and hair were soaking wet from cava. He had a cigar in one hand and a bottle in the other.

He remembers why it was that Luís Figo decamped to Real Madrid in 2000. He believes it was about *amour propre*. 'It was not just for the money. Always the excuse, the explanation that the player has is: "OK, my club is not valuing me. They don't appreciate my contribution. They don't love me too much. There is another girl that loves me more than you who is my wife!" he says, thumping the table. "'What's going to happen? I gotta go. They love me, and you do not love me. Do you love me or not?" It's a question of love. I respect his decision. In the case of another player, who had come from our youth system – that would be, oh, that would be different.'

Laporta has been a Barça fan since he was five years of age. He used to sit on his grandfather's lap at the Camp Nou eating *Darling* sweets. He was incorporated as a *socio* in 1973, the year Cruyff, his hero, joined the club. Like many of his classmates, he took to wearing his hair long and unkempt like the Dutch star, whose bohemian airs, at the fag end of Franco's dictatorship, were intoxicating. Years later, when Cruyff was manager of Barcelona, Laporta and his mates used to run from the stadium to their cars after the final whistle of a match so they could hear his football philosophy at press conferences on the radio. 'It was delicious,' he says.

When he was president, Laporta was also fond of holding forth to the media after Barça matches. If you watch football on TV in Spain, it's customary to be subjected to post-match interviews with the presidents of the country's premier division football clubs. Though not all of them carry on at it, as Tomás Roncero once pointed out to me. 'Well, Florentino doesn't speak,' he said. 'Florentino just shakes hands. Other presidents do it. Laporta and Ramón Calderón [Real Madrid president, 2006–09] spoke. They always wanted to be in the public eye. They say to their friends, their wives, their lovers: "Did you see me on TV? Did I look handsome?" They feel important and Laporta was fond of women.' Barça fans loved Laporta because he defended the club's honour; in contrast to his successor Sandro Rosell who is colourless in his media exchanges.

The most conspicuous feature of Laporta's presidency, apart from the fleet of Lear jets his key staff whisked around in for junkets, was his politics. He's an incorrigible populist. He used the club as a parish pump, as an adjunct to further his aspirations as a Catalan separatist politician, particularly in his final years. A month after he left Barça, he set up his own political party, Catalan Solidarity for Independence, which won four seats in Catalonia's 135-member parliament in

November 2010. He left the party he founded a few months later for another Catalan separatist party.

While president of Barça, he promoted the club as a national symbol, encouraging fans to think of it as a substitute for Catalonia's national team. (The Catalan team, incidentally, is older than the Spanish national team and has played more than 200 'international' matches, but does not have official FIFA status. The team was managed by Johan Cruyff until January 2013. It beat, for example, Argentina 4–2 in December 2009 with a starting XI that included Víctor Valdés, Joan Capdevila, Carles Puyol, Gerard Piqué, Sergio Busquets and Xavi.) Barça's Laporta makes no apology for disenfranchising non-Barça supporting constituents by his simplified identification of the club with Catalonia.

'It is history,' he says. 'From the beginning of the twentieth century, Barça has always been considered the club of Catalonia. Why? Because the board of directors in a general assembly supported the *Estatut de Catalunya* [a statute which defines its self-governing rights] in the 1930s and during my presidency, in 2006, we supported the new *Estatut de Catalunya*. Since democracy, Catalan rights are not being promoted, and if we don't promote our rights, who is going to? Of course under the dictatorship, the repression was more evident. The Catalan language was forbidden. But today we are in the same process. Barça is a representative of Catalan culture, a symbolic church for our country. It is a way to promote our feelings, the best possible tool to promote the image of Catalonia to the world. It's very important because we are giving a cause, a sense to our club, a reason to exist.'

Not many people outside Catalonia appreciate Laporta's politics. Few around Spain – outside the Basque Country – sympathise with Catalonia's push for independence, which is so ardently promoted by FC Barcelona. It offends their notion of a unified nation. 'Spain is a very complicated country, politically speaking,' says Julián García Candau, the writer and former *El País* sports editor. 'There is no great sympathy for the Catalans. There is more sympathy for Madrid, for political reasons.

A few years ago, there was a campaign in Madrid against buying Catalan products such as cava. Is it possible that there would be a campaign in London urging people not to buy products from Liverpool?'

A curious thing happened when democracy came to Spain in the late 1970s. The new constitution created 17 'autonomous communities', with Catalonia being one of the most distinct culturally. With the freedom of expression that was ushered in, the country's rich diversity began to bubble to the surface. Andalucía, Galicia, the Basque Country and the other peripheral regions, repressed for so long, were keen to re-establish their customs. Possibly the biggest cultural renaissance occurred, however, in Madrid. It felt threatened by the flowering of so much culture beyond its extremities.

'Madrid was a city of *funcionarios*, of civil servants,' says Alfredo Relaño. 'It hadn't any special characteristics. There was a sense that it had just kept the rest of Spain's money. Madrid felt very harassed ideologically. Madrid then created its own instruments or not so much created as it exalted its own differentiating elements. One of them it promoted vigorously was bullfighting. Antoñete, "*el torero*", a famous local bullfighter, was lauded. It was during "the transition", the shift into democracy, when Las Ventas, the bullfighting stadium in Madrid, was again full of people. All the big companies wanted a subscription so they could take their guests. Another of them was *la movida*, a modern and advanced musical movement. The mayor of Madrid at that time, Enrique Tierno Galván, got in on the act. He made edicts written in the old Spanish language. Real Madrid, as a symbol of the city, was another. As its enemy symbol it found *El Barça*. The club continued to be strong – it always was strong – but it began to represent for *madrileños* the fact that the periphery slanders us. It insults us. This increased, or focused, a mutual antipathy between Madrid and Barcelona.'

This was the background in which Laporta came of age. He attended some titanic Madrid-Barça clashes over the years, including 'the Guruceta match' in 1970, but his favourite encounter was Barcelona's 6–2 win at the Bernabéu stadium in 2009. 'It was the best match in history,' he says, repeating the scoreline with a can-you-imagine-it expression on his face: '6–2 and I,' – disbelief again registering on his face – 'was the president of Barcelona, enjoying the VIP area of our rival. It was very satisfying.'

He says his counterparts at Real Madrid, such as Florentino Pérez, never got offended with his overt pro-Catalan positioning of Barça. 'Florentino is a very respectful man and he understands all these questions of national identity, but, you know, it is easier being Spanish. They are condescending. Spaniards feel comfortable because they have a state. It is a different level. We are working for our independence, for our freedom, to become a state of the European Union. In my case, I'm from Barça. I express my ideas. There are some of them that are respectful and there are a few people that I met who are disrespectful to our ideas. But in Florentino's case, he always respected our way to understand Barça. But it is easy to say, "Well, football is not politics." That's not true,' he says banging the table. 'When a Spanish person tells you "sport is not politics", don't believe them. Only people who have a state feel comfortable with their structures, with their national teams. In that case there is no politics. But in our case, I couldn't support my national team – the Catalan national team – playing in the World Cup. Then football is politics. Of course it is!' he says, giving the table another thump. 'I've been involved in using football and sport in politics. Think about Cuba or think about the United States. Sport is not politics? My God!'

There is a Teflon quality to Laporta. One of his club directors was outed as a member of the *Fundación Nacional Francisco Franco*, an appreciation society for *El Caudillo*, in 2005. The director was Laporta's brother-in-law; he has since been known as *El Cuñadísimo* (supreme-brother-in-law), the title the husband of Franco's sister used to go by. Laporta survived a no-confidence motion in 2008. At the time of writing, Barça's president Sandro Rosell, his friend-turned-bitter-enemy is investigating a huge hole left in the club accounts by Laporta's dissolute administration. But, of course, where it counted most, Laporta delivered four league titles in seven seasons. He also made one of the boldest managerial appointments in top flight football of recent times, opting for the unproven Pep Guardiola, who was coaching the club's B team, over José Mourinho in 2008.

Mourinho was between jobs at the time. He got his agent, Jorge Mendes, to sound out Barça about the club's managerial position, as the time had come to remove Frank Rijkaard. Laporta was keen to hear more. He proposed a meeting, but his suggestion that Johan Cruyff should tag along vexed Mourinho. The Portuguese questioned why the Dutchman, who belittled his football philosophy and held no official position at the club, should be involved. 'Why shouldn't he?' said Laporta. In the end, Barcelona dispatched one of Laporta's vice presidents, Marc Ingla, to Lisbon to interview Mourinho. Among the slides of his 27-page PowerPoint pitch, there was one which mentioned Guardiola, among four former Barcelona players, as an option as his number two. The support Guardiola had, however, of kingmakers like Cruyff and the club's technical director Txiki Begiristain, as well as Mourinho's refusal in the interview to reign in his aggressive media style, swung it for the 37-year-old Catalan.

'I had spoken to Frank Rijkaard,' says Laporta, 'and told him that if we didn't win any titles that season, I would replace him with Pep Guardiola. Frank understood the situation perfectly. Then I went to Pep. I had a very nice lunch with him. I said I'm taking this decision. And he said: "You won't have the balls to do it." He was managing in the third division! I said, "Pep, it's done. I've decided this and I will do it." He had played in all of FC Barcelona's youth teams. He is "original denomination", a product of La Masia. He was the extension of Cruyff on the pitch; he was the midfielder who controlled the system. He won six leagues, the European Cup at Wembley in 1992. He was captain; he was coach of the second team of Barça. I explained to Pep that we were creating a very nice story. And I said, "Why do you think I'm taking this decision?" He said: "Presi, because you are sure I'll win the Spanish league if I'm the coach," and I said: "Only the Spanish league?" He said, "Step by step, Presi." And he won six trophies in his first season!'

9

CANTERA VERSUS CARTERA

After Barcelona beat Real Madrid 5–0 in November 2010, Pep Guardiola dedicated the victory to Johan Cruyff and Charly Rexach and to the work they had done at La Masia, Barça's youth academy. Cruyff and Rexach were the Clough & Taylor of Barcelona's Dream Team in the early 1990s. They played together for Barça in the 1970s. When Cruyff returned to manage the club in 1988, he sought out Rexach to work as his assistant manager. Several of their old comrades from the championship-winning team of 1974 – Mora, Asensi, Antonio De La Cruz – trained the club's reserve and under-age teams. Cruyff made sure that each of their teams was fitted with the *tiki taka* template. Everyone was on message. From then on, Barça – whether under-8s or senior – aspired to play a similar, keep-ball style of play. No one is sure who coined the phrase *tiki taka*, but its onomatopoeic jingle perfectly captures the pam-pam, possession-based football philosophy that has become synonymous with Barça, since Cruyff's time as manager, and more lately with Spain's national teams.

Rexach first started playing for the club when he was 12 years of age. He's now 65 and still works for Barcelona as an advisor to the president. To get about the city, he locks his tall frame onto a scooter. His nose has the prominent bridge of a Roman, although he has many quintessential Catalan traits. 'I think the first bonus he received as a player is still in his savings bank,' says his friend Joan Golobart, the former Espanyol player. 'When it came to tackling, his gear was never dirty from throwing himself to the ground. Barça was playing Real Madrid at the Camp

Nou one time. There was a Real Madrid central defender called Benito, who was *una bestia*, a beast. Rexach was running for the ball, he was five metres away. Benito was 15 metres from it, but he got to the ball before Rexach. Rexach is very lazy. He used to say that running was for cowards. But technically he was a great player.'

Rexach spent 17 years playing as a winger for Barça, but he never cared much to do the running for the Spanish national team. He spent a decade playing for Spain, but only accrued 17 caps. He mentions a contemporary, Luis Suárez, possibly Spain's greatest player, who only won 32 caps in 15 seasons on the Spanish team. Over the same period, Bobby Charlton amassed 106 caps for England.

'Historically,' says Rexach, 'the *selección* hasn't got *espíritu*, spirit. You go to Brazil and ask a child, "Who's your favourite team?" and he will say, "Brazil." He won't say Botafogo or Santos or Corintians. In Argentina, people's first team is Argentina, and after that River Plate, Chacarita Juniors. You go to Portugal and people's first team is the national team, and after this, Porto and so on. Here in Spain, if you ask someone, "What's your team?" the first answer is Barça or Madrid. The *selección* has never had cachet. Until now. Now it has changed, but I think that they have done well because the *selección* today is cohesive. It has got 30 players that have really gelled as a group. In my time, Catalan people didn't like to play with Spain. I went to the World Cup in Argentina in 1978, for instance. The club said "Five players from Barça? No, only two will go. That's enough." In the old times, it was a Solomonic decision, to do with politics – "two from here, two from there", to please everybody. In 1962, Spain went to Chile with Helenio Herrera as manager. Di Stéfano, Puskas, Gento, Kubala, Suárez were all playing and they finished bottom of their group, because they weren't a team. Everybody went *a su aire*, not all together, but individually.'

So, I asked, the players' reluctance to sweat for Spain back in the day was due to ambivalence about Franco? 'Yes,' he replied, 'but apart from this there was also a problem. There was no money. Now to play with Spain means a lot of money.'

When Rexach started playing for Barça in the mid 1960s, the rivalry with Real Madrid was all-consuming for the club. A season was often defined by whether they won their *clásico* matches or not. Coming second in the league, forfeiting it to Real Madrid, was rationalised, he says, because so many of their other matches were, in his words, 'robbed'. The rivalry was more intense than today, he adds. His dad was left wing and fought on the Republican side in the Civil War. 'Barça was his flag,' he says. 'My support for Barça comes from my father, who instilled in me what it meant to be from Barcelona. It was a political matter. From me to my son, it's only sport, although I explain him the history. But if you were to talk to my son about Franco, he wouldn't know who he is.'

As well as being a player, Rexach has had all the major portfolios in the Barça cabinet, including shifts as technical director of La Masia and as manager. He held the managerial reins a few times, usually on a care-taker basis, but took over full time in 2001. In April 2002, Barça met Real Madrid in the semi-final of the Champions League.

'The pressure was terrible,' he says, 'because it's not only a clash in this country. The whole world is looking on. In these matches, you try to relax the players because if not some of them would be climbing up the walls.' His team, he laments, was dogged by injuries – Rivaldo missed both legs – suspensions and the woodwork. In the end, they went down 3–1 on aggregate. The defeat cost Rexach his job, but, as he likes to joke, his rank improved – the club made him a director instead.

One of Rexach's protégés, Pep Guardiola, went a couple of steps further in his first season in charge. In 2009, he became the youngest manager of a Champions League-winning team. There is a priestly quality to Guardiola. John Carlin reckons he's like the head of a seminary. Born in 1971, he grew up in the shadow of a religious retreat – a Francis-can hermitage towers over Santpedor, his hometown in the flatlands of central Catalonia. Football became his vocation. He entered La Masia at 13 years of age where he stayed for six years before his ordination with Barça's first team in 1990. He likes to dress in well fitted but sombre clothes. His suits, like his view of this world, tend to be black. He once wrote in an article, while still a player, that he shared the opinion of a friend: 'I arrived to try to change the world. Now, all I hope for is that the world will not change me.' He feels comfortable using religious metaphors, once suggesting that Johan Cruyff painted Barça's chapel; subsequent managers must merely restore and add to it.

Rexach remembers him when he first arrived at the club in 1984. He describes him as being '*muy poca cosa*' – a very, little thing – and clever. As a player, he says Guardiola was slow; he couldn't shoot, dribble or score goals. He understood football, though. More than play himself, he made others play. He was quicker even, mentally, than Xavi, his successor on Barça's team, says Rexach. He describes him as the extension of the manager on the pitch. 'When Cruyff and I were managers, we would think of a strategy and explain it to the players. When the players left, we would call Pep and say to him, "We are going to play so and so, but, in the 20th minute, I'll signal to you, and you change to this other strategy." And he was the only one who had the information; because there are players that with too much information will go mad.'

After leaving Barça in 2001, Guardiola played in Italy and Mexico and endured the desert heat of Qatar. Free from the entrenched politics and insularity of Barça, he began to acquire different perspectives on the game. For intellectual sustenance he rocked up at the doorsteps of former Argentine coaches Marcelo Bielsa and César Luis Menotti for late-night tutorials on the nuances of the game. Menotti, who managed Barcelona in the 1980s, remarked that in Guardiola he met a man who 'reads, studies, listens and shows an enormous capacity for observation'.

Guardiola is an intense man, though not in an intimidating way like, say, Roy Keane. He has greater emotional intelligence than the moody Irishman who shares many of his hallmarks – successful playing career, drive, wit – but has floundered in management because he can't cajole others. Guardiola can connect with people. 'He has his own personality and he knows that it's not necessary to shout at people to make them work,' says Rexach. 'Imagine that a waiter comes over here and spills a glass of water on you. Pep would make a polite comment to relax the waiter. He wouldn't shout. He knows how to transmit what it is he wants people to do.'

Jordi Cotrina, a photographer with *El Periódico de Catalunya*, once told me that in 25 years of snapping pictures of Barça matches, Guardiola is the only player he has seen getting sick from tension before a match. There is a marked restlessness about him. Since assuming the mantle of leadership at Barça, moments of relaxation must have been an alien pleasure for him. When a journalist asked him if he would prefer to manage in England where he would have more control of day-to-day issues, he blurted: 'but I don't want more responsibility! I've already lost my hair and got a bad back.' He witnessed first-hand the rot that set in during the final years of the Cruyff management era. Perhaps it informed his decision to work at the club based on rolling one-year contracts.

Guardiola's in-laws own a line of high-end clothes stores in Barcelona, which probably accounts for his taste in fine clothing. He isn't, however, flashy. Ronald Koeman made the point in an interview recently that when Guardiola first broke into the Barça squad, he was driving a second-hand Volkswagen; three years later, he was still driving it. (Barça's first team players are barred from driving their sports cars to training today.) He is bookish, which leaves him open to lampooning in the laddish world of football. *Crackòvia*, the satirical Catalan football TV show, often depicted him wandering into the dressing room immersed in a book of poetry, sending his players scampering for cover. 'Everything is for doing and everything is possible,' he would say sanctimoniously, reciting the words of a famous Catalan poem.

Like many of the players schooled at La Masia, Guardiola tries to be humble. When Gerard Piqué and Víctor Valdés raised their hands in *manita* fashion to fans after the 5–0 filleting of Real Madrid in November 2010 they were quickly censured by Carles Puyol. Their team captain gestured frantically towards the stand with his eyes. Guardiola had sent out a message – he didn't want any gloating. However, traces of Guardiola's personality that seep out occasionally suggest he is not completely dry. When a Madrid newspaper dispatched a journalist to ask him if he pissed perfume, he thought for a second and then replied deadpan: 'Maybe they are right; maybe I do piss perfume.'

He is such a powerful presence at Barcelona that the club president Sandro Rosell says he could have his job one day. Santiago Segurola said to me in March 2011 that Guardiola already was the real president of the club. Guardiola's Catalan pedigree is interesting. He says that he doesn't like nationalists, even moderate nationalists, yet he has never been slow to promote Catalonia's independent cause. As a player, he petitioned to have Catalonia's national team recognised officially. When Barça celebrated its 1992 European Cup win at a city centre square in Barcelona, the callow 21-year-old made a play on Josep Tarradellas' famous speech from the same balcony in 1977. Tarradellas was returning to the city after four decades of political exile. '*Ja sóc aquí*' – 'I am here now', he kept repeating during his speech, a pretentious phrase that Catalans made fun of when it was first uttered in the 1970s; it was something to be said when you turned up at a bar. Over the years, however, the phrase has taken on a more solemn air, something Guardiola picked up on with his tinkered version fifteen years later: '*Ja la teniu aquí*' – 'Here you have it'.

How great a manager is Guardiola? He has worked with a prodigious collection of players in his own backyard. How would he fare elsewhere? 'I'd like to see him try,' says José Mourinho.

The winner of the 2010 FIFA *Ballon d'Or* award was announced in Zurich on 10 January 2011. Three short players made the shortlist – Andrés Iniesta, Leo Messi and Xavi Hernández. They all play with Barcelona. It is the first time that all three shortlisted players for this prestigious award came from the same club since the days of Arrigo Sacchi's great Milan team. When the trio line up alongside David Villa and Pedro – or Pedrito, little Pedro – for Barcelona's Famous Five attacking line, they average 5ft 7in, the height, as it happens, of Alexis Sánchez, the Chilean striker who joined Barça in July 2011.

It would be difficult to find a football analyst outside Madrid who does not think that the Barcelona of Xavi and co is one of football's finest teams. Commentators have breathlessly installed them on the same hall of fame as the sport's great sides, alongside di Stéfano's Real Madrid, Cruyff's Ajax and the Milan of Van Basten. Their pinball brand of football is a marvel to watch. Since Guardiola took over in the summer of 2008, they have been making short work of the best teams that Spain and Europe can throw at them. Every team they play is taller than them. In a 2013 study by the Professional Football Players Observatory of 31 top division leagues from UEFA member associations, Barcelona's squad registered as the smallest in height. (Interestingly, Real Madrid has the tallest collection of footballers in La Liga.) But Barcelona is happy that its players are short. It's part of its distinct football philosophy.

'In Barça, we look first for talent. When Messi was 11 years of age, he was this height,' says Carles Folguera, resting his fingers on the edge of a big oak table in one of the meeting rooms in La Masia, the stone farmhouse where Barcelona's football academy originated, 'but it was obvious he had talent.' Folguera, a former roller hockey player at the club, is now the director of La Masia. He says that a Napoleon complex feeds into the selection criteria of their 40-odd scouts. 'If Messi was going to grow up or stay small nobody knew for sure,' he adds. 'The physical part of a player like Messi is important but it's not the most important thing. If I have two players with the same technical skill, one big and one small, I will keep the small one because the small one will overcome the big one. He will have to work harder and he will be more resourceful. He will need to come up with clever strategies to compensate for his lack of size. The bigger guy won't try as hard. Messi, Xavi, Iniesta, Pedro are all like this.'

They might be onto something at La Masia. In that demographic study of UEFA football leagues, it was found that the most picked players in a squad tend to be shorter than their teammates. This wasn't always the case. There is a shortage of room in football today. Players are fitter than they used to be. They close down space quickly. In a

90-minute match, the Real Madrid midfielder Xabi Alonso will run almost three times further than his father Miguel Ángel 'Periko' Alonso did when he played in Barcelona's midfield in the early 1980s. Most of the frenetic running in football is done in the middle of the pitch. Midfield, as Jorge Valdano, Real Madrid's sometime guru puts it, is 'a good place to meet people'. Until a few years ago, big, hulking players with boundless reserves of stamina were prized assets in this hunting ground. Men like Patrick Vieira, Michael Essien, in his days at Chelsea, and Yaya Touré stalked the midfields of the Champions League like human wrecking balls. It was all about knockdowns and rebounds. But in a short space of time, Barça has introduced a corrective to the ideal physique of a football player. Their game is played on the ground. In short, it moves the ball amongst its players so rapidly that big, strapping opponents can't get at it.

Other teams in Spain, like Villarreal, and abroad, like Arsenal, try to emulate Barcelona's style. Barça's success, the result of over 30 years indoctrination at La Masia, has also filtered through to the Spanish national team, where at underage and senior level its teams are peppered with Barcelona's short players. Spanish teams practice their *tiki taka* technique with unrivalled results for a European country. Fernando Hierro, the former Real Madrid player, worked as a sporting director for the Spanish Football Federation from 2007 to 2011. He looks with a withering eye on those who have come lately to herald the rise of the short player. 'People used to think that the Spanish type of player – small, skillful, technically good – would not make it at the professional stage. However, now that we've won [European Championships] and the World Cup, the world loves these types of players and says: "Look how well these people play football!"'

The winner of the 2010 FIFA *Ballon d'Or* was, of course, Leo Messi. He is 5ft 6½in. He wasn't always so tall. When he arrived in Barcelona as a 13-year-old from Argentina, he was 4ft 6in, nearly one foot shorter than the average height for a boy of that age. As a child, Messi was diagnosed with a rare growth hormone deficiency. The condition affects one in 20 million people. It is not a family affliction. His younger sister, María Sol, for instance, is a tall young lady. The average cost of treatment, which involves subcutaneous injections every day for three to five years, is over £100,000 a year. This kind of money was beyond the means of Messi's parents. Messi began his treatment in 1998. (He used to administer the injections into his legs himself every night.) At the time, his father worked in a steel-making company; his mother at a magnet manufacturing workshop. The medical insurance they used to cover the costs of the treatment ran out after two years. Messi's club, Newell's Old Boys, had initially offered to pay for every second injection, but when payments started arriving late, Messi's parents got the hump and took their talented son for a trial to Barcelona when the opportunity arose.

What is, perhaps, the most arresting thing about Messi is not his size (for Diego Maradona is an inch and a half shorter) but his speed. Frank Rijkaard, who gave Messi his league debut for Barcelona in 2004 at 17 years of age, says that Messi has better acceleration than Maradona, who, of course, Rijkaard played against many times. In fact, Messi's running speed is 4.5 strides per second, which is faster than the 4.4 of Asafa Powell, who, at the time of writing, has broken the 10-second barrier in 100-metre races more times than anyone else.

Barça's most famous fairytale nearly never happened. Messi initially came to the club for a trial period in September 2000. Charly Rexach was heading to Sydney for the Olympics when he landed. 'I told the club to watch him for 15 days,' he says. 'He had to be very good to justify the money. It was a big investment. When I came back, I asked about him. Some people said that he dribbled a lot, he was small; some others said he was a table football player. There wasn't a quorum. I said, "Tomorrow there's a match at 5 p.m. I'll come and decide yes or no" because the family was waiting for an answer. When I arrived at the pitch, the ref whistled for play to begin. I walked around the pitch, talking to a fellow, watched a bit of the game and, when I arrived to the manager's bench, I said, "You can sign him up. He is *fuera de serie*, a phenomenon."

'I phoned the club and said that the next day a boy will come with his father to sign a contract. Messi's father had gone to the club several times without solving anything. The father called me to talk. We were in a cafeteria in Montjuïc. He said, "I'm fed up. You sign a contract or we leave." To please the father, I asked for a piece of paper and the waiter gave me a paper napkin. I wrote, "I, Carles Rexach, as technical director of FC Barcelona, promise to contract this player, Leo Messi." I signed it and I told him to keep it. If the club at the end didn't sign, I'd have felt ridiculous. The contract was signed and I forgot the napkin. I thought it was thrown away. I was surprised to hear it has reappeared. They are talking about putting it in the Barça museum.'

Messi's family joined him in Barcelona when he arrived to take up his apprenticeship in February 2001. They knew so little about their new city that it came as a surprise to them that it was by the sea. Suffering from homesickness, however, his mother and his siblings returned to their hometown, Rosario, birthplace of Ché Guevara, later that summer. Messi, who summered in Argentina, was asked repeatedly what he wanted to do; he decided to return to Barça of his own volition. Messi's father, Jorge, who looks a ringer for his son and manages his financial affairs to this day, stayed in Catalonia to chaperone him. The young prodigy admits that he was so miserable at times that he used to cry in his house, alone so that his father wouldn't see.

Messi looks as if he's shy, but apparently he's as much of a trickster off the field as he is on it. 'People who know him in the dressing room know that he's *cachondo*. He's a kidder, a real scream,' says Carles Folguera. Messi's from the famous class of 1987, a contemporary of Gerard Piqué and Cesc Fàbregas. In his early days with the big boys, the little Argentine nearly chose the wrong path. He used to traipse after Ronaldinho when the Brazilian hit the town. One day he was pulled aside. 'You've two options,' said Guardiola, who was manager of Barcelona's B Team at the time. 'Either you keep on partying, and you'll be out of here in days. Or you start eating properly, quit the alcohol, go to bed early and come to practice on time. Only then might you become the best in the world.'

Messi loves to dribble. He's great at winning 'the second ball'. When he's tackled sometimes, the ball bobbles in the air between himself and his tacklers. Because he has such a low centre of gravity, he is invariably the one who lures it back to earth. It helps to be short. He plays with the wonder of a child. Barcelona played Real Sociedad a couple of weeks before Christmas 2010 at the Camp Nou. In the 86th minute, he gathered the ball at the edge of Real Sociedad's box. He ran straight across the box with it, parallel with the 18-yard line. Four Real Sociedad players followed him. The first defender half-attempted a tackle, but withdrew his boot, realising he would be too late to get anywhere near the ball. Instead of trying to tackle, the other three players just ran across the box after him, waving their arms like they were trying to shoo him away from a house fire. Messi eventually outpaced the last of the defenders just before he reached the other side of the box and then slotted the ball with his left foot back across the goalmouth into the bottom corner of the goal. We leapt to our feet to give him a standing ovation. It was ridiculous. I'm sure people could see what he was going to do when he set off on his jaunt, but probably discarded the childish thought immediately. When he pulled it off, you could hear the laughter in the applause. It was the kind of goal that you would see in a schoolyard.

Earlier in the half, he scored an archetypal Barça goal. Gathering the ball near midfield on the right hand touchline he set off on a dribble but immediately found his path blocked by Real Sociedad defenders. He passed inside to Dani Alves and ran forward to receive a return pass. The next few seconds were dizzying. The Barça pair was outnumbered eight to two. With the aid of three one-twos with Alves, Messi somehow managed to turn up on the edge of the six-yard box with the ball, where he calmly stroked it into the goal.

In Spain, a debate rages as to whether Messi is better than Real Madrid's Cristiano Ronaldo. The Portuguese star is a peculiar man. He is the ultimate *galáctico* and one of sport's great narcissists, seen as often in celebrity magazines as he is on the back pages. He once bragged that he does a thousand press-ups a day to maintain his rippled abs. He's a dandy when it comes to clothes fashion and confesses that shopping is his greatest vice. Off the pitch, he owns a couple of boutiques; on it, he likes to pop his collar, wear a pink strap for thigh strains and unveil experiments in hairstyle every other week. He is petulant when things don't go smoothly for him during matches, a childish practice which he has never managed to kick. His mother said that his nickname was 'cry baby' as a child; that he used to cry if his friends didn't score when he passed the ball to them, which might explain why he loves to dribble so much. During the award ceremony for the 2007 FIFA World Player of the Year, he was on the verge of tears when it was announced that he had trailed in third behind Messi and the winner, Kaká.

Despite the arrested development and the sappy exterior, he is, however, a resilient man. On the pitch, he is courageous, has largely forsaken his youthful habit of diving, and is strong in the air. Xabi Alonso, his teammate at Real Madrid, points out that he's a workhorse when it comes to rummaging for the ball, something that is uncommon for players of his ilk. 'When a team loses the ball, some superstars wait for their teammates to get it back for them. Not Cristiano. He fights, he runs, he helps us in midfield.' People wonder at his self-love. 'I think that being rich, handsome, being a great player, people are jealous of me,' he said recently in a post-match interview, trying to account for why opposition players like to hack him down in matches. It was as if he were listing some of the chemical elements from the periodic table. This kind of arrogance might offend some; others are grateful for his spikiness, for having the personality to provoke while most of his peers in Spanish football excel at saying nothing.

A defining moment came for Ronaldo at the 2006 World Cup. In the quarter-final match between England and Portugal, he winked conspiratorially towards the Portuguese bench after Wayne Rooney was sent off for stamping on Ricardo Carvalho's groin. The English tabloid press blamed him for the sending off – for pressuring the ref – and labelled him 'the most hated man in England'. Making up with Rooney, his Manchester United teammate was one thing; facing down the vilification that awaited him on his return to England's Premier League grounds was, for a 21-year-old, quite another thing. Alex Ferguson, his club manager, flew to Portugal to help assuage his fears. Ronaldo toyed with the idea of leaving United. He told the Spanish press he wanted to move to Real Madrid. In the end, he decided to return to England, and ride out the opprobrium, which he did and swept the boards in the league's Player of the Year awards in the ensuing season. He had shown steel. Neither is he naive when it comes to the charades around transfer time. After Manchester United beat Chelsea in the final of the 2008 Champions League final in Moscow, he chatted with English reporters. He assured them he was 'definitely' staying at Old Trafford. Then he walked a few steps and spoke to Spanish reporters and told them he had 'yet to decide' about his future. It was only a matter of time before he left for Spain.

His bloody-mindedness owes something to his childhood. He was born in February 1985 on the island of Madeira, which is about 600 miles from Portugal, closer to Africa than to mainland Europe. He was named after his father's favourite actor, Ronald Reagan. He's the youngest of four siblings. One of his sisters eked out a career in music on the back of his subsequent fame by using the stage name, Ronalda. The family wasn't impoverished – his father, who died of an alcohol-related illness in 2005, was a gardener; his mother, a cook – but money was scarce enough that they lived in a bungalow so small that the washing machine was kept on the roof.

At 12 years of age, he was picked up by Sporting Lisbon and took his first plane ride to the Portuguese capital to enrol in its football academy. It was a brutal, lonely experience for him, the kind familiar to millions of boarding school boys. Suddenly thrown into a dormitory with nine other boys, he was mocked for his strange accent. He, in turn, had trouble understanding everyone else. When it came to phoning home, he used to tearfully watch the units bleeding from his phone cards. He was eventually so homesick that the club sent for his mother to be with him. But there was a determination that drove him to succeed. As a teenager, he used to tie weights onto both feet and practice his drib-bling, believing it would help him to be even faster with the ball.

Ronaldo's goalscoring stats are the measure of Messi's. Ronaldo, to his credit, has scored most of his Real Madrid goals for a team in transition. He knows his importance. Late in the 2010–11 season, he told a Real Madrid fan site that 'if it were not for me, you would be at least 20 points behind Barcelona'. He's more powerful than Messi. He's a better header of the ball and has a unique, banana-leaf trajectory to his long-range shots. He has become a more effective player under Mourinho, who has taught him to forage closer to goal. In the white heat of the most pressurised matches, however, differ-ences between them become apparent. Ronaldo, at 28 years of age, is only just learning to do one-twos. In that crowded middle space of the field where Messi usually gathers the ball, he often looks for passes, with an eye for looking round corners beyond his Portuguese rival. Messi creates more goals than Ronaldo, as he did for Villa's brace in the famous *manita* match. To pass the ball is an attribute of La Masia boys.

Spain's football academies are called *canteras*. *Cantera* is the Spanish word for quarry. The players of Barcelona's *cantera* train at Sant Joan Despí, a new complex on the outskirts of the city. It is also where the first team trains. It is big and spacious like any modern training campus. The gate into it is surprisingly wide, about 100 feet, like something you might find at the entrance to a factory, which is fitting. Barcelo-na's production line is the envy of the world. Ten of the 14 Barcelona players who saw action against Real Madrid in the *manita* match were carved from the stone of Barcelona's *cantera*. That night only two of Real Madrid's players, Iker Casillas and substitute Álvaro Arbeloa, came through their youth system. The days of the *Quinta del Buitre*, when five *cantera* graduates – Míchel, Manolo Sanchís, Emilio Butragueño, Martín Vázquez and Miguel Pardeza – backboned Real Madrid's team for a decade, have long passed.

Albert Puig, who has been technical director at La Masia for the last couple of years, says the most impressive thing about Barça's operation is its consistency. Trainers come and go, but the style of football has remained the same since Guardiola's time there as a teenager during the 1980s. At Real Madrid's *cantera* each coach imposes his own vision. All of Barça's teams, from the seven-year-olds to the first team, play the same way; this is not the case at Real Madrid. Each year there are 60 pupils, 12 of whom are basketball players, the rest footballers. One or two of these will make it as professional athletes with the club. Barcelona looks after their academy stars around the clock, like at a boarding school. Their education is through Catalan. Real Madrid has a less hands-on system – it outsources accommodation and education to external institutions. There is such an emphasis on education at La Masia that Barça's youths spend, on average, half the time of their counterparts at top English football academies playing organised football – only 90 minutes a day, plus a match at the weekend. A notable byproduct of Barcelona's inculcation, of its marshalling of a kind of benign military school or what would be called formation in a seminary, is the forcefield it exerts on its graduates. The good ones that slip away are often drawn back like prodigals, most recently in the case of Piqué, Arsenal's former captain, Fàbregas and the tearaway fullback Jordi Alba. Three Catalan boys who boomeranged back to Barcelona once they became men.

Since the summer of 2011, trainees no longer live at La Masia, the eighteenth-century building on the grounds of the Camp Nou which served as a hall of residence. It is where Barcelona's football academy started in 1979. La Masia's walls were draped with school year-type photographs of its players when they were kids. Carles Puyol, Barcelona's captain, had the same shaggy-haired mullet as a teenager as he has today. Puyol is famous for his intensity. He often shouts 'Geri! Geri!' during matches just to make sure that Piqué, his central defensive partner, is alert. Puyol is from La Pobla de Segur, a Catalan village of a few thousand inhabitants close to the French border. 'When he was dropped off here by his father for a few days' trial,' says Carles Folguera, 'he said to him: "If you come back to our town, it won't be because you didn't give everything."'

Barça's players don't do physical training until they are 16 years of age. It is all ball work. *Rondos* (piggy-in-the-middle ball exercises) are the fulcrum of Barcelona's philosophy. When you wander around Catalonia, you'll see kids in dusty parks or wherever there's a bit of asphalt concrete playing variations of the game. Girls mixed in with the boys. Whoever's in the middle is the subject of derision – someone to be laughed at. Every Barça match you watch is an extended game of *rondos*. Round and round the ball goes. Johan Cruyff is credited in the Barcelona museum with introducing the practice to the club. It has become a staple of training sessions for teams – whether Sunday League or Champions League – the world over. Most Spanish premier division clubs, even Real Madrid on occasion, do *rondos* for warm-ups before kick-off in matches. They're a feature of Barcelona's regular training sessions. If there is an exemplar of *rondos*, it is Xavi. Guardiola calls him *maqui*, the machine. He's unlike any other midfielder who has played the game in bearing. When he has the ball nestled at his feet, he keeps his head upright and swivelling, like a periscope scouting for a target. He has an obsession with *lebensraum* – with finding more space on the pitch, and a mathematician's appreciation for the geometry of it. Somebody calculated that the *gematria* values (where a numerical value is assigned to a letter) of 'Xavi' (56) and 'pass' (55) are almost identical. He completes more passes than any other player in the Spanish league, almost twice as many as Xabi Alonso, Real Madrid's current playmaker.

'Barcelona's idea is simple,' says Puig. 'They try to keep the ball until the opposition make a mistake. They even use the ball to defend – by tiring the opposition out. The training mantra at La Masia is "receive, pass, offer". They try to think of where they will make a pass before the ball arrives at their feet.' Dani Alves once quipped that Xavi plays 'in the future'. Historically, Barça used to buy *galácticos* – such as Ladislao Kubala in the 1950s and Diego Maradona in the 1980s – and adapt the team to their style. Periko Alonso told me they were ordered to give the ball to Maradona. Now Barça players do the opposite. Not all of their stars can adjust. According to Michael Robinson, Thierry Henry and Zlatan Ibrahimović 'looked clumsy' while playing in Barcelona's colours. Eidur Gudjohnsen, who played for Barça from 2006 to 2009, doubts if the club would be able to fit Wayne Rooney into their system. Similarly, he questions whether many from Barça's ranks would cut it elsewhere; Barcelona's sum, he argues, is greater than their parts. 'I don't think Pedro, for example, is the best right winger or striker in the world. I don't think Busquets is the best defensive midfielder in the world. I'm not sure Puyol is up there with the best in his position either, but this team are just perfect the way that they're moulded together. Maybe I'm being harsh, but if you put Busquets in a mediocre side in England – or elsewhere – he'd struggle, but together with Iniesta and Xavi that midfield trio works perfect.'

There is something admirable about the project at La Masia – the production of home-grown players who adhere to an aesthetically pleasing type of football. It is applauded by Michel Platini, the UEFA chief. You can see the continuity at work. The playmaker on Barça teams is revered. Pep Guardiola directed traffic in that position for a decade. Xavi took over from him. Andrés Iniesta is waiting to do the job once Xavi passes on. Guardiola had a premonition about this when he first took a proper look at the pale-faced Iniesta. He said as much to Xavi. 'You see that? You'll push me towards the exit, but that guy will send us both into retirement.' Barcelona has a mission to play the way they do. Jorge Valdano says that Guardiola took it 'to the point of exaggeration'. Real Madrid's objective is first to win, then to provide the spectacle. It uses a chequebook in this pursuit. *Sport*, one of the Barcelona-based sports newspapers, coined the term *cantera versus cartera*, academy v. wallet, to capture their ideological differences. Laporta used to like saying that Real Madrid buys *Ballon d'Or* players whereas Barcelona prefers to make them.

It is naive, however, to think that Barcelona is at the mercy of Real Madrid's superior spending power. According to Sid Lowe, Barcelona spent £600 million over a decade on players, which is not far off the £870 million spent by its nemesis over the same period. It actually outspent Real Madrid during the summer of 2011, as Mourinho, eschewing the *galáctico* philosophy of his president, sought to build a more workmanlike team. In fact, Barça pays its players more. The 2012 Global Sports Salaries Survey ranked it ahead of franchises like the LA Lakers as the best-paid team in the world. The average wage of a Barcelona first team footballer is £101,160 a week. It pays well to be miserly with possession of a football.

I once asked Alain de Botton, the popular English philosopher, if he bought into the notion of national stereotypes. 'I think,' he said, 'if you took all the English babies that were born this year and you brought them up in Germany they would end up as Germans in their character. I don't think there's anything ethnic about any country that makes it this or that. It's obviously a cultural thing. Society helps to nurture those sides of human beings which are there in everybody, in every country but don't get that much attention in other countries. What happens in countries is a little bit like what happens in families. There's a kind of self-identity. It's like, "How come Brazilians know how to dance?" When a Brazilian child does his first dance everybody is looking at him. Everybody's telling him how to make the moves. Everybody's clapping him. He sees his mother doing it. It develops. It's not inherent. It's a cultural thing, but it ends up being true.'

What about the cultural differences between Madrid and Barcelona, the two great cities of Spain and *Països Catalans*? 'The thing about *madrileños*,' says John Carlin, who has been living in Spain for over a dozen years, 'is that they're much more difficult to pin down than Catalans. Madrid is a bit like the Spanish New York. It has a more dog eat dog, concrete jungle feel to it. It's a place where people have come from all over the country. Everybody in Madrid you talk to will have some hometown village they refer to, which they might have left five, ten, twenty, forty years ago – or even that their parents have left. It's a much more uprooted, dynamic sort of place.

'So in Madrid, because you've got people from all over, there isn't the same sense of belonging to the place as there is in Barcelona. It's more chaotic. It's dirtier. People double park and nobody cares too much about other people. You have to look after yourself. Compared to Catalans, they're more anarchic, more irresponsible and more fun, open, *simpáticos*. In Barcelona, there's much more of a sense of an ordered, civic society with a sense of pride and belonging. People are more careful with money. People are more withdrawn. They are more thin-lipped and uptight.'

Could these distinctions feed into the type of football their teams play? In Barcelona, where every peseta is a prisoner, their footballers hate to cough up the ball to opponents. Their play is cerebral, more northern European than their dogged, cavalier Castilian kin. Real Madrid teams, extroverted and invariably packed with outsiders from around Spain and overseas, are famous for the fight in them. Their history is littered with epic comebacks, *remontadas*. They try to match this fighting spirit with artistic flourishes, to be flamboyant like the Spanish character, but above all they like a scrapper.

'It comes from di Stéfano – half artist, half warrior,' Alfredo Relaño told me. 'Madrid likes the *luchador*, the fighting player, the one who wants to win. It doesn't matter whether he's good or bad just that he never yields, who receives kicks and doesn't complain, the player who plays well in any pitch, even if it is Elche's one in the second division, covered in mud. Madrid wants its players to resist defeat, that if they lose, they're bleeding with a broken leg. Not that they're aggressive, but the Madrid that pleases is a heroic Madrid.'

Sid Lowe points out that there's a contradiction at the heart of both clubs. Barcelona's identity is hung on Catalan nationalism yet its footballing identity is a Dutch one, whose origins can be traced to former coaches Rinus Michels, Johan Cruyff, Louis van Gaal and Frank Rijkaard. Until recently, they've also sprinkled their teams with more international superstars than Real Madrid, most notably with Brazilians. Over the last two decades, for instance, Romário, Ronaldo, Rivaldo and Ronaldinho have lit up the Camp Nou. 'It is reflected in Barcelona as a city,' he says, 'which is tremendously proud of being Catalan, but is much more international than Madrid. It's a port city. It likes to project its Catalanism internationally, rather than to Spain. At the same time, Real Madrid has this universal appeal where it is supposed to stand for Spain; yet it represents something a little more insular than Barcelona does, even though theoretically it represents something much more expansive.'

There is nothing absolute, of course, about the clubs' identities and their players' characteristics as footballers. Stereotypes are loose fitting, but to what extent do teams take their nature from recent, influential managers – José Mourinho and the priestly Pep Guardiola? Ramón Besa makes the point that when Messi won the FIFA *Ballon d'Or* in January 2011, the abiding image was a photo of him smiling with his two teammates, Xavi and Iniesta, the runners-up. There were no complaints. They congratulated him. They were happy for him. He's their mate. 'In any club there are problems due to jealousy,' says Besa. 'But Guardiola thinks Barça is an ecosystem of socialised management, a collective, where the individual is subservient to the group ethic. There must be no egos in the dressing room. The idea is that it's a team game, not a self-worship game.'

Guardiola axed several stars from Barça's roster – Ronaldinho, Deco, Samuel Eto'o and Zlatan Ibrahimović – because he felt they were upsetting harmony in the squad. Humility is a central tenet of the La Masia creed. In contrast, Mourinho, the game's greatest ego, is happy to work with big personalities, including Cristiano Ronaldo, who generates more search queries on Google than any Hollywood film star. Real Madrid, the biggest club in the world, is built to cater for men with attitude. 'Real Madrid,' says John Carlin 'is more of a bunch of thugs and braggarts – Sergio Ramos, Pepe, Cristiano and Ricardo Carvalho. Barcelona's guys – Messi, Xavi and Iniesta – are all awfully good. They're well-behaved boys. They're like worthy seminarians. You could imagine them shuffling behind the cardinal in their little sacrosanct robes.'

10

BRING ME THE HEAD OF GARCÍA CORTÉS

Rafael García Cortés had the most memorable fresh air in Real Madrid's history. The club reached the final of the 1981 European Cup. It was the first time in 15 years that they were back at that stage of the tournament they believe is theirs by birthright. The final was in Paris, scene of their first triumph in 1956. They played Liverpool. It was a filthy, tense match. In the 81st minute, Liverpool had a throw-in by one of Real Madrid's corner flags. The ball was flung towards Liverpool's full back Alan Kennedy who chested it forward as he ran into the box. The ball bounced in front of García Cortés. He had time to draw aim. He swung at it with his left foot, his good peg, but missed it completely. Kennedy bypassed him and rifled the ball into the net from an acute angle. Liverpool won 1–0.

García Cortés works out of an office from the Bernabéu stadium. He's a director of the club's youth foundation, *Escuela de Fútbol del Real Madrid*. Like Barcelona, the club has schools scattered around the globe for children, which cater for all skill levels, for a fee. It's good to keep kids off the streets and it's good to spread the brand. Real Madrid boldly opened their first such school in Barcelona a decade ago, but fell out with the local franchise owner and withdrew their name from the school's masthead.

García Cortés is whippet thin, like a lot of former Spanish footballers, and spirited by nature. He invariably winks or pinches your shoulder when delivering the punch line to one of his anecdotes. He's friendly or, as the Spanish say, *muy simpático*. He's also *muy tranquilo*, at peace, about the Alan Kennedy incident. He actually had a fine game, having kept the shackles on Kenny Dalglish, Liverpool's danger man. It was one of those freak moments that swing a match and one he is not allowed to forget. The pitch was lined for rugby. It was full of '*montañas*' he says. The ball landed on one of these craggy mountains just as he took his unfortunate swipe at it. Real Madrid had only watched one video of their opponents before the final. 'It was a great adventure,' he says.

I saw Alan Kennedy play when I was a kid. It was in a league game at Anfield in 1983. His car was parked within the grounds of the stadium. It was a red Ford – Liverpool, of course, play in red kit – and it had a white facsimile of his autograph emblazoned along the side of it. Kennedy, along with others from the Liverpool team of that era, including Graeme Souness, Jimmy Case, Mark Lawrenson, Steve Highway, Bruce Grobbelaar, David Johnson, David Hodgson, Ian Rush and Terry McDermott, sported a moustache and brown, shaggy hair. I think I understand now why Kennedy felt compelled to write his name on his possessions.

There was a homogenous feel to Real Madrid's team in that 1981 European Cup final, too. They were known as '*equipo de los García*' because five of them, including Rafael García Cortés, were named García, even though the stars of the team were the German Uli Stielike; José Antonio Camacho, the guy who lasted three league games during his two rides on the Real Madrid managerial merry-go-round; the striker Carlos Santillana and the iconic Juanito. Traditionally, the shorthand for Real Madrid's teams comes from their players. There was di Stéfano's team in the 1950s; the *Yé-Yé* generation during the swinging 1960s; the Garcías; the *Quinta del Buitre* in the 1980s; the Ferrari Boys in the 1990s; and Zidane and the *Galácticos*. The present bunch, Alfredo Relaño assures me, will be known as Mourinho's team, and Barcelona's all-conquering team as Guardiola's team, just as previous Barça ones were known by their manager – from Frank Rijkaard, Guardiola's predecessor, back as far as Helenio Herrera in the 1950s.

Born in 1958, García Cortés is a *madrileño* and a product of Real Madrid's *cantera*. His first Madrid-Barça match at the Camp Nou was a bone-rattling experience. 'I never heard a noise as loud,' he says. 'Every single person in the stadium seemed to be whistling. It was such a hostile atmosphere. I remember when I was going out onto the pitch I held onto my shorts. One of my teammates said, "What are you doing?" I said, "I'm holding onto my shorts to make sure they don't fall down from all the noise." I have never, ever heard a noise like it before or since. I suppose that it must have been something similar for Figo when he played there for his first match for Real Madrid.'

García Cortés has fonder memories of playing *clásicos* at the Bernabéu, where he scored a free kick during a 3–1 win in 1982. He played for Real Madrid at the time their fans first began chanting, '*¡Así, así, así, gana el Madrid!*' – That's how Madrid wins. He says Barcelona's famous politically loaded rallying cry – '*¡Visca el Barça, visca Catalunya!*' – doesn't bother him. 'I think there is a political component that is stronger in Barcelona. Here, you're a *madridista* and that's it. There you're from Barça and also Catalan. I know they are part of Spain. Even if they don't want it, they will still be part of Spain,' he says with a laugh.

Vicente del Bosque also played for Real Madrid in the 1981 European Cup final. He marked Ray Kennedy, the Liverpool player whose throw led to Alan Kennedy's goal. There have been many great characters in Real Madrid's history. Del Bosque is one of the most interesting. He was born in Salamanca, the old university town, in 1950. Salamanca is a charming little city close to the Portuguese border. Its city centre is a clutch of narrow, medieval streets knotted around a few palaces and plazas. Del Bosque is loved in his hometown. In early 2011, he was awarded the honorary title of *marquis* by King Juan Carlos I. In October 2010, Spain played its first competitive fixture in the Euro 2012 qualifiers at home against Lithuania in UD Salamanca's stadium. I went to the match. It threatened rain beforehand. Patrons could pay a euro to leave their umbrellas in umbrella stands dotted around the belly of the old stadium. You could almost touch the players on the pitch. During the match, fans held '*Gracias Vicente*' banners aloft and broke into chants of 'Vicente! Vicente! Vicente!'

Del Bosque's father was a clerk in Salamanca for RENFE, Spain's national railway company. The man was a trade unionist with a head full of radical, progressive ideas. Politically, he was a Republican. During the Civil War, he was captured by Franco's forces close to Mingilla, in the Basque Country. He was charged with being a *rojo*, a red. Nothing else, this was enough to get him arrested. He remained in captivity in the Basque town of Álava for three years where, according to del Bosque, he had a rough time of it. Del Bosque has spoken out, as recently as March 2011, in favour of people who are looking to find out what happened to ancestors who 'disappeared' during the Civil War.

According to the Real Madrid player Sergio Ramos, who plays for him on *la selección nacional*, del Bosque is 'psychologically refined'. Del Bosque inherited his father's inquiring mind. He cites Miguel de Unamuno as one of his intellectual heroes. Unamuno was twice suspended as rector of the University of Salamanca, and spent time in exile, for his anti-Falangist sentiments. José Millán-Astray, the one-armed founder of the Spanish foreign legion, had a famous spat with Unamuno. The pair locked horns – in front of Franco's wife – during a public ceremony at the University of Salamanca a few months into the Civil War. Unamuno was a pacifist. He denounced Millán-Astray from a podium for his bloodlust, telling the assembled crowd that Millán-Astray was a war invalid who wanted to add to the list of Spain's invalids. Millán-Astray responded, drawing applause from his Falangist supporters, by screaming: 'Death to intelligence! Long live death!'

Del Bosque has spent most of his life at Real Madrid. He joined the club as a teenager. When he graduated to the first team, he remained ensconced on it for a decade. He was a defensive midfielder. Joan Golobart, the former Espanyol player and journalist, says he was 'an organiser'. On his retirement from playing, del Bosque put his organisational skills to work in Real Madrid's *cantera*, living in an apartment so close to the club's former training ground that he could clock which players arrived early to practice. Twice during the mid-1990s, he acted as caretaker coach of the first team while the club shopped around for managers. In 1999, after John Toshack got sacked, he took over full time as manager. He was a revelation, guiding the club's *galácticos* to two Champions League titles and a brace of league trophies.

He has a collegiate management style. His lack of ego was useful, during the era of Figo, Zidane and the Brazilian Ronaldo, for soothing a dressing room of larger egos. During half-time, he might only speak for a minute or two. Players say that he never raises his voice or singles out a player for criticism. To try and analyse his emotions when he's on the touchline is a pointless exercise. He's inscrutable. You might as well be looking at a cow in a field. Effective though his quiet industry was, he still fell out of favour with the club. At the end of four seasons – the evening after Real Madrid had been crowned league champions – he was fired. He was dispensed with because he was an unfussy, old-school coach who didn't fit with Real Madrid's marketing-driven business plan. Pérez fawned over the image rights of his star assets like a Hollywood studio boss. The club had just signed David Beckham and was selling replica jerseys with frenzied zeal. Del Bosque, a loyal, humble soldier from another era, was passé. 'Del Bosque's profile is a traditional one,' Perez told a news conference. 'We're looking for someone with more emphasis on tactics, strategy and physical preparation. We believe that the squad we are building would be more powerful with a coach with a different character. Del Bosque was showing signs of exhaustion. I want to be sincere about this – our belief that he was not the right coach for the future.' Del Bosque avows that he will never return to work for Real Madrid. The reasoning proffered at his exit interview incensed him. 'The fact,' he said, 'that some smart-arse dressed in a pair of braces comes up to me and tells me I've got to get "modern" really pisses me off.' Del Bosque was swapped for a man with multi-linguistic skills and a good tan – Carlos Queiroz, Alex Ferguson's former No. 2, who failed to deliver Pérez a trophy, as was the case with five subsequent chosen successors until the construction chief decided to try his luck with José Mourinho.

*

I went to Las Rozas, home to the Spanish Football Federation, to interview del Bosque. Las Rozas is a dormitory town about 20 kilometres north-west of Madrid. It was scene to some of the most vicious fighting during the Spanish Civil War. There are still concrete bunkers, a hangover from these battles, on the Guadarrama river that runs alongside the town. Many inhabitants fled Franco's marauding forces by taking refuge in caves in the surrounding Sierra Mountains. They were known as *cucos*, the sly ones, for their preservation instincts. The Spanish Football Federation's facilities comprise several pitches, including a specific one for goalkeepers, and accommodation for the players. The federation's museum is also on the grounds. It houses the World Cup and, amongst other attractions, a white Fiat sports car that used to belong to Alfredo di Stéfano. The organisation's security guards – in keeping with security staff at many Spanish football stadiums – dress in Stasi-style uniforms as old as the car.

Del Bosque is a tall man, over six feet. I had met him briefly five months beforehand. I was waiting to interview his deputy Fernando Hierro, the former sporting director of the Spanish Football Federation, who left to take up a job as general director of his hometown club, Malaga, in July 2011. I was sitting by a coffee table outside del Bosque's office. There is a panel of glass instead of a wall between his office and the meeting area outside it so he could see me waiting. He came out to ask if I was OK, and to see if I was waiting to see him. It was a thoughtful thing to do, a kind of come-in-out-of-the-cold gesture. He is universally respected in Spanish football circles for his decency, for being a *señor*. His most distinguishing feature, of course, is his moustache. He dislikes it when the press makes fun of it. On this day, it is tightly clipped. We sat at a coffee table by the window while his assistant Paloma remained in the office, sitting at his work table. Before starting the interview, I explained my two objectives. I wanted to chat to him for a newspaper profile and for a book on the rivalry between Real Madrid and Barcelona. He sighed. 'I work for the Spanish national team,' he said, adding wearily, 'For me to talk about Real Madrid is not easy. It is very complicated.'

I wasn't surprised by his caginess. Hierro had been just as wary when I sat with him in the adjoining meeting room months earlier. Hierro was one of Real Madrid's great dogs of war. He was an inspirational footballer, a hero even to Barcelona's Gerard Piqué. He spent 14 years badgering referees and opponents all in the cause of giving Real Madrid an edge. I was keen to speak to him about his war stories from Madrid–Barça battles but he, like del Bosque, was in a compromising position when it came to the subject. Both left Real Madrid under a cloud. Hierro, a bolshie figure in the club's dressing room, had been culled, even though he was the team's captain, on the same day as del Bosque. 'Hierro is nearing the top age limit and we believe it's the right moment to break our relationship,' was all that Jorge Valdano, who was in charge of player contracts, had to say on the matter. Del Bosque was brought back into the fold in March 2011 when he was awarded honorary membership – along with Rafael Nadal and Plácido Domingo – but for several years he had felt awkward going along to matches at the Bernabéu stadium with his family, given the circumstances of his departure from the club. His left-leaning politics had complicated membership of the tribe, too.

'Del Bosque is loved because he represents values of moderation, prudence and cohesion,' Santiago Segurola said to me. 'He is a very interesting figure because he is a *madridista* to death. He served the club for over 30 years. He coached the team, won leagues and Champions Leagues, the World Cup, but he is accepted more by the rest of the world than he is by the core of Real Madrid. When Florentino Pérez awarded him the honorary medal, the normal thing would have been to present it to him in the middle of the pitch at the Bernabéu and people would have risen to applaud a *madridista*, but this didn't happen. I think that Real Madrid is a club that divides.'

I had, however, been careful to flag the subject of the book to Paloma when requesting the del Bosque interview. But maybe she had forgotten. It had been four months since I made the initial interview request and the Spanish Football Federation had been harried of late. In January 2011, the federation's website inadvertently posted a note that the referee for an upcoming *Copa del Rey* semi-final would be operating 'under the watchful eye of José Mourinho, who considers himself to have had decisions go against him lately'. The item was taken down after ten minutes, but it was too late – the press had picked up on the gaffe. Real Madrid fired off a statement saying it confirmed their belief that the federation was biased against them. The Spanish Football Federation explained that it had been the fault of a work experience girl.

Despite his early retiscence our discussion was interesting. His answers were discreet although he cracked the occasional joke. I think he found the way I did violent things to the Spanish language amusing. We chatted about the 1981 European Cup final. He answered my queries about the national team and his time working at Real Madrid's *cantera*, where he mentored players like Iker Casillas and Raúl. He insisted that Real Madrid and Barcelona's football styles are similar – both teams leave a lot of space in defence in their relentless push to attack and dominate teams. He reminisced about his days as a player, of clashes with Charly Rexach, a teammate on the Spanish team, and the 'tall, thin and very agile' Johan Cruyff, but he didn't remember anything of great consequence from his *clásico* encounters. We spoke about Figo's torrid times at the Camp Nou as a Real Madrid player. He explained they decided not to let him take corners in 2000 in case he got injured by a missile. After 30 minutes, Paloma rose from her chair and started hovering nearby. It was her signal to wrap things up. We never got to talk about his family history or the dark politics at the heart of Real Madrid's institution with the exception of one exchange towards the end. I asked him if it was true that Florentino Pérez interfered with team selection when he was manager of Real Madrid.

'Nah, no, no,' he said.

'No?' I asked again.

'No.'

I inquired about Steve McManaman. The former English international joined Real Madrid in 1999. He spent four seasons at the club, the final two of which were spent as a bit-part player. McManaman knew that Pérez, who became president in 2000, wanted shot of him. His first signing was Luís Figo, who played in McManaman's position. McManaman's salary was a drag on the club's balance sheet, but he'd been Man of the Match in the 2000 Champions League final and was determined to stay and fight his way back onto the team, particularly when he could see Figo was struggling with injury and form at one stage. In *El Macca*, the co-authored memoir of his time at the club, he says that del Bosque sympathised with his predicament but 'at one point effectively told me his hands were tied. They were the rules set from above.' I explained to del Bosque that I had read McManaman's book. Del Bosque was interviewed for the book by McManaman's co-author. I asked if Pérez interfered in team selection in the case of McManaman.

'No,' he replied. 'Never. Steve McManaman wasn't his favourite *hombre*. He came with Lorenzo Sanz [former Real Madrid president]. Like any president, he had his favourite people, but no, no… He never told me to do anything about people to play.'

11

ANOTHER DIMENSION

Three days after the 1981 European Cup final, Vicente del Bosque and his Real Madrid teammates were dumped out of the *Copa del Rey* by Sporting de Gijón. The side from Asturias went on to meet Barcelona in the final. By this stage, the Spanish league race had already been concluded. It was an incredible saga. On Sunday 1 March, Barcelona beat Hércules 6–0 at the Camp Nou. It kept Barça two points behind the league leaders, Atlético de Madrid. Two of Barcelona's goals were scored by star striker Enrique Castro, or 'Quini' as Pep Guardiola's childhood hero was commonly known. He was tall and gangly with a head of short, curly brown hair. He joined the club in the summer of 1980 for 82 million pesetas, a huge sum at the time, from Sporting de Gijón. His nickname was *El Brujo* – The Wizard. Like all great goal-poachers, most of his scores came by stealth. He was never there; he was always arriving.

After the rout against Hércules, Quini left the Camp Nou alone in his car. He had spoken to his wife on the telephone. She was in Asturias, holidaying with their kids. She was about to fly the family back to Barcelona. Quini arranged to pick them up, but he didn't make it to the airport. His car was found abandoned near his house, which was close to the highway leading out to the airport. He was kidnapped at gunpoint by two men and whisked to Zaragoza, about 300 kilometres away.

These were dicey times in Spain's fledgling democracy. On 23 February 1981, a few days before Quini's abduction, there had been an attempted right-wing coup d'état. Brandishing a pistol, Lieutenant Colonel Antonio

Tejero, a disaffected Francoist, and 200 military cohorts stormed Spain's parliament while it was in session. They held 350 deputies, including the country's prime minister, at gunpoint for 18 hours, before surrendering. Unbeknownst to the rebels, someone from Televisión Española kept a camera rolling so the Spanish public watched the drama unfold at home on their TVs.

Nobody knew of Quini's whereabouts until the following day. At 3 o'clock on the Monday afternoon, a hoax call was made to *La Vanguardia*, Catalonia's main newspaper. A group called the Catalan-Spanish Battalion claimed they held Quini. They announced they would release him after Barça's next league game against Atlético de Madrid, but not before then, they said, 'Because a separatist [team] can't win the league'.

Four hours later, *La Vanguardia* received a call from another gang called PRE. They had Quini. To secure his release, they wanted 100 million pesetas, about £500,000 in today's money. They threatened to cut off his finger. Negotiations went nowhere. Quini's ordeal dragged on. The national and international press corps camped outside his house in Barcelona. Meanwhile in Zaragoza, he was kept in a basement room of an apartment building, with only a mattress, one meal a day and some music by the failed Real Madrid goalkeeper Julio Iglesias to sustain him. Barça pushed to have the match against Atléti postponed, but their request was denied by the Spanish Football Federation. Bernd Schuster, Barcelona's rampaging German midfielder, made another stand. He refused to play the match out of solidarity, but was eventually forced to, claiming Barcelona's hierarchy said to him dramatically: 'If you do not play and something happens [to Quini] you will be solely responsible for his death.'

Barça's challenge for the title quickly unravelled. The squad was deflated. Helenio Herrera, who was back coaching the club after a 20-year hiatus, curtailed training. Atléti beat them 1–0. Quini's No. 9 jersey was retired for the game. The following week they lost to Vicente del Bosque's hometown team UD Salamanca, who were later relegated; they drew against Zaragoza; and lost 3–0 in the *clásico* at the Bernabéu stadium. Towards the end of the month, a 26-year-old accomplice of Quini's three captors was apprehended in Geneva while trying to collect the 100 million pesetas ransom money deposited in one of the city's banks. He confessed to the whereabouts of Quini. With his face covered in stubble, the striker cut a bedraggled-looking figure when he emerged after 25 days of captivity.

Quini resumed play ten days later in a 2–1 win against Valladolid. He finished the season as the league's top scorer with 20 goals. Barcelona trailed in fifth in the standings. He also helped himself to 11 goals in the *Copa del Rey*. Two of these came in the final, both of them whistling past his brother, Sporting de Gijón's goalkeeper, in a 3–1 victory. Although Quini, in a fit of Stockholm syndrome, dropped the charges against his captors, his employers hunted them through the courts. The club demanded 35 million pesetas in compensation for scuppering their title chase. In January 1983, the kidnappers were sentenced to ten years imprisonment. Quini was awarded personal damages of 5 million pesetas, which he never claimed.

When I asked Ramón Besa about the Quini kidnapping in the context of Barcelona's history, he smiled at the memory of it. He was working as a cub reporter for the Catalan newspaper, *Avui*, at the time. 'It was Barça's fate – *victimismo*. When it wasn't a ref, it was a kidnapping! We have always had an excuse.'

The league title was decided on the last day of the 1981 season. Real Madrid defeated Valladolid that day, throwing down the gauntlet to their closest rivals Real Sociedad, who needed a point from their away game against Sporting de Gijón to pip them. One of the Real Sociedad players that day was Miguel Ángel 'Periko' Alonso, Xabi Alonso's father. I spoke to him about that match during a conversation in a Madrid restaurant. Although he later played with Barcelona for three seasons – and scored a goal in a *clásico* match – in 1981 he was a Real Sociedad player. The San Sebastian outfit is his local team. Squatter than Xabi in build, he was in the mould, I'm told, of Claude Makélélé. He used to like tackling. Rafa Arias, a Televisión Española commentator at the time, made a crashing sound when I enquired about him. He spends a lot of his spare time these days shooting partridge, when he's not travelling to see Xabi playing every other weekend at the Bernabéu stadium. He favours neither his old club Barça nor Real Madrid these days. 'A son pulls you a lot,' he says.

About 6,000 Real Sociedad fans made the journey along the Cantabrian coast for the Sporting de Gijón match in late April 1981. There are a couple of things that stood out about the afternoon for Periko. The pitch was hard like an airport runway. It was cold and teeming with rain. He said he could feel the goosebumps on his arms as he recalled the final play of the match. Real Sociedad were losing 2–1. With a few seconds remaining, a miscued long-range shot by a Real Sociedad player fell to Jesús Zamora inside the box. He pulled the trigger and it flew in. Real Sociedad won the title on goal difference. It was only the second time in seven seasons that Vicente del Bosque had not won a league winners' medal with Real Madrid.

The morning after meeting Periko Alonso I travelled up to Gijón, which is in the principality of Asturias, to watch Barcelona play against Sporting de Gijón in the league. It was the second weekend in February 2011. It was a bright, slightly windswept day. Gijón is a port town with a population of about a quarter of a million. It has a long promenade that looks out onto the Atlantic Ocean. Like a lot of inlets in the Bay of Biscay, it is a haven for surfers. The region is one of Spain's black diamonds. Its most notable moment in the last century came when its miners staged a military uprising in October 1934. A general strike escalated into armed insurrection. The miners seized several towns and cities in Asturias, including Gijón and the capital Oviedo, but were overrun within a few days by Franco's troops. The revolt had an anti-clerical bent to it – churches were razed and dozens of priests were slaughtered. The reprisal was vicious and included looting and rape. A couple of thousand miners were killed, around 18,000 were imprisoned, many of whom were tortured, and thousands more – of the wrong political hue – lost their jobs.

David Villa, who was signed by Barça just before he scored five goals in Spain's victorious World Cup, is from rebel Asturian mining stock. His father's grandfather, a *rojo*, was named Trotsky. Villa's father is a retired miner. Villa's family worried every day about his safety. He survived two serious accidents down the pits. Villa is from Tuilla, where his father and mother still live. It's a town of 1,900 inhabitants about 30 kilometres inland from Gijón. He started his professional career with Sporting de Gijón. Villa, like many of the Spanish squad, has a well-developed political consciousness. He has lent his name to a campaign to get the Asturian tongue equal status with the languages of the Basque Country and Catalonia. His nickname is *El Guaje*, which is Asturian for The Kid. He is a hero to all of Spain, but he is also proud of his region's distinct identity. Most Spaniards have an ability to serve a couple of masters. Nowhere is this more evident than the way in which the country's football people support their local team, but also pay fealty to either Barça or Real Madrid. If anything, it ensures they always have a stake in the title race.

Before the match, I hooked up with three members of various local Barça *peñas* (supporters' clubs) in a hotel in the centre of the city. Born in 1951, Matías Álvarez, who has a pencil moustache, is their ringleader. He's president of the 'Julio Alberto' *peña* and an FC Barcelona delegate for Asturias and Cantabria. Even though Gijón is 900 kilometres from Barcelona, it has five Barça *peñas*. There are 36 in Asturias and hundreds more in the outlying regions. The original Barça *peña* was founded by a bunch of ex-players in Barcelona in 1944. It was called Solera. The *peñas* really took off as a concept after Cruyff's time as a player with the club in the 1970s. Many of them take their name from Barça players. The *peña* of Matías, for example, is named after Julio Alberto, a defender with Barça in the 1980s, who hails from a town in Asturias.

Lorena Alba is president of the 'Gamper' *peña*. It was founded in 1983 and owes its name to Joan Gamper, the Swiss co-founder of FC Barcelona. Gamper stopped going by his German name Hans Kamper on settling in Barcelona; he instead adopted the Catalan spelling of it. The 'Gamper' *peña* is based in Santander, the Cantabrian port city, halfway along the coast between Gijón and San Sebastian. It's an outpost in the *clásico* land wars, says Lorena, as Santander '*es blanco*'. Lorena is blonde, very elegantly dressed for a football fan and 42 years of age. When she asks if I think she looks older, I get confused and respond with too much enthusiasm: '*Sí, sí – mucho.*' When we get chatting about Quini, she shows me pictures of him in that morning's newspaper. He looks gaunt. He's been battling cancer for the last few years. The photos were snapped at a function of the Quini Foundation. He had asked not to have any taken, Lorena tells me in dismay.

Manolo Lahera is aged 70 and is accompanied by his wife. He is self-effacing but exudes a quiet authority. The others defer to him. He is a *socio* of Racing de Santander and trained the club's youth team for six years. At the moment, he coaches the Cantabrian Football Federation's youth team. He's been a fan of Barça – going against the grain in a city that has more Real Madrid fans – since the days of Ladislao Kubala and Sándor Kocsis in the 1950s. In over half a century of watching Barça, his most memorable *clásico* encounter was the last one – the *manita* game in November. He's re-watched it a few times. He tells me the Football College of Coaches in Cantabria analyse it for use in their coaching instruction. He gets along to the Camp Nou three or four times a year for matches, travelling to Barcelona by plane. They are all veterans of several Champions League expeditions overseas, including recent finals in Paris and Rome. They are also united in believing that José Mourinho is '*un sinvergüenza*', that he's shameless, a crook. He's not welcome in town, they stress, by *culés* and non-*culés*.

Manolo has a dual affinity for Racing and Barcelona. He supports his local team on the Spanish scene, but Barcelona gives him an international outlet. 'I'm strongly attached to Barça,' he says. He admits, if put to it, that he prefers Barça. They're more important; they are, he says, '*otra dimensión*' – another dimension. Lorena also has a place in her heart for both Racing and Barça. I ask her why she supports two teams and she says it has no rational explanation. When I press her on it, she says in exasperation: '*Ay, hijo*, what you do you want me to say!'

Manolo interjects: 'What happens is that with Barça, there is something… a feeling. It's special. It's hard to explain…'

'I don't know, Manolo,' says Matías. 'You are a bit older than me. Why are we with Barça? Everybody supported Real Madrid when we were young. I'm talking about 1960. I was nine years of age. If all the people were with Madrid, we were with Barça as a reaction against that.'

'I've an opinion,' says Manolo in response. 'Let's see if we agree with it. Spain at that time was a dictatorship. Franco–Madrid, Madrid–Franco. Real Madrid's stadium was full of *Franquistas*. It's for that reason that the Bernabéu stadium is still full of fans waving Spanish flags. I always say that the flag belongs to everybody, not only to Madrid.'

'They have appropriated the flag,' says Lorena.

'Then if I go to Racing's stadium,' continues Manolo, 'and Real Madrid supporters come with the Spanish flag, I say: "What the hell!" Why do they have to bring it, if it's also our flag? They could bring the flag of Madrid, or the Catalan flag, or Asturias has its own flag. But the Spanish flag belongs to all Spain.'

'I'm a Barça fan,' adds Matías, 'because I have left-wing views and Barça's stadium was the only one in which you could make any kind of political statement against Franco. In that stadium there was always someone who showed the Catalan flag, even though doing this meant you risked going to prison. What was good for the flag was that Spain won the World Cup. Then the flags meant we were all Spanish. Before this, if you wore the Spanish flag on your watchstrap, for example, that meant you were right wing. People called you "*facha*" – you were a person from the right. The Spanish Football Federation gave me a "*banderín*", a little flag, which hangs in my car. One day in Bilbao's airport car park, the attendant in charge said to me that it would be better to take it off because someone would probably scratch or vandalise my car.'

In Spain flags are contentious. They are important markers for the country's cities. Take Valencia, one of Spain's outlying regions, which isn't politicised or separatist like Catalonia or the Basque Country. Three of it main football teams are Valencia, Villarreal and CD Castellón. Each of the clubs' crests contains the four red bars across a yellow background of the Valencia flag. Barça, of course, has the Catalan flag and the St George's cross on its crest. Barcelona's separatist posturing, the chanting of '*Visca el Barça, visca Catalunya*' – and the waving of Catalan flags – irritates the majority of Real Madrid's supporters. It is an affront to their belief in a unified Spain, as it is to most of the people from other parts of Spain, such as Andalucía, Galicia or the two Castillas. The flipside also applies.

'It is the same when *madridistas* defend the unity of Spain. It annoys Barça fans,' Alfredo Relaño said to me in his Madrid office. 'If Valencia comes here, Madrid supporters wave flags of Madrid. If Barça or Athletic de Bilbao comes, besides Madrid flags, there are Spanish flags, as if it was Bayern Munich. Of course, if Bayern Munich comes, it's normal that people would wave Spanish flags, but not if the team is Barça, or one of the two teams from the Basque Country – Athletic de Bilbao or Real Sociedad. These Spanish flags are saying, "You are in Spain". I don't really like this because it's a kind of reverse separatism. You are saying to the Catalans that they are not Spanish, when really you pretend they are Spanish. The Spanish flag is not used against Sevilla or Deportivo de la Coruña. And, by the way, neither can you go to the Camp Nou with a Spanish flag!'

Ramón Besa says the nationwide Madrid-Barça wars of allegiance stem from the idea of 'a broken red Spain'. It is the legacy of a country that has experienced a civil war – one half of the land supports Barcelona; the other Real Madrid, except in regional areas that are strongly nationalist. It is a split that is reflected in the political parties of Spain. There is the conservative party, *Partido Popular*, and the socialists, *PSOE*. Only in places where nationalism is buoyant – such as the Basque Country, which has its own separatist parties – is there a divergence from this dichotomy. According to a study by *Centro de Investigaciones Sociológicas* in 2011, 41 per cent of FC Barcelona supporters are left-wing voters, twice the rate of Real Madrid fans; while 50 per cent of those from the right are Real Madrid aficionados, compared with 20 per cent allied with their Catalan rivals.

When I left the Barça posse after our chat in the Gijón hotel, Matías and Lorena give me Barça business cards, embossed with their *peña* logos, both of which contain the colours of the Catalan flag. 'If Barça has to lose a match,' says Matías, 'I hope it is tonight.'

It was unlikely Barcelona would lose. The previous weekend, the club broke a 50-year-old record held by di Stéfano's Real Madrid team by winning 16 league games on the trot. Because of Real Madrid's January wobble, they had pulled seven points ahead of their rivals. Villarreal, in third place, languished 17 points behind. The table had a familiar feel to it – Barça and Real Madrid were cantering ahead of the rest. The season before, third-placed Valencia was almost as close to the relegation zone as it was to the two behemoths out in front. The Madrid–Barça axis has won the league each season since 2004 when Valencia won the last of its five crowns. The worry is that the gap is widening. It is difficult, except for Barça or Real Madrid supporters, to think seriously about challenging for the league title anymore. The other 18 teams that make up the *Primera División* are resigned to their positions as also-rans. They squabble over European competition places or survival in the top flight. La Liga has become a two-horse race. It is dispiriting. The economics of it are atrocious. Their annual budgets are four times more than any other team in the league.

Simon Kuper, the football writer, makes the point that sports economists have long trumpeted: most fans support big clubs. They prefer Goliaths. They don't want equality. They like dynasties, and they don't care much for upsets. Even supporters of the minnows like being able, in the case of Spanish club football, to try and sock it to the Big Two. The buoyancy of overall television viewing figures and match attendances, even as Barça and Real Madrid surge ahead of the pack with each passing year, confirms this disturbing contentment.

TV money is at the root of the problem. Spain differs, for example, from the Premier League in England regarding the honey pot generated by television rights. There is no collective bargaining for the money divvied up on the domestic scene. Each team negotiates individually. Few of the other teams in Spain have a strong bargaining position. According to the Spanish Football Federation, one recent premier division game that didn't involve Barça or Real Madrid had 47 pay-per-view customers. In a season, the Big Two trouser about £110 million each (about £50 million more than Manchester United). Valencia gets £37 million. The other Spanish teams get dwindling fractions. Racing, Manolo and Lorena's second team, gets about a tenth of their takings. This takes no account of the money the two *clásico* teams rake in from televised action of their Champions League exploits or ticket sales or merchandising or sponsorship. Attempts to split the domestic TV money up more equitably have, to date, failed. The majority of the other La Liga clubs are cowed. 'The thing is, when Madrid and Barcelona stand before them, when Florentino starts to talk, the other clubs shit themselves,' said one renegade Espanyol director, after a failed roundtable attempt in September 2011 at redistribution along similar lines to Europe's other big leagues.

In the meantime, the money funds their extravagant squad purchases. Real Madrid's bench would beat most international teams. It invokes a despotic clause when loaning (and sometimes in selling) its players to other clubs – if the player excels with his new team, he isn't allowed to play against Real Madrid. Over the years, Spain's bankers, fat from lots of *jamón* and state profligacy, have always treated the country's two marquee clubs indulgently. As far back as the 1970s, when Barcelona pulled off the transfer coup of the decade in coaxing Johan Cruyff to the Camp Nou, Banca Catalana registered the deal as an agricultural import, which legally entitled the club to a low interest rate.

The Spanish media is also in cahoots with them. One of the most jarring things about watching a *clásico* match in the press box is that it's full of Spanish and Catalan journalists who do little to hide their emotions when fortune or misfortune befalls their team. Both Barcelona (*Sport, Mundo Deportivo*) and Madrid (*Marca, AS*) have two daily sports newspapers devoted to their exploits. They have vested interests in the wellbeing of Spanish football's two giants. *Sport* is blatant about its allegiance. Its motto is '*Sempre amb el Barça*' – 'Always with Barça'. They go to ridiculous lengths in their propaganda wars. A week after the Barcelona match in Gijón, for example, *AS* loaded a photograph onto its website which showed Dani Alves clearly offside as he set up a goal for Barça against Athletic de Bilbao. Someone had photoshopped the defender who played him onside out of the picture. They are newspapers, but I've heard them called different names – newsletters, bulletins, fanzines. They wield a lot of power. *Marca* is the biggest-selling newspaper in Spain. It was founded in 1938 during the dog days of the Spanish Civil War with an agenda to promote Franco's vision of muscular nationalism. The front page of its first issue displayed a picture of a blonde girl giving the fascist salute 'to all the Spanish sportsmen and women'. These days it salutes Real Madrid.

'Whether they're good, bad or indifferent is one debate,' says Sid Lowe. 'The other debate is, "Who do they support?" Spanish people will say about the British press, "Oh, your tabloids are pretty bad." Yes they are, but they don't have teams. The *Sun* doesn't support Chelsea. The *Mirror* doesn't support Man United. It just doesn't happen. It's not like the *Guardian* or any newspaper in England wants a team to win because it creates a good story. In Madrid, a good story is Madrid winning. The editor of one newspaper admitted that every Madrid win is 10,000 more in sales. The prism through which everything is seen is very deliberately biased. I wouldn't go as far as to say unashamedly so because there is a pretence at objectivity, but it's nearly so.'

This is the case even though they have some great writers. The best of them is Santiago Segurola, who writes for *Marca*. 'The Madrid–Barça rivalry is generating lousy journalism,' he concedes. 'It's combative and entrenched around the two clubs. It is journalism which encourages confrontation. It seems to have perverted the values of both clubs rather than accepting that they are just engaged in an intense sports rivalry. It is obsessed with creating more conflict.'

Their only saving grace is that they ultimately serve the team's fans who are, of course, their paying customers. They can be very critical about management issues, and quite vindictive in skewering personalities. *Marca* hunted Real Madrid manager Manuel Pellegrini, Mourinho's predecessor, out of town. '*Marca* had this guy as an editor – Eduardo Inda – who decided to destroy Pellegrini and managed to do it,' says Miguel Aguilar. 'He's built Mourinho as a hero. His newspaper has got a very big readership, probably over a million people every day, and a lot of young readers who will believe what they say, who think, Hey, if you need to insult referees to beat Barcelona, let's do it, et cetera.'

When Johan Cruyff was manager of Barcelona, he coined the shorthand *entorno* – or environment – to describe the array of forces that made life stressful for the Barcelona football team. These included supporters, the club's hierarchy but most of all the press. 'Clubs like Real Madrid and Barça live in a very aggressive environment,' Manolo Sanchís said to me. He spent almost two decades as a player trying to shelter from the twisters that circulated the Bernabéu stadium. 'Every day you face journalists looking for a headline or fans telling you how good or how bad you are. There's almost no place where you could be out of this. So you end up creating a kind of shield.'

Cruyff spent a lot of his time as manager at loggerheads, if not boycotting *Sport*. That was 20 years ago. The media has mushroomed since. Today, *Marca*, for instance, has 200 staff – across print, internet, radio and TV – exclusively focused on football. It creates enormous pressure on the two teams to succeed. It makes losing a single match unacceptable, a 'moral aberration', says Sid Lowe. It feeds the clubs' paranoia about referring decisions and it is exacerbated by the relentlessness with which they pursue each other. The two clubs won't let up. 'They drive each other,' says Lowe. 'If Barcelona weren't so brilliant, Real Madrid wouldn't feel obliged to spend so much money. If Madrid weren't closing in on Barcelona so much, Barcelona wouldn't need to keep saying, "Let's just add a little bit to our squad." They're McEnroe and Borg, Coe and Ovett. They're producing unbelievable statistics, partly because they have to.'

Real Madrid is run by one of the country's canniest businessmen, a man who has an intuitive feel for the marketing potential of his livestock. The club sells its replica jerseys at £70 a pop. It shifts around 1.5 million of them each season, according to *Time* magazine, some 300,000 more than Barcelona. The billion-dollar Real Madrid Resort Island in the Persian Gulf is its latest imperial project. It taps into the Asian market, which makes up more than half of its fans. Opening for business in 2015, it expects to attract a million visitors a year, who, according to Florentino Pérez, 'will become part of the legend of Real Madrid', while getting to frolic among attractions such as a club crest-shaped marina and a 10,000-seater stadium with one side open to the sea.

Barcelona is equally grasping, having overtaken Real Madrid as the most popular club in Spain. In 2011, an *AS*/Ikerfel survey of fans from La Liga's 20 premier division clubs found that it leads its Madrid rival by seven percentage points, a swing of 14 per cent from a similar poll conducted by the *Centro de Investigaciones Sociológicas* in 2007. 'We do tend to mythologise things like the Spanish Civil War and FC Barcelona,' says Ardal O'Hanlon, the comedian who made a six-part television documentary series on European football rivalries entitled *Leagues Apart*. 'The club itself has won the propaganda war about how it is different to other football clubs. But that's not exactly true. They've always had sponsorship to some degree. We don't see it, but it's on the shoulder or somewhere.' In late 2010, Barça's club president, Sandro Rosell, a former Nike executive, agreed a sponsorship deal with the Qatar Foundation, which will bring it £25 million a year for the next five years. It was a controversial move, distasteful for the romantics among its *socios*, as it ended the hundred years plus of the club going without official shirt sponsorship. It is hard to know where its colonisation will stop. It has five times as many *socios* as Espanyol, its city rival.

'The supporter of Espanyol thinks that Barça would prefer it if Espanyol didn't exist,' says Joan Golobart, the *La Vanguardia* columnist who once ran for president of Espanyol. 'Barça would like to monopolise everything. It is powerful because it has the protection of the media and of the referees. It is rich. It's like a feudal lord. In an important city like Barcelona, there is only Barça and Espanyol. This doesn't happen in London where there can be four or five teams. Why? Because Barça has eaten it all up. L'Hospitalet is a town next to Barcelona. It has about 700,000 inhabitants. Its club plays in Segunda B, a four-group, 80-team third division league. Why? Because L'Hospitalet has got 20,000 *socios* of Barça. If all these people were supporters of their town team, L'Hospitalet would be the eighth largest team in Spain in its number of members.'

Whenever Barcelona visits Espanyol's ground, the home team's fans always display a banner around the halfway line: 'Catalonia is more than a club,' a play on Barça's motto. It may not be long before Spanish football is little more than two clubs – Barcelona and Real Madrid.

El Molinón, Sporting de Gijón's ground, is one of the few – if not only – big football stadiums in Europe designed by a female architect. Like Gaudí's *Sagrada Família* in Barcelona, it remains, over a century after inception, an unfinished place of worship. It has a shell-like feel to it. One side is full of glass and steel; another is gridiron like a tiered car park. There are two gaps, wide enough to drive a car through, where the stands fail to meet each other at two ends. I moseyed around the stadium 45 minutes before kick-off. There is a river that hugs one side of it. At this side, 20 people were pressed up against a gate at one of the openings between the stands. Another 20 were standing back about 50 yards and looking onto the pitch from the riverbank. I asked a lady with a pram who was standing on the riverbank if the people would remain there for the duration of the match. 'I don't know,' she said, 'but you can see the goal.'

The goalmouth she was referring to was the end where Sporting's *ultras* were stationed. They fluttered about seven Spanish flags during the match. The game was a cracker. Fifteen minutes in, Leo Messi lost possession during a Barça attack on the edge of the box. Sporting swept up the left flank in counter attack. David Barral took the ball towards the corner flag before slaloming his way back inside towards the penalty spot. Gerard Piqué and Gabriel Milito, deputising in defence, watched as he worked a way past them and slotted the ball into the corner of the net.

Barcelona were out of sorts. Ibrahim Afellay, recently acquired from PSV Eindhoven, tried an ambitious dribble through the middle at one stage later in the first half but was easily dispossessed. It was a foolhardy raid, untypical of the *tiki taka* school. As expected, Barça put on a cavalry charge in the second half, but still struggled in execution. By the touchline in front of me, Andrés Iniesta and Maxwell failed to control long-field crosses, allowing the ball to spill out of play. On one of these occasions, Manolo Preciado, Sporting's coach, did a little twirl of the ball behind his back, before handing it to Piqué.

Preciado, the guy who called Mourinho a *canalla*, a creep, earlier that season, was one of Spanish football's beloved, stoical characters. Born in 1957, he lost a wife to cancer and a 15-year-old son in a car crash, and died himself in June 2012. He was a player with Racing, the club he twice managed. He took Sporting into the premier division in 2008 and did magic tricks with a small budget (until he got the sack in January 2012). 'This is a cheap team,' he liked to say, 'but one with a pair of bollocks like General Espartero's horse.' After breaking for a rare counter-attack in the second half, he turned and exhorted the home crowd to roar his team on. They obliged. At another moment, one of their defenders hoofed the ball upfield. Milito had to run back into Barcelona's half to retrieve it. No one else, except Víctor Valdés the keeper, was home. The clearance was greeted almost as if a goal had been scored. After 79 minutes, Barça's equalising goal finally came. It was genius. Messi, foraging around midfield, won possession just inside Sporting's half. He shirked off a tackle, and while surrounded by four players, threaded the ball 20 yards forward between two more Sporting defenders to an on-running David Villa. Villa took one touch to take the sting out of the ball before checking on the edge of the box. He raised his head a fraction and then clipped it over the keeper for a goal into the *ultras'* end. They would have appreciated its artfulness on the riverbank outside. Sheepishly, he refrained from celebrating. The game ended after five minutes of extra time. Sporting held out for a heroic draw. Preciado had big hugs for Villa, Pep Guardiola and Sergio Busquets as they left the field.

In the press room afterwards, he plonked himself down in front of the assembled media. With his moustache, he looked the image of Sam Torrance, the former Ryder Cup captain. His voice was hollowed out by too much screaming and smoking. He was known for occasionally sneaking a fag in the dugout during games. He was shattered. Two bags hung under his eyes. He knew his people were drained, too. 'The fans,' he said in one of the curious constructions the Spanish have for cursing, 'had a prostitute's mother of a time.' After Guardiola spoke, Villa stepped onto the podium to answer a few questions. In a final act, Quini, wearing a Sporting blazer, emerged from behind some curtains to hand over an award to Villa, his heir. It was from Barça's local *peñas*. The headline on one of Gijón's newspapers the following morning bellowed: 'And David Stopped Goliath'.

12

COMANCHE TERRITORY

There was another interesting incident when Real Madrid beat Vall-adolid 3–1 in the final league match of the 1981 season. The game was played in Valladolid, a city about halfway between Madrid and Gijón. Real Madrid started their match at the same time Real Sociedad, their rivals for the title, kicked-off against Sporting de Gijón up in Asturias. They didn't, however, finish at the same time. Convinced that they had done enough to win the title, Real Madrid's players started their celebrations on the pitch. Juanito, their feisty winger, had promised if they won the league he would return to the dressing room on his knees. He had waddled as far as the touchline when word filtered through that Real Sociedad had scored in injury time. The Basques were champions.

Juanito is one of Real Madrid's iconic figures. He was christened Juan Gómez González, but like many Spanish players he went by a nick-name. Born in November 1954 in Fuengirola, a tourist resort in Málaga, he joined Real Madrid in 1977. The following year, he was banned from European competition for two seasons for assaulting a linesman during a game against Grasshopper Club Zürich. He got into more trouble at the tail end of his career in a game against another Swiss side, Neuchâtel Xamax. He was caught spitting in the face of Uli Stielike, the German midfielder he soldiered alongside for eight league campaigns with Real Madrid. They talked about the incident on a beach sometime afterwards and agreed to make up. Former players say Juanito wasn't a thug; he was just full-blooded. He was uncompromising, driven by scratch-your-eye-out determination. He was also generous. Joan Golobart, who played for Espanyol against him in the 1980s, said he used to conduct running commentaries while playing. 'If I won the ball,' says Golobart, 'he used to say: "Very good, very good!"'

Juanito came to enshrine Real Madrid's resolve. Fans loved him for his tenacity, for embodying Real Madrid's indomitable will to win. The club mourned deeply when, a couple of years after retiring from the game, he died in a car crash. He was asleep in the passenger seat of a car on the way home from watching Real Madrid play in a UEFA Cup match. The driver of his car swerved to avoid logs that had fallen off an overturned truck on a highway and hit an oncoming truck. He wore the No. 7 jersey as a player. To this day, the *Ultras Sur* at the Berna-béu stadium occasionally chant '*Illa, illa, illa, Juanito maravilla*' on the seven-minute mark of matches to commemorate him.

Juanito was buried in Málaga. There is a picture of his tombstone in the basement room of the 'Juanito' *peña*, which was founded in 1992, the year of his death. Real Madrid has some 1,800 *peñas* around the world. 'Juanito' is one of the most curious. It is one of several Real Madrid *peñas* in Barcelona. Coming across its clubhouse, which is in the Sant Martí quarter of the city, is like finding a Masonic Lodge on the Falls Road in Belfast or, as alluded to in José Miguel Villarroya's book *The Catalonia of Real Madrid: Chronicle of a Resistance*, a mining camp deep in Comanche Territory. There are, in fact, quite a number of Real Madrid supporters in Catalonia. Some put the total at about 800,000. This makes Real Madrid, stress its embattled fans, the second biggest team in the region. They feel besieged. They resent the overbearing separatist politics of Barça, particularly when it leaks into the school curriculum.

'In a lot of public schools in music class, the Barça anthem is taught to the children as if it was a Catalan folk song,' says Villarroya. 'This is a problem. It's the anthem of the Barça team, like the German anthem or the British anthem. It's not a traditional Catalan song. People in Catalonia support other teams than Barça, like Espanyol and Real Madrid.' Villarroya was born in Barcelona in 1966. His father, who was a Barça fan, worked for FC Barcelona. They used to go to matches together at the Camp Nou.

Villarroya saw Real Madrid play there for the first time in the 1970s. He cannot account for his own attachment to Barça's great rival. It is, he says, 'without logic'. He writes for *AS* and does radio work for *Marca*, but has not been back to the Camp Nou since his father died in 1999.

'Now there is an agenda,' he adds. 'A lot of politicians, bankers and industrialists are trying to create a homogenous society. They say a good Catalan person loves Catalonia. Barça is the image of Catalonia. It is a great team. It wins a lot of trophies. The most important thing in Catalonia is Barça. It's the central column of this feeling. So if you're not from Barça, you're not a good Catalan. If you're from Real Madrid, you're the devil incarnate. Real Madrid is the foe, not only against Barcelona but also against Catalonia. For these people, not all the Catalans, Real Madrid represents the old orthodoxy, old Spain. It represents the old enemies – Franco's time, centralism and restrictions on Catalans' liberties. This makes it more difficult to be from Real Madrid at the moment. The resentment towards Real Madrid supporters is stronger now. They say, "Are you a Real Madrid fan? Well, then you are a fascist." When I was a child in Franco's time, this was not a problem because there was no democracy. People couldn't talk about politics. Real Madrid, Barcelona, Espanyol were only football teams.'

I asked him how he felt when people refer to Real Madrid as Franco's team. 'We fight every day about this idea,' he says. 'Real Madrid is a great team and it has *socios* who have different ideologies. We have people in Real Madrid who are fascist, from the right, but also now people who are communists. Like in Barça, which has members from the right, from the left, ultra left, ultra right, *independentistes*. It's in the interests of Barça fans to say Real Madrid is Franco's team because in Franco's time, Real Madrid normally won leagues, European Cups, but Barça won, too – the *Copa del Generalísimo*, which today is called the *Copa del Rey*. It won leagues also. But Barça always say that Real Madrid just won their titles because it was Franco's team. It's just a cliché that has become a reality, but it's a piece of fiction.'

*

I boarded a bus with 60 members of 'Juanito' outside their clubhouse a few minutes after midnight on 22 February 2011. We headed across the French border bound for Lyon to watch Real Madrid's first-leg last-16 Champions League tie with Olympique Lyonnais, the side who knocked them out of the competition at the same stage the previous year. Pepe Ribó, the president of Catalonia's Real Madrid *peñas*, organised the trip. Aged 58, he is from Barcelona. He's a Real Madrid fan by chance. When he was eight years of age, he and his classmates wrote letters to Barça and Real Madrid. Only the Madrid club replied – it posted back some T-shirts. Pepe was hooked even though all his family are Barça fans. When he was young, he jokes, he had to always eat in the kitchen, although his choice of club made life easier in other respects. 'Barça are like Indians,' he says, using an old line, 'because they're always running behind the white ones.'

Antonio Feijoo is another passenger. He works as a football agent for Espanyol. He's from Galicia, but is living in Barcelona and has been a member of 'Juanito' for the last decade. He's known Andrés Iniesta since the Barcelona star was a 13-year-old. The World Cup final scoring hero rustled up two tickets for him for Spain's Euro 2008 final in Vienna. The ages of the people on board the bus ranged from about 17 to 72. There were only a few females in the mix. After a while, people took turns to tell bad jokes on a microphone. In a variation on the topical 'Who's better – Cristiano or Messi?' debate, Michael, who sat in front of me, tried to get a rise from a gay couple sitting near him by saying that 'a woman's magazine' in the UK suggested that the Argentinian is better looking. Everyone seemed confident about a good Real Madrid result later, even though Real Madrid had failed to beat Lyon in six previous encounters, and they'd never scored against them in France.

Bleary-eyed, we poured off the bus in Lyon sometime after 8 a.m., and broke up into groups to wander around the city. There was nothing like the number of Real Madrid fans who travelled for the corresponding fixture the previous year. Everyone put it down to 'the crisis', the global financial one that is, not that fact that the club had been in the shadow of Barcelona for the last couple of years. Lyon's main square, the Place Bellecour, is where most fans congregated. It's a huge public square. It must be the size of three football pitches. The year before it was mobbed by Real Madrid fans, seemingly, and local and Spanish TV crews. There were a few other Real Madrid *peñas* who had made the journey, including Peña 'Berne' from Switzerland. There were 40 of them who had come across the Alps by bus. They travel to every one of Real Madrid's Champions League games, both group stages and knockout.

I spent the day with José García, whom I had sat beside on the overnight coach ride. He was born in Zaragoza, 'right in the middle of Barcelona and Madrid,' as he puts it, in 1950. His family moved to Barcelona when he was four years old. He spent 30 years of his working life in London as a banker, but moved back to Barcelona three years earlier on retirement. He has an impressive command of languages. He speaks Catalan, and after little or no sleep on a sweaty bus, he spent the following day casually slipping between Spanish, English and French. His dad, who was from Madrid, was an Atlético de Madrid fan. By occupation, he was a Civil Guard, part of Spain's elite military-style police force, as was his grandfather. Shortly after José finished school, he made his first forays overseas, stopping over in England and Holland. It was around 1968. He said he was bemused when people challenged him about how oppressive life was supposed to be under Franco's rule. 'I told the English,' he said, 'in Hastings, "You call Spain a dictatorship when at 11 o'clock you cannot have a drink on a Saturday night in a disco. What do you call this, eh?" The English girls agreed with me. There was more freedom here in Spain.'

Like a good *madridista*, José likes fighting his corner. He reminded me of Edward G. Robinson. They share the same short, sturdy frame and have a similar demeanour – like the characters the Romanian-born American actor often played, José has unshakeable conviction in his beliefs. He has a long media career of accidental TV punditry. On the same trip the year before, he was interviewed by Marca TV for a match prediction. While living in London, he told me about a time he locked horns with the broadcaster Eamonn Holmes in a football debate. Then there was another confrontational interview with Sky during Euro 96. He was fed up with the derogatory Spanish stereotypes in the British tabloids before England's quarter-final against Spain. 'All this nonsense was in the papers,' he said, 'like "Why do all Spanish players have moustaches? Because they want to look like their mothers."' When he was collared by a Sky TV crew for a street-side opinion about the clash between the two countries, he used the opportunity to unload some of his own stereotypes of the English, but, he said lamentably, his broadside was heavily edited.

I asked him why he decided to support Real Madrid even though he grew up in a hotbed of *catalanismo*. 'Because I'm a rebel,' he said. 'I am always against the establishment. In those days, there was not the fanaticism there is these days. I grew up when Real Madrid won the first European Cup in 1956. I listened to the match on the radio. Real Madrid beat Stade de Reims. I was five years of age. Growing up your principles and feelings are being formed and I thought this is a good team – the team of Puskas and di Stéfano.' Puskas gave José a ticket for his first Madrid–Barça match when he was eight or nine years old. He was playing truant from school with a classmate when they met the Hungarian major in the Hotel Manila on Las Ramblas and he gave them two tickets for the game. The league match was played later that day at the Camp Nou. José has been to the Camp Nou about 200 times, but he stopped going there in the late 1990s.

'Obviously there was rivalry in the 1960s,' he said, 'like as if Manchester United played Liverpool but not with this hatred that there is now. Things started to change after 1975, after Franco died and the regional governments started to be introduced. The last time I went to the Camp Nou, Figo was playing for Barcelona. In the metro, the Barça fans started insulting us. I had a ticket amongst Barcelona fans. I was surrounded by ignorant people, most of them from Badajoz. They couldn't even speak Spanish properly, but they were still there with their copies of *Avui*, the daily Catalan newspaper. They were shouting,' he said, mimicking their garbled Spanish accents, "'*¡Hijo de puta!*' On the big screens they were showing black and white film of the 1974 game at the Bernabéu when Barcelona won 5–0 with Cruyff and Sotil. This night, they won 3–0. Figo scored for Barça. The referee was a bastard because, being 1–0 down, in the last minute of the first half, Real Madrid's Clarence Seedorf was on his own in front of the Barcelona goalkeeper and the referee pulled him up and whistled for the end of the first half. It was like that. I had crossed a line. We say, "*cruz y raya*." It means this relationship is over – I won't come here anymore. You wouldn't believe the hate in there. I will never go to the Camp Nou again even if I'm taken by a limousine.'

Lyon's stadium, which holds 40,000, has been rebuilt but it has held onto the shell of its old ground as an outer perimeter. It makes a cool design feature. All the Real Madrid fans were corralled in one corner of the stadium, beside the Kop Virage Nord. The fans from Lyon's north end conducted a running chant during the match, alternating song verses with their Lyonnais kin in the south terrace. They also spent the match hopping up and down. It may have been to keep warm. It was cold, cold like an outhouse on a winter night. I took up my seat with the other 'Juanito' members, some of whom were sporting 'Juanito Maravilla' scarves. Like at all Real Madrid games, some of the fans brandished Spanish flags. Invariably, these flags have bulls imprinted on them in black, ones with drooping, oversized balls and a fluttering tail.

The first half wasn't enjoyable for the travelling fans. Lyon, or 'l'ol' as they're called, were on top. The Brazilian Michel Bastos on the left wing for Lyon, in particular, was causing all kinds of difficulty. He was playing just in front of us and had Sergio Ramos, who got booked for a late tackle after ten minutes, in a truss. Real Madrid started to get on top in the second half, though. The famous Chelsea chant 'José Mour-INHO, José Mour-INHO, Jooooosé Mourinho' got an airing. The Portuguese man is the first Real Madrid manager to have his name serenaded from the terraces of the Bernabéu. He introduced Karim Benzema, the local Lyon lad, on the 63-minute mark. He got a charitable, rousing reception from his old fans on entering the fray. A minute later, with his first touch of the ball, he scored, having popped up in the box at the end of some neat skill by Mesut Özil. Real Madrid's fans launched into choruses of '*¡Que viva España! ¡Que viva España!*' A few fans also started chanting, a bit incongruously, '*¡Puto Barça, Puta Catalunya!*' Benzema's name also got a few hosannas. I read later that Florentino Pérez, who had personally closed the deal on his signature, jumped to his feet in the VIP box to celebrate his goal. Benzema, however, looked bashful amidst his celebrating teammates. Any guilt he might have been feeling was assuaged when Lyon stole an equaliser with seven minutes left, the goal coming as a result of idle defending from a long-range free-kick. A knockdown header found Bafé Gomis in acres of space on the six-yard box, which allowed him to sweep a volley past Iker Casillas.

As we reconvened on the bus after the match, after wolfing down some *bocadillos*, a cargo of the traditional Spanish sandwiches having made the journey with us, the atmosphere was muted, one verging on disappointment. The general consensus was that Real Madrid didn't play well but they were unlucky not to win. There was no live-mic joke session as we meandered our way back to Barcelona through the night. Everybody was whacked. There was still work to be done in the return leg.

13

THE LION AND THE DAGGER

Real Madrid beat Lyon 3–0 in the second leg. It was a significant stake in the ground for José Mourinho. He called it 'historic'. The club hadn't won a knockout round in the Champions League in seven years. The Portuguese man knew how much the competition meant to the supporters and the club. The essence of Barça is a flag, that of the putative Catalan nation. Real Madrid's identity is tied up with its pursuit of a jug-eared cup. The Champions League is its grand obsession. Fans talk about '*la décima*', the tenth European Cup that awaits the club at some indeterminate date, in reverential tones. It is a Holy Grail. The most popular terrace song of the *Ultras Sur*, their hooligan quarter (or 'the End Zone Guys', as Magic Johnson calls them) is a schmaltzy number which concludes with the line: 'We have to love you so much because you gave us the ninth European Cup.' It is always a strange sight, given their diabolical, hate-filled ideology, to see the *Ultras Sur* break into the love song during league matches at the Bernabéu. They have a dance routine to go with it. It involves marching backwards and forwards across their rows of seating, arms outstretched and resting on the guys' shoulders in front.

The club's seventh Champions League win in 1998 was their sweetest, more gratifying for fans than Spain's triumph in South Africa. 'There's this notion in Madrid,' explains Miguel Aguilar, 'that we won the first five European Cups. Then we won a sixth one in 1966. For many years, we were the club who had won it the most. It was a trophy that was ours. For 32 years, we hadn't been winning a cup that was owed to us… that we had a right to. Whereas I thought I was going to die without Spain winning the World Cup. I could live with that. The Champions League was something that I thought we were entitled to, but had never won in my life. Fulfilling that need was much more satisfying than this other thing.'

Manolo Sanchís was Real Madrid's captain for that final in 1998. It was played at Ajax's stadium in Amsterdam. Predrag Mijatović scored the winning goal in the 67th minute. 'There was a special moment,' says Sanchís, 'and it was right after Predrag scored. There was almost 25 minutes until the end of the game. There was a look among all of us that was very conspiratorial, especially between Fernando Redondo, the other defenders and Bodo Illgner, our goalkeeper. It was a look that said, "This match is over". It was a special sensation. People who were watching the game tell me that those 25 minutes lasted forever, like as if they were two hours. To me, they went like that,' he says, snapping his fingers.

I interviewed Sanchís at his office in Madrid on the morning before Real Madrid's return leg against Lyon. He runs an event management business, but also moonlights as a commentator for Televisión Española, amongst other football punditry gigs. He is one of the lions of Real Madrid. As a sweeper, he spent 13 seasons as club captain. Sanchís graduated onto the team in 1983. He was part of the *Quinta del Buitre*, a quintet of players including Míchel and Emilio Butragueño, from the club's *cantera*. They carried the team for a decade, both on the field and politically off it. They wielded enormous power for players, serving as a kind of kitchen cabinet for Ramón Mendoza, their club president. On getting fired as manager in 1990, John Toshack said of Sanchís that he was 'the worst person it has ever been my misfortune to meet.'

Sanchís appears as if he could still line up for Real Madrid. He looks much as he did when he was a player, with a slight hardening of his features with age. He has a long scar that runs between his lip and nose, which has the look of a childhood wound. A portrait of his father, also Manolo, hangs in the Bernabéu stadium. They look like brothers. They have a rare distinction – as father and son – of having both won European Cups. Sanchís Senior is a veteran of Real Madrid's 1966 team. Sergio Busquets and his dad Carles at Barça and the Maldinis at Milan are the others in the select club. 'My father is *Ultras Sur*,' says Sanchís. 'At first, when you're a player your vision of the club is very elemental: you have a professional relationship, with a lot of commitment. Later on, when you retire, you change that professional relationship for an emotional one. Today my father's relationship with Madrid is 100 per cent emotional.'

Sanchís is one of the most decorated players in Real Madrid's history. He saw great times at the club. Apart from the couple of Champions League medals he picked up, he was also part of a five-in-a-row championship-winning team during the *Quinta del Buitre* years. Perhaps no other Real Madrid player, though, has witnessed so much managerial roadkill – 18 appointments in as many years. 'It is very curious and hard to explain,' he says, surveying the carnage, 'that Jupp Heynckes won a Champions League title after 32 years and still had to leave the club. It's hard to explain that Lorenzo Sanz [president from 1995–2000] after winning two Champions Leagues and an Intercontinental Cup lost the presidential elections. But the club is like that. It's a very demanding club. It's not only about winning, but also what matters a lot is how you get things done. Real Madrid is unbelievable with everything. It gets to the maximum with its virtues and with its defects. That's the thing about being the best club in history. And it is very difficult to live for a long time with a club as complicated as this one. It is a machine so big, so powerful and so merciless that sometimes in its way it often ends up trampling an occasional life.'

Sanchís got a *bocadillo*, a sandwich – the colloquial expression for a dead leg – which forced him out of his first *clásico* after 15 minutes. It resulted, he says, from a 50–50 clash with Barcelona's Alexanco. There were no other matches, he says, to compare with the Madrid–Barça encounters, not even the epic European Cup nights he experienced. 'There was a time in which we got a lot of bad results away from home in the Champions League and we would overcome them all at home. There was a special spirit at the Bernabéu. People say it was the spirit of Juanito, of great comebacks. That lasted for two or three years. Great matches against teams like Milan and Bayern Munich. But none are comparable – neither for good; nor for bad – to a Madrid–Barcelona game. Madrid–Barça is always special. It is incredible because a match lasts 90 minutes, but *El Clásico* doesn't last 90 minutes. *El Clásico* is being played the week before. Statements are made here and there. There are hugs here and there. Then match day comes. The intensity is huge. It is played, and after that there are three or four days of "digestion of the match". They end up being almost two-week long affairs. Every time there's a Madrid–Barça game, you'll always hear the same thing: "This is the match of the century". Until the next one comes.'

He thrived on the tension they wrought. He used to relish the coach ride to the matches, even when under fire by 'brainless' hooligans on the way to the Camp Nou. It helped him focus. Managers, paradoxically, were calmer on the day of a *clásico*, he says. There was never a need for blood-and-thunder speeches. The players were self-motivated. And the teams were so intimate with each other that nothing had to be pointed out about opponents. He refused to be drawn on specific sledging that went on between players on the pitch, except to say that more of it goes on than imagined. Even back in the days of his father the hectoring between the rivals was unceasing.

'There were always those who wanted to mix it all up with politics, and those of us who just wanted to get on with playing football,' recalled former Barça midfielder and skipper Josep Maria Fusté in an interview. His career, in the 1960s, overlapped with Manolo Sanchís Senior. 'As a Catalan I felt that they screamed phrases at us which I didn't like and which affected me, even though I still enjoyed the games. In a sense I felt proud that they felt the need to insult us. It made me feel that we did really represent another country, another nation, even though the words they used were pretty horrendous. From 1941, the year I was born, until the day I retired from football, they always screamed the same insults.'

I mention to Sanchís that I had arranged to interview Hristo Stoichkov, the former Barcelona striker, the following morning. They had some memorable tussles in the 1990s. I ask if the Bulgarian spoke much on the pitch. He goes cold. 'I don't care about that character,' he says. 'Barcelona has had, and will always have, great players, and some of them are great characters. Characters that you like to talk about, that are interesting. There are others that are not interesting at all.'

Hristo Stoichkov is an interesting character. They know him at Sandor, a cafe restaurant around the corner from where he lives in Barcelona. It's a hangout for people used to the good life. It has a canopy outside for patrons who lazily sip coffee or martinis while a shoeshine guy hunches over their footwear. When Stoichkov enters, their tranquillity is briefly disturbed. '¡Venga!' says one old guy in greeting mode. Another slaps him on the shoulder. Someone whispers, 'Is that Stoichkov?' The Bulgarian laps it up. He leans in to one table to sign an autograph and exchange a few words. He's like an old prizefighter.

He makes his way to the back of the restaurant, which is empty and dimly lit. He's followed by some of his entourage. Tanev, his agent, is described as 'a confidential man for the Dagger in Bulgaria' in Stoichkov's official biography, *That's Me: Stoichkov*. As well as keeping his confidences, Tanev also played alongside him in the Bulgarian national team. He now runs his successful football agency business out of Stoichkov's old apartment. Joan Capdevila, Spain's World Cup-winner, is one of the players on his books. Lubo, one of Tanev's staff, is also in train, and Tanev's son, who must be about 15 years of age. The boy acts as a useful foil for Stoichkov's pronouncements about the enervation of youth today. He won't play football on the street, Stoichkov complains, he only has time for fiddling with his mobile phone.

Stoichkov is equally unimpressed with the modern footballer. 'For me, money is very important – for the family, for the kids,' he explains. 'At the same time, this money is a big problem. People go crazy. They pick up cars. They pick up jewellery. Publicity comes very quickly.

Tattoo, very quickly. Gel, very quickly. They forget the first principle: why do you play soccer? Are you a good player or do you come to the field only for the money or to pass the time or because you're looking for a girlfriend in TV?'

Stoichkov's 'formation' – it's the word he uses – happened in the old Eastern Bloc. He was born in February 1966 in Plovdiv, a city some believe to be the oldest in Europe. Half his life was spent living under communism. It was a world which had 'two faces' he says. One face was very tough, very closed. No one spoke second languages like German or English. 'Only Russian!' says Tanev. On the other hand, it instilled useful values such as organisation and discipline. The latter is something Stoichkov struggled with as a player and coach.

In June 1985, his authorised biography records that, 'destiny played another trick on the ambitious and fearless Stoichkov.' He was banned from football for life because he started a brawl in the Bulgarian cup final. After the match, he stormed into the opposition's dressing room and smashed the trophy they had just won by throwing it against a wall while they celebrated in a communal bath. He was still a teenager. He was banished to a military base in Stara Zagora, but returned to the game within a year, having received a pardon on the eve of Bulgaria's departure for the 1986 World Cup.

He came to Johan Cruyff's attention in 1989 during the semi-final of the European Cup-Winners' Cup. Stoichkov banged in his club CSKA Sofia's three goals against Barça over two legs. The Barcelona manager told his people to get him. Josep Maria Minguella, the agent who has lured everyone from Maradona to Messi to the club, was tasked with the job. It took six months of trucking backwards and forwards to the Balkans. Soldiers kept guard outside meeting rooms while Minguella carried out his negotiations. Unusual hurdles had to be jumped. One of them involved drinking vodka with yoghurt at the insistence of the generals who ran CSKA Sofia, before Todor Zhivkov, Bulgaria's head of state, finally agreed to ink the deal. It made many people a lot of money. Stoichkov's monthly wages jumped from £600 to £20,000, but ostensibly his objectives were framed in different terms. Manolo Sanchís and his Real Madrid teammates had been winning the Spanish league title on the bounce for years. 'At this moment, Real Madrid is the best team in Spain,' explains Stoichkov. 'Five times, they have won the league. Five times, Hugo Sánchez has scored the goals. In June 1990, I said in my first interview: "Real Madrid is finished. Real Madrid's hegemony is over. Barcelona will be the best."'

His first tilt at silverware came six months later. Barcelona met Real Madrid in the final of the *Supercopa de España* at the Camp Nou in December 1990. It was an incendiary battle. Johan Cruyff was sent off for insulting the referee. Stoichkov took things a step further. 'There was a discussion with the ref. He was nervous. He gave too many frees. I was pissed off with him. I stood on his foot. Bam, that's it,' he says, clapping his hands. The incident happened by the touchline in the middle of the pitch. A trench-coated Barcelona official tried to intercede during their parlay when Stoichkov stomped on the ref's foot. It was like a manoeuvre by one of the Three Stooges. The ref hobbled away gingerly, bent over with his right hand reflexively resting on his backside. Stoichkov was banned for three months.

'The referee was crazy. Why did he come close to me? Why am I the best player? This is why. This is the best moment in my history. It is a memory. Like Eric Cantona when he was with Manchester United and he was kicking the fan. It's no big deal,' he says happily. Stoichkov sits back when a big smile comes on, like now. The muscles around his cheekbones spring into action and a light dances from his eyes. It's a bit like the grin of Robert De Niro, one of his favourite actors. It announces to those in his company: I'm smiling now.

Barcelona lost 1–0 and ultimately 5–1 on aggregate. Real Madrid's lap of honour was confined to a little bit of hand-clapping over their heads in the middle of the pitch. Objects and bottles rained down on top of them. Real Madrid's Hugo Sanchez also incurred a four-match ban for grabbing his crotch provocatively in front of one of the stands.

Stoichkov spent the best years of his career with Barça, scoring over a hundred goals for the club. 'I die for this jersey,' he tells me.

He helped the club win five leagues and its first European Cup. Individually, he won the *Ballon d'Or* in 1994, the same year he got the Golden Boot while at the World Cup with Bulgaria. His hatred of Real Madrid became legendary. The antipathy is mutual. Every time a *clásico* match rolls around, he's door-stopped by the world's media for a warmongering quote. It's usually a variation on the theme that talking about Real Madrid makes him physically sick. His hatred for *madridistas* is proportionate to the love he has for his adopted city. Like Barcelona's international idols from previous generations – Ladislao Kubala in the 1950s and Cruyff in the 1970s – Stoichkov has settled in the Catalan city.

'Why do I love Catalonia so much? Because it is the first place that opened my eyes,' he says. 'Barcelona is the first big team in the world that signed me. My family came to the best city in the world. My daughters went to the best schools. The mentality of the Catalans and Bulgarians is the same. I very, very quickly adapted. Catalans receive foreigners very well. They open the door. If I'm walking down the street, people stop me to say, "Hello." They receive me as one more Catalan here.'

Tribal loyalty sits comfortably with Stoichkov. Rivalries are easy to understand for him. After scoring four goals one time for CSKA Sofia against their city rival Levski Sofia, he wore the No. 4 shirt in their next derby match. Everything is black or white. You are either for him or against him. When I ask about Michael Laudrup's defection from Barcelona to Real Madrid in 1994, he is visibly sad. 'It hurts inside,' he says. He's like a *padrone* from a Mediterranean village. I can imagine that he's always surrounded by a close circle of colleagues, that he inspires fierce loyalty. He is instinctively generous and prone to grand gestures of charity for those who follow him. In 1992, when the Bulgarian government couldn't afford to pay for broadcasting rights to televise the finals of the European Championships, Stoichkov footed the bill. He loves to defend his people's honour. Before a World Cup qualifying match with Bulgaria in 1993, he bent down to tie his shoelace during the French national anthem in revenge for a perceived slight.

Barça's fans see the way he defends their honour. They love the way he runs down Real Madrid. He won't travel to the Bernabéu stadium for matches, only to play. 'Real Madrid is the team of the government. This is the reason why I don't like Real Madrid,' he says. Many people describe themselves as being from 'the Stoichkov generation'. I know of one Barça fan that carries a photo of Stoichkov – a couple of decades after the Bulgarian's pomp – in his wallet alongside one of his girlfriend. They love his crazed, irreverent passion. Barça returned to Plaza Sant Jaume in 1992 to show off the European Cup. When Stoichkov got out onto the balcony, he lifted Jordi Pujol, Catalonia's president, up off his feet from behind in a bear hug. It drew raucous laughter. They are proud of the pro-Catalan political stances he has taken over the years. During the 1998 World Cup, for example, he hung a Catalan flag outside the window of his hotel room before Bulgaria's match with Spain. He has led from the front in the fight to have Catalonia's football team accorded full FIFA status at the expense of Spain's *selección*.

But he doesn't despise all Real Madrid people. He says proudly he has three Real Madrid jerseys in his house – those of Emilio Butragueño, Míchel and Hugo Sánchez. Manolo Sanchís, he says, 'is a little different'. He has a lot of time for José Mourinho, who he worked with at Barça in the late 1990s. 'He is a very good guy. People don't understand his character. He is direct. This is the problem for journalists. The Spanish journalists try to provoke him. This is the reason why Mourinho is ignorant for the journalists. They say, "Mourinho is a translator. Mourinho is FedEx." Fuck you. He is a very good guy. He is correct. I'll tell you a story. In one press conference, the same journalist who was telling him in 1996 that he was just a translator was telling him 15 years later – the same journalist – that he was only a translator. Mourinho said, "I have changed after 15 years. I am one of the best managers in the world. You are still doing the same job. I have new clothes, new shoes. You are still in the same clothes."'

14

'I'M WITH MOURINHO *A MUERTE*'

José Mourinho was crotchety. The season had drifted into March and his side had just leaked two more valuable league points by drawing 0–0 with Deportivo de la Coruña. A few days later, during a press conference at Real Madrid's training ground a reporter asked him if all this whinging – about referees and kick-off times that supposedly favoured Barcelona – was getting out of hand.

'They are truths not complaints,' he shot back. 'Are you a hypocrite?'

When the journalist said he wasn't, Mourinho pressed him: 'Then tell the truth. Are they truths or complaints?'

The journalist suggested they were complaints. 'Then you're a hypocrite,' he spat.

'This is a hypocritical world,' he added, turning to address his audience. 'Everyone knows what is truth and falsehood. I'd rather I was a punching ball for cowards than a hypocrite. But I was born to grow up well and to die well. With head high. *Contento*. And without fear of telling the truth. Without fear that tomorrow a gang of cowards would come to attack me. What can I do? I have no fear to tell the truth.'

Then he digressed, absentmindedly, apparently alluding to Pep Guardiola's brother, Pere, who is a football agent: 'I, for example, don't have a company to represent football players. If I had a real estate agency, I would sell houses [but I don't].'

When someone brought up the subject of Real Madrid's next match against Málaga, who were trained by his predecessor, Manuel Pellegrini, a man that had accumulated more points for Real Madrid at the same point the previous season, Mourinho was dismissive. If he checked out of Real Madrid, he wouldn't go to a lowly club like Málaga; he'd coach a big club in England or Italy, a slur that later prompted Málaga's mayor to call him 'a clown'.

When Mourinho was asked if he felt supported by his club, he got enigmatic: 'Why go to complain about others if I'm going to complain about myself?' Having dazzled momentarily, he guided the assembled journalists towards the nub of his existential angst. It was an old beef with him – the club was disjointed and malfunctioning. Only he was taking the fight to the world: 'There are people who, when something has to be said, won't say it and will get others to do it. There are clubs that have a communications strategy. There are clubs where the players play very well in a communication strategy, where the coach is protected, where he can be calm and do a different role. Here, no. Here, I am the one who comes out to defend [the club's honour]. No more.'

The hacks were flummoxed. Was he going mad? He wouldn't have been the first man to go charging around Spain tilting at windmills. Was he trying to engineer his own dismissal? It was said that he had hassled his players after the draw with Deportivo to bitch about the fixtures schedule to the press, but, going from evidence, they had demurred. He had been badgering Miguel Porlán 'Chendo' to plague the fourth official during matches. Chendo, a former player, has spent most of his life at the club, since his schooling began at its *cantera* in the late 1970s. As match day delegate for the club, he falls under Mourinho's remit. According to Real Madrid's players, Chendo had been sidestepping the handiwork Mourinho had tasked him with. Instead of pressuring the fourth official he'd been asking him anodyne questions like: 'Do you know the time? Is *El Corte Inglés* [the shopping centre] open today?'

The bulk of Real Madrid's fans, however, loved Mourinho's dirty tricks campaign. 'He is a kind of rescuer for *madridismo*,' explained Tomás Roncero, Real Madrid's most colourful TV football pundit, who was wearing a lime green suit the day I spoke to him. 'He appeared in a moment full of doubts after two years of Barça hegemony. He is a *tipo*, a good bloke, who comes and says what [pro-Real Madrid] journalists had said a long time ago but the club didn't dare to say. Mourinho has put on the Madrid hooligan's T-shirt and says what supporters want to hear. He defends the club, says the truth about referees, criticises the schedule of matches, recognises the favours granted to Barça. He attacks Barça. He is not politically correct. He is not diplomatic. He is *madridista a muerte*. The *barra brava*, the hooligan quarter, would kill for Mourinho.'

When I asked Roncero, keeping up a bloodthirsty line of enquiry, if Mourinho's mercenary streak as a manager unsettled Real Madrid's fans, he said they had no illusions he was a soldier of fortune. 'The *madridista* knows it,' he said, 'but thinks that he is so professional that as long as he is in Real Madrid, he will kill for it. They don't want him for 15 years. They know that the two or three years he is in Real Madrid, he kills for it. Real Madrid prefers this arrangement better than if it had a moderate and wise manager for seven years. What they want is a *tío*, a geezer that will front up for Real Madrid; that will fight for it, whether he stays one year or two.'

Florentino Pérez, the club's president was also taken with the street fighter he'd signed up as manager. The construction boss first made his way in the world as an underling in the mayor's office of Madrid, seven years that taught him the value of a poll. He regularly conducts market survey tests of his Real Madrid constituency to canvass their opinions. A couple of weeks after Mourinho's latest press conference tantrum, Pérez addressed Real Madrid's members at a club ceremony. He used the platform to endorse Mourinho's polemics.

'For many years,' intoned Pérez, 'this institution has showcased what we've come to define as "class". Class is earned by acknowledging the merits of our opponents, but also by defending what we believe is just. Class is also earned by denouncing irregular behaviour both on and off the pitch. It is also an example of true *madridismo* to defend Real Madrid from what we believe to be unjust, irregular or arbitrary. And that is exactly what our coach, José Mourinho, does. What José Mourinho says is also an example of *madridismo*.'

It was a remarkable concession. By tethering himself to Mourinho's ethics, Pérez effectively ceded control of the club's public image. It was a desperate roll of the dice, an unprecedented political move by a man who, hitherto, had treated coaches with disdain. Manuel Pellegrini said that Pérez never spoke to him after August during his season in charge. Pérez was now so enamoured with his successor, Mourinho, he was allowing him to speak for him. Were Mourinho to fail, it would leave Pérez in an almost untenable position. It clearly sprung from desperation. 'Mourinho is a man who knows very well the world of football,' said Santiago Segurola, 'and he's a man who adores power because he's an egomaniac. He doesn't admit any competition, not even from the president. He knows that he is in a superior position in relation to Real Madrid, because it's sick. It is *enfermo de urgencias*, very ill.'

Fernando Carreño, the author of *La Historia Negra del Real Madrid*, a book on the underbelly of Real Madrid, told me that some of his colleagues at *Marca*, the pro-Real Madrid daily sports newspaper, were worried that their kids were starting to support Barça. 'The problem is that after Mourinho there is no one better,' he said. 'What do they do next? Do they get Guardiola?'

The only other manager to have acquired such authority was Fabio Capello, during his first reign as manager of Real Madrid in the 1996–97 season. But it was short-lived, and lacked Mourinho's shamelessness in style. 'Capello had a lot of similarities with Mourinho,' said Segurola, 'but he also had something that made him more human. He was a manager who looked for fewer excuses than Mourinho, who didn't need to corrupt everything that surrounds football. For example, Mourinho says that all rival teams surrender to Barcelona, when the only one that has surrendered has been Málaga. He has also said that there is a referees' plot on behalf of Barcelona and against Real Madrid, that there exists a fixtures schedule in favour of Barcelona and against Real Madrid. And Mourinho's last lie is that

Barcelona takes dope. He speculates about it, and Real Madrid hasn't refuted this in any official note.'

The doping allegation was a story that blew up at the time of the Pérez speech. It was aired by Cadena Cope, a right-wing radio station, which is owned by the Spanish Catholic Church. The media organ incurred a legal action as a result of its slander. Joan Laporta, the former Barcelona president and politician, took a swipe at Real Madrid for its alleged role in stirring the scandal, even going as far as to name Pérez. 'It is abundantly clear,' he said, 'that Real Madrid is behind the accusations of doping against Barcelona.'

One preposterous story followed another. 'I think that this is poisoning football,' lamented Segurola. 'I think that Spanish football, which came from winning the World Cup, instead of enjoying a great year and excellent teams, has found a spiteful and despicable atmosphere generated from only one side, because Barcelona has never thrown a discourteous or suspicious message. It has always been Real Madrid that has done it.'

The media battles were absorbing Spain. A few weeks after Pérez lauded Mourinho's idea of 'class', Esperanza Aguirre, the president of Madrid's parliament, rowed in. In one of her first public pronouncements after an operation for cancer, she said that Mourinho was the best manager of the twenty-first century. 'I'm with Mourinho *a muerte*,' she pledged. The speech sent Spain's intelligentsia into overdrive. The Portuguese interloper had become an icon of the Spanish right. For deconstruction, *La Vanguardia*, Catalonia's main newspaper, rolled out a Harvard sociologist, José Luis Álvarez. Aguirre, the politician, loved Mourinho, he pointed out, because of his popularity and, as he had seized control of Real Madrid's public speech and image, he had won a political battle that was to be admired.

Mourinho had rescued Real Madrid from its past. The club was hung up on its *señorío*, its grandeur. Real Madrid had an idealised pre-feudal notion of itself. Its knights had brought the club incomparable glories – having plundered nine European Cups on its crusades. Ideally, argued

Álvarez, Real Madrid would like to freeze time. It hated having to risk these victories. The club would prefer to play outside the rules so it could go on winning, as Spain, the coloniser, had been able to do at one stage during history. It despised having to measure itself against inferior armies. It disguised this loathing in distant elegance. But the masses of Real Madrid had chosen Pérez for his money, not for his *señorío*. They wanted to win again, more than anything they wanted to win *la décima* – that elusive tenth Champions League title, the crown that Mourinho had won, only months beforehand, within their city walls. Barcelona, too, had its grand aspirations. Pep Guardiola embodied *seny*, common sense and restraint, the conduct becoming of a gentleman, an approximation of *señorío*. He wasn't given to rhetorical flourishes. In press conferences, he would blandly repeat again and again what worthy opponents the other teams were. In discarding the facade of *señorío*, Mourinho had made Real Madrid more antithetical to Barcelona.

The enmity was set to come to a head. In a quirk of the fixtures' list that Mourinho didn't complain about, Real Madrid were to play Barcelona four times in three competitions over 18 days – in the league at the Bernabéu on 16 April; in Spain's cup final and in a two-legged semi-final of the Champions League. The press billed it as football's World Series. For an arch tactician like Mourinho, it offered an ideal opportunity to fell Barcelona, who had carefully carried on a war on three fronts with fewer quality resources in its squad, in one swoop. Critically, two of the four games would be in Madrid, one on neutral ground. The pressure and scrutiny would be huge, unparalleled. The last time the clubs met in a run of four games over a similar timeframe was in 1916. Santiago Bernabéu, a man who personified *señorío*, scored a goal in one of the matches for Real Madrid. A Catalan newspaper, prefiguring a long era of Barça *victimismo* in *clásico* exchanges, groused about being 'robbed'. Much had changed since then.

Mourinho started his media war by saying nothing. On the eve of the sides' league match, word was delivered to the world's press assembled in

Madrid that he wasn't going to talk in the pre-match press conference. His assistant, Aitor Karanka would field questions instead. It was stated Mourinho was tired of having his comments 'blown out of proportion'. Karanka, a veteran of Real Madrid's successful 2000 Champions League final, had represented him before at several press conferences during the season. But this was the *clásico*. A chunk of the press corps – predominately the local journalists – was livid and threatened to boycott.

Mourinho turned up for the press conference, but Karanka sat centre stage, Mourinho to his left. Real Madrid's press manager reiterated that Mourinho would not be speaking. A block of about 30 journalists stood up and walked out en masse. Mourinho winked as they departed, many of them awkwardly carting their unclosed laptops. Mourinho sat quietly throughout, only intervening to help with translation for foreign correspondents. His ruse – a new take on an old practice of drawing attention away from his players onto himself – worked, of course. The match-day headlines were all about his ventriloquist manoeuvre. And his players were under pressure. They were eight points adrift of Barcelona, who had only dropped ten points all season, with seven matches to go in the league. Toe to toe, they had lost the last five *clásico* matches; the latest one the 5–0 caning at the Camp Nou, a match they weren't allowed to forget. Over the preceding few weeks, a fleet of buses had been parading around Barcelona remembering *manita* – the little hand. As part of an advertising campaign for a private health insurance company, the buses were plastered with a picture of five Barcelona players – Xavi, Carles Puyol, Víctor Valdés, David Villa and Sergio Busquets – in white medical gowns over their Barça jerseys. Each smiling player was holding a hand up, fingers spread, in *manita* fashion.

There's always a lot of horse dung around the Bernabéu stadium on match days. Before and after games, mounted police cut a dashing presence outside the ground, as they saunter along the streets that hug it. The Bernabéu is a magnificent building. One corner of it looks out onto Castellana, the long, wide avenue that cuts across the centre of

Madrid, like the bow of a ship. On the evening of the match, which kicked off on a Saturday at 9 p.m., a police helicopter circled overhead for a couple of hours beforehand. But there wasn't much lawless behaviour. At around 6 p.m., a TV crew foolishly tried to film the *Ultras Sur* who had convened, as usual, on Marceliano de Santa María, a pedestrian street that runs perpendicular to the south end of the stadium. The filmmakers got to the top of the street before retreating under a hail of bottles and glasses. The tree-lined street is leafy and benign looking on a spring evening. It has functional, Eastern Bloc-style apartments that overhang street-level commercial units such as hairdressers, as well as low-end diners and booze cans. Thirty riot police arrived about half an hour later and stationed themselves at the top of the street, with newly minted tear-gas rifles cocked as the *Ultras Sur* continued singing their battle hymns. When the *Ultras Sur* spotted a professional photographer taking pictures of them high up in one of the apartments, they started chanting '*Periolisto*,' a play on the words *periodista* and *listo*, which roughly translates as 'smart-assed journalist'. Like Mourinho, they are suspicious of the press.

The couple of hundred Barcelona fans who had travelled to the match were nestled amongst the eaves of the north stand. There is possibly no finer theatre in which to watch football than the Bernabéu. It's smaller than the Camp Nou. It holds 85,000 people, but its stands rise sharply towards the sky, like 'the teeth of a monster', as Jordi Cotrina, the sports photographer described it, which creates an incredible, closed-in atmosphere. The pitch was dry and bony. Apparently, Mourinho told the groundstaff to let the grass grow three inches longer than normal to disrupt Barça's passing game.

When the teams were announced on the loudspeaker, the biggest jeer went up for Pep Guardiola. He had surprisingly picked Carles Puyol at centre half, rushing him back after a three-month layoff from injury. The woolly-headed defender bossed his domain, however, until he limped off with a hamstring strain two-thirds of the way through the match. By that stage, Barcelona had taken the lead, having predictably dominated the possession stakes. As David Villa broke free in the box early in the second half he was rugby-tackled by Raúl Albiol, which earned the central defender a red card. Messi converted the penalty. It was the first time he'd scored against a Mourinho-trained team. The stadium was convulsed in whistles, although a strange kind of quiet took hold once the teams kicked off again. With the exception of the *Ultras Sur* who upped their chanting, Real Madrid's fans were momentarily dazed, as if they'd sensed a death foretold.

Then something great happened. The next 40 minutes were a whirlwind. Both sides attacked in unyielding waves. Xavi clipped a shot just over the bar from the edge of the box. Messi, after jinking through a forest of defenders, set David Villa free in the box only for him to shoot tamely into the keeper's arms. We saw the best of Real Madrid, the *luchador*, the fighter. Pepe crashed through Messi and another Barcelona player to get at the ball on the halfway line at one point like a man possessed. Messi, who was flung sideways like he'd stepped on a landmine, appealed in vain to the ref for a free-kick. It was another marker. Pepe swarmed all over the centre of the pitch during the match, cutting out Barcelona's attacks at source. Deploying him as part of a three-man midfield, where he occasionally plays for Portugal, was a crafty move by Mourinho. Pepe is a wildcat. He plays on the edge. He is infamous in Spain for a heinous episode during the dying minutes of a league game against Getafe, another Madrid team, in April 2009. After pushing over a Getafe midfielder in the box, he launched two kicks at him while he was prostrate on the ground. The second kick would make you wince. He was deranged looking and had to be escorted off the field by Iker Casillas. During a bout of depression afterwards, he wondered whether he would ever play football again. He did, of course, and his battling performance in a ten-man team 1–0 down to a rampant Barcelona side was inspiring.

A few minutes after Barcelona's goal, Mesut Özil came on as a sub for Real Madrid and began his usual sorcery along the right flank. Cutting inside with less than ten minutes to go, he passed to Ronaldo on the edge of the box. The Portuguese star trapped the ball and ferried it immediately onwards to Marcelo who was haring into the box at such speed that he enticed Dani Alves into a late sliding tackle that won Real Madrid a penalty. Ronaldo converted it. Like Messi, he'd also got a monkey off his back – he'd never scored in a *clásico*, and his strike helped him in his private goalscoring duel with the Argentinian. In Real Madrid's dressing room, they were calling Ronaldo 'The Anxious One' because of his obsession with the shootout the press had been hyping all season. When his penalty flew in, thousands of white flags billowed around the Bernabéu. The coliseum was sated. The late, spirited come-back had momentarily beguiled them. When the ref blew for full time, cries of '*¡Madrid! ¡Madrid!*' echoed around the stadium; even though Barcelona had effectively sealed a third league title in succession.

Mourinho was spitting mad. Someone had let the cat out of the bag. At 5 p.m., a few hours before kick-off, a television reporter announced Real Madrid's ploy to play Pepe alongside Xabi Alonso and Sami Khedira in the centre of midfield. In the dressing room afterwards, Mourinho let rip. 'You are traitors!' he shouted. 'I asked you not to leak information about the line-up and you have betrayed me! It's obvious you are not on my side!'

His players had never seen him so upset, according to journalist Diego Torres, whose fly-on-the-wall accounts of Real Madrid's camp, harvested from insider sources, have kept *El País* readers titillated during the Mourinho era. Insults poured out of his mouth. He eyeballed each of them before settling on Granero, the most servile amongst his legions. 'The only friend I have in this room is Granero, but I can hardly trust him! You have left me alone. You are the most treacherous squad I've had in my life!'

He took a can of Red Bull and hurled it against the wall. It smashed, spraying gunk over some of the assembled players. A few, including Iker Casillas, drifted off into the showers. Mourinho was inconsolable. Sobbing, he said he'd talk with Florentino Pérez and José Ángel Sánchez, the club's general manager, to make sure the mole would be smoked out. Then, according to one witness, he compared their circumstances to a platoon fighting in the jungle. 'If I'm in Vietnam and I see that someone ridicules a comrade, with my very hands, I'd take a gun and kill the guilty man. Now you have to look for the person who leaked the line-up.'

Mourinho answered questions in the press conference afterwards, but not for everyone. When a journalist from *AS* who had walked out of the press conference the day before, opened the questioning, Mourinho responded with his own query: 'Are you the managing editor of *AS*? If not, I can't reply. Because according to your philosophy, if you won't speak to my number two, I will only speak to the editors.' There were stifled giggles around the press room. The journalist stayed rooted to his seat as Mourinho moved loquaciously onto the next questioner. 'I will answer you,' he said, 'because *Punto Pelota* showed respect [yesterday], and you, sir, are a fine professional who also deserves respect.'

He continued in sombre mood. His clairvoyant powers were as strong as ever – his pre-match training routine with ten players had proved useful – but he pined for the day when he could play Barcelona with 11 players. 'I would really like to but I know that in Spain and in Europe that is mission impossible. They are a team that controls every situation that surrounds the game. When we got off the bench, we were told to sit back down. When they did it, they could do whatever they like. I would love to have the control of football that they do. I do not understand why they dominate the situation but they do.'

There had been positives to take from the game – Real Madrid had stopped its run of *clásico* defeats. It had fought back gamely with ten men, but the critics were appalled at Mourinho's defensive tactics. Hundreds of millions of pounds had not been spent assembling a squad that was afraid to come out and play at the Bernabéu. It was not the Real Madrid way. Two former club managers said they'd have got the sack for such servility. Johan Cruyff called Mourinho's anti-football a 'eulogy' to Barcelona's might. 'Madrid is a side with no personality. They just run back and forth constantly, tiring themselves out,' blasted Alfredo di Stéfano, Real Madrid's honorary president, suggesting his heirs were like a mouse to Barcelona's lion. 'The whites were cornered all game,' he said. 'Barcelona play football and dance.'

There was only four days to the next instalment – the *Copa del Rey* final at Valencia. When asked how he saw the matches panning out, Mourinho continued dancing to an old tune: 'I hope that all three teams play well.'

15

MR MO MENTUM

The Vatican believes the Holy Grail is in Valencia. It certified the chalice that sits in the city's cathedral as being the one that Jesus Christ used at the Last Supper. It's a gaudy-looking goblet. It has been fiddled with over the centuries – gold and pearls have been added to it as well as a pair of love-heart handles not unlike the shape of the ones on the Champions League trophy. The *Copa del Rey* – or the King's Cup – has nothing of its lustre. It has been slowly discredited in Spain over the years even though it's older than La Liga. A Spanish TV presenter described it as a tournament with a drip on its arm. It's rigged in favour of big clubs. First division teams don't partake until the last 32 stage. As an extra little sweetener, second legs are played at home for the bigger teams. Still, the competition has struggled to engage Real Madrid.

When José Mourinho landed at the gates of the club, it hadn't won the cup since 1993. The Portuguese man set his sights on it from the off, though. The cradling of a chalice, even if it's not the real thing, can be uplifting. His focus resulted, of course, in a classic line-up for the 2011 final – Real Madrid and Barcelona at Valencia's Mestalla stadium, scene of their first *Copa del Rey* final together in 1936. That final, which was held a few weeks before the Spanish Civil War broke out, is largely remembered for a goalkeeping save. In the dying minutes of the game, Ricardo Zamora dived to the bottom left corner of his goal to keep out a shot by Barcelona's star player, Josep Escolá; half the stadium had risen prematurely to acclaim a goal. His acrobatics preserved Real Madrid's 2–1 lead. At the final whistle, Zamora, who had won two *Copa del Rey* winners' medals with Barcelona in the early 1920s, was carried shoulder-high off the pitch by Real Madrid's delighted fans. It was his last game for the club.

His name is on the trophy for Spain's goalkeeper of the year award. He was a hulk of a man. Apparently, he once played on during a Spain v. England match with a broken sternum. He was a flamboyant character by nature; he made a cloth cap and white polo neck de rigueur for goalkeepers for a generation. He liked cognac and was lax in his tax affairs. His political allegiances went with the wind. He played several times for the Catalan XI and was happy to receive a medal from Spain's Republican government, but declared his sympathies for Franco once the Civil War set in. During the war, he was arrested by anti-Franco forces and imprisoned without trial in Madrid's Modelo prison. He was spooked by the experience. Prisoners' names were called at random and those selected were taken out and shot. The practice was called *sacas*, or unexpected callouts. His name was shouted out regularly so he could do some dressage for visiting dignitaries. Every time he heard his name, he recalled years afterwards, his knees shook in fear. After an international campaign on his behalf, he was released and fled the country until the war was over, leaving for France, as it happened, via the port at Valencia.

The next time Real Madrid and Barcelona met at the Mestalla for a *Copa del Rey* final was in 1983. Diego Maradona was playing for Barcelona. He ran onto a 60-yard pass by Bernd Schuster that landed in Real Madrid's box for the game's opening goal. He controlled the ball with such alacrity that it threw the two men marking him. Then he nonchalantly rolled the ball, like Pelé to Carlos Alberto in 1970, to an on-running Barça teammate, Víctor Muñoz, who finished from 15 yards.

Santillana equalised for Real Madrid following a defensive cock-up. In the last minute of the game, Marcos got on the end of a cross with a diving header to secure a win for Barcelona. It was a sublime header. He was at an acute angle in between the back post and the edge of the six-yard box. He levitated for what seemed an age with his neck craned before making contact to direct it back across the goal. When it flew in, the mix of emotions – joy, relief, hatred of Real Madrid – was overwhelming for Schuster. The German, who was practically on the Real Madrid goalline when it hit the net, wheeled away with his arms in the air in triumph until he got to the edge of the six-yard box. Still on the run, he tried to make eye contact with Real Madrid's disconsolate defenders. They were oblivious to him. Undaunted, he twice jerked his left arm violently, gripping the inside of his elbow with the other arm in an 'up yours' gesture, until he took off in another direction to join his teammates in celebration. In the stands, Barcelona's president, Josep Lluís Núñez was in floods of tears at the final whistle seconds later.

Schuster's manic behaviour is a notorious moment in the history of *El Clásico*. People still talk about his *cortes de manga* gesture. When I brought up Schuster with Manolo Sanchís, who played with him at Real Madrid for two seasons when the German crossed the great Spanish divide, he shook his head and smiled. 'Very German,' he said. 'I have many German friends and they all are very alike in their personalities. Just like Spaniards, we're all alike. Bernardo, as a player: exceptional. As a mate in the dressing room: exceptional. And very German.'

His German humour caused all kinds of headaches for his managers in football. *Der Blonde Engel*, as the midfielder was nicknamed, retired from international duty at 24. On being substituted by Terry Venables during the 1986 European Cup final, he walked out of the stadium in disgust before the match went to a penalty shootout, which Barcelona lost. Núñez, Barça's tyrannical little president, ordered that he be banished from the team for his insolence, which led to a one-man, season-long boycott by Schuster. He was 26 years of age, at the peak of his powers and one of the finest players of the 1980s, yet he wasn't playing football for club or country.

He lounged around in Barcelona city while his lawyers fought an unfair dismissal case. He came back into the fold the following season but his legal squabbling threw up some my-oh-my evidence for the

Spanish tax authorities. It turned out he had signed two contracts with the club, only one of which was for the taxman's eyes. Half of Barcelona's squad were on the same type of deal. The club was running its players' payroll like a Follow the Lady table at the fairground. When tax inspectors looked for their money back, Núñez brazenly demanded that the errant players settle up rather than the club. A stand-off ensued, prompting Schuster and the bulk of his teammates to stage a players' mutiny. In late April 1988, they issued a statement demanding that Nuñez resign.

The diehard supporters of the club denounced what they perceived to be money grabbing by their pampered stars. Two days later, the team faced Real Madrid in a league match at home. Disgruntled Barça fans jeered as their team emerged for the warm-up and whistled cynically when they scored to take the lead. Real Madrid, in a rare outbreak of respect for a Castilian team at the Camp Nou, was applauded. It was only in the second half when Barça had run Real Madrid ragged – a display crowned by a Gary Lineker goal to make it 2–0 – that the home fans' scorn petered out.

The sedition, which coincided with Johan Cruyff's appointment as manager later that summer, led to a clear-out of most of the mutineers – ten in total. Schuster was picked up by Real Madrid, although his departure, given its circumstances, didn't arouse the type of opprobrium accorded Luís Figo, for instance, a dozen years later.

He appeared in Real Madrid's midfield in 1990 at another *Copa del Rey* final between the two clubs at the Mestalla. He was the only survivor from the 1983 match, although he was wearing different colours. The game was spoiled by the sending off of Real Madrid's Fernando Hierro for a second bookable offence in the first half. Barcelona won 2–0. During their players' lap of honour, goalkeeper Andoni Zubizarreta, who is currently the club's sporting director, was felled by a missile. He had been jogging along, holding one of the handles of the cup, when he was struck. He crumbled in a heap on the pitch after being hit. Schuster was also in bits. He sensed referee betrayal. 'After this match,' he sniffed,

'Mr Loza will go to spend a very happy holiday in the Costa Brava, in a little chalet there, for sure.'

The 2011 final was played on Adolf Hitler's birthday – 20 April. To mark the occasion, Real Madrid's *Ultras Sur* draped a black banner on one of the railings in the ground which said, 'Happy birthday 18' (the neo-Nazi code for 'AH' is 18). The city of Valencia rolled out 2,000 troops for security duty on the day of the match. Valencia is roughly equidistant from Madrid and Barcelona, about four hours' drive down the Mediterranean coast from Barcelona. Each army of supporters was guided towards its own fan-zone near the stadium; dedicated areas thronged with revellers taking shade under marquee tents, like a music festival. Live bands provided music and merchandising stores a range of officially branded accessories. They were also stocked with food stalls and family-orientated entertainment distractions, like the Bucking Donkey in Barcelona's mini-city. Across town at Real Madrid's one, there was even a fake Cibeles fountain, a reproduction of the goddess of fertility statue in Madrid which Real Madrid's players always end up straddling to celebrate their trophy wins.

With so many fans wandering about the city, there were inevitably disturbances. The sides hadn't met on neutral territory in over two decades. There is YouTube footage of fans taking 'scalps' – hit-and-run attacks where one fan belts another and makes off with his scarf or flag. I was caught in the middle of a police swoop about two hours before kick-off. Some 500 Barça fans had convened outside various bars on a cross-section of streets close to Avenida Cataluña. They were singing Barça songs and setting off the occasional flare when a fleet of police wagons suddenly descended. I couldn't see what provoked the police, but they certainly ended the dispute, wading in with batons as they dispersed the fans. For a couple of minutes bottles and chairs flew overhead, coming from two street ends, which put a lot of people in the line of fire. Several windows were broken. The police launched a volley of shots into the sky. One of their helicopters hovered above us. There were several bloodied fans and one was so outraged that his face was contorted with rage.

The fracas was a far cry from the reverential scene a few streets away. The Mestalla, which holds 55,000, is always a bottleneck on match days. The stadium is a charming, crumbling old shell – originally built in the early 1920s – which lacks the vast underground car parks of Spain's more modern constructions. Its antiquated infrastructure meant that the clubs' dignitaries and officials and guests from the Spanish Football Federation were deposited a few streets from the stadium before kick-off. Men like Real Madrid president Florentino Pérez, his right-hand man Jorge Valdano, Spanish manager Vicente del Bosque and nondescript directors and their families made the last leg of their match-day journey on foot. A passage to the stadium, lined with fans, was carved for them. Occasionally a fan or two broke the cordon and ran to hug a hero or get a photo taken.

Inside the stadium, the atmosphere was *increíble*, buoyed by a younger, prepared-to-travel demographic than is normal at *clásico* games. The Mestalla's stands are sheer. They rise sharply like the ramps in a skate park. One half of the stadium was whitewashed, the other a mosaic of *blaugrana* and the yellow and red of the Catalan flag. I was sitting in the Barcelona side. Their fans greeted the Spanish national anthem with disdain. Toilet rolls spilled onto the pitch. Beside me, a teenage girl stood with her thumbs turned down throughout it. I took a coach to Valencia earlier that morning with *Almogàvers*, one of Barça's supporters' clubs. When I raised the subject of the Spanish national anthem later, Albert Yarza, their president, had, wordlessly, plucked a referee's whistle from his pocket and smiled.

The talk of the day had been about goalkeepers. Iker Casillas had a great yen for the *Copa del Rey* – it was the only bauble missing from his trophy cabinet. Barcelona, in keeping to custom, rested their first choice keeper Víctor Valdés, as they had done all through the tournament, and started José Manuel Pinto. Born in Andalucía in 1975, Pinto is another in the tradition of eccentric goalkeepers. He has long black hair, which is braided, and runs a hip hop record label. He caused a pickle earlier in the season during a Champions League group stage match against FC Copenhagen at the Camp Nou. A winger from the Danish side had beaten Barcelona's offside trap and was bearing down on goal when he pulled up suddenly, believing the ref had blown for offside. Pinto had faked the whistle. The FC Copenhagen boss was apoplectic. As play resumed, Pinto smiled devilishly and wagged his finger in the air towards the Barça bench. It was only after the game that his actions were noted and he incurred a two-match ban from UEFA for 'gross unsporting conduct'.

There were three acts to the *Copa del Rey* final. Real Madrid allowed Barça to massage the ball deep in their own half, but once the leather found its way towards the halfway line, they sprung into tackles. There was a sustained aggression to their play, bordering on the illegal, which unsettled Barça's rhythm. Midway through the half, Álvaro Arbeloa and David Villa fell over each other when turning to run onto a long ball over the top of Real Madrid's defence. While springing back to his feet, Arbeloa, a former Liverpool defender, stepped maliciously if not with great force on Villa's calf. The Barcelona striker was only allowed to make one roll of a foetal-position cry to the heavens before being hoisted onto his feet by both shoulders by Arbeloa and his teammate Sergio Ramos. They wanted no playacting. The ref, who was immediately surrounded by several screaming players from each team, left his cards in his pocket. Play started again with a free kick to Real Madrid, who carried on bullying. On the cusp of half-time, Pepe was unfortunate not to put them ahead with a long-range header which crashed off a post.

Barça had failed to get a shot on target in the first half, but that changed after the break as Messi started finding room where there had been none before. Operating in the kind of crowded spaces where pickpockets prosper, he created several chances. The first was for Pedro. Gathering the ball on the halfway line close to the right-hand touchline, he ran towards goal only to find his way blocked by three Real Madrid players. He stopped, drew a tackle and set off on a different, diagonal course, leaving two of them waylaid. Seconds later and still dribbling, he was again surrounded by three defenders, only one of whom, Sergio Ramos, was facing him. He brushed off his challenge, which diverted him again slightly off course. The other two pursuers gave up their pursuit. Still running across the pitch, as if he was headed for the touchline 40 yards out from the goal, he laid off an angled, inch-perfect pass for Pedro to run onto in the box, from where he slotted the ball into the corner of Iker Casillas's net with his first touch. The goal was disallowed, however, for offside.

Messi persevered. Four minutes later he put Dani Alves through, but he fluffed a goal chance. Messi tried for himself the next time, drawing a diving, one-handed save from Casillas after unleashing a shot from 20 yards out. Fail again. Fail better. Moments later, he gathered the ball by the halfway line. Skipping over a tackle by Marcelo, he was heading away from goal towards the centre circle, when he dramatically doubled back with the deftest of chops. The move took him past Xabi Alonso, who was left standing like a ticket collector at a turnstile as he swept past. With three other defenders all set to gobble him at the same second, he laid off a pass to Xavi who shovelled it onto Pedro whose chip brought a spectacular save from Casillas. The Spanish international keeper had hardly drawn breath when Andrés Iniesta charged into the box after working a one-two with Messi. His low shot on goal, which took the slightest deflection from Sergio Ramos, demanded the finest yet of Casillas on the night.

The final whistle arrived; Real Madrid had survived. They came out fighting in extra time. Again the pendulum swung. Eight minutes in, Xabi Alonso gathered the ball on the edge of the centre circle in Real Madrid's half. Looking up, he released one of the passes of the season, a 40-yard pathfinder along the turf between Sergio Busquets, Gerard Piqué and Adriano – all of whom were back-peddling and caught off guard by his vision. It arrived at Cristiano Ronaldo's feet in behind the defence and he shot first time but his effort whistled just wide of the far post. His time would come. Just before the break, Messi was dispossessed in a midfield pincer movement by Xabi Alonso and Marcelo. Marcelo found Ángel di María. They exchanged passes, the last of which put Di María goal-side of Dani Alves by the corner flag. He whipped in a half-goal cross which Ronaldo finished with a scorching header that flew in over Pinto's head from 12 yards out.

To celebrate, the Portuguese star cantered over to the corner flag, just in front of where I was sitting, gesturing to his teammates to follow him. He came to rest in front of the baying Barcelona masses by sliding on his knees with his chest pushed out. There were people around me jigging like jackhammers with rage. Anything that was to hand was pelted down on top of him, including beer cans, Coke bottles, lighters, and – presumably from a clandestine Real Madrid fan – an unlit cigar. While Ronaldo was engulfed by his teammates, Pepe reprised Schuster's infamous *cortes de manga* gesture. It was the only, decisive goal of an invigorating contest.

A couple of hours later, the Real Madrid squad waited at Valencia airport to board a flight back home. Madrid, one of Europe's great all-night party cities, was already ablaze. The television viewing figures in Spain for extra time in the match – over 15.5 million – was a record. Mourinho was in reflective mood. Over the hills, some critics were saying nasty things. They said Mourinho was an enemy of football; that his Real Madrid side had smothered Barcelona. They despised his pragmatic brand of play. Coincidentally, it was a year to the day since he masterminded Inter's 3–1 win over Barcelona in the Champions League semi-final. Their bad faith made Mourinho smile. 'This is football,' he said.

Barcelona's football was only a work of theatre. It was flimsy, an illusion concocted by the media. When put to the test, they wilt. Strangle Barcelona of space in the middle third of the field, he said, and they flounder. In the run-up to the *clásico* series, he had been bombarding his players with slogans to assure them that it wasn't necessary to have the ball. '*¡Pelotazo!*' he kept screaming. '*¡Pelotazo!*' The wonder of this word. In Spanish, it has two meanings. In business, it means to quickly pull off a profitable deal, usually with insider information. In football, it roughly translates as 'long ball'. What cunning. This was their secret weapon. '*¡Pelotazo!*'

Mourinho knew, pointed out the *El País* journalist Diego Torres that the vulgarity of this strategy was 'a countercultural message' for his gilded players. They were proud men – many of them were World Cup-winners, who were raised to believe that a football was to be cherished, that it shouldn't just be rashly thumped up the other end. This was why he needed to keep repeating his idea, especially now in the hour of victory. There were other ways to win a football game. Besides, there was no turning back now.

A month beforehand, according to Diego Torres, he convened his troops. It was an important moment. They needed to be as one. There was still dissension in the camp. He wasn't a hypocrite he told them. At the end of the season either Valdano went or he did. 'I can't stand him,' he said. It was tantalising – if he stayed, he explained, he'd be responsible for all of sports management in the club except for marketing and basketball. 'You have the key to everything,' he told them. 'If you win a trophy, I'll stay and he'll be cast off. If you fail, he'll stay and I'll go. From now on, I'll see who's with the team and who isn't.'

The players were in a bind. One of them said as much in a meeting: 'He plays with our will. He makes us his accomplices. If we run and win trophies, he'll say to the president we are with him and against Valdano. If we have a bad day, we'll become his enemies.'

What were they to do but run for him. And it worked. Most of them had just won their first medal with Real Madrid. It was the club's only trophy in three years. It was the end of an eight-year drought for Pérez. And they had put Barcelona to the sword. In a flush of excitement, Alfredo di Stéfano was converted. He had become a disciple. 'Madrid's appetite for victory doesn't happen with the flick of a switch,' he wrote in his column for *Marca*. 'It was the result of the work headed up by Mourinho since he arrived. I hope he stays for many more years.' Real Madrid was renewed. It faced into the future emboldened. Barcelona was no longer invincible. Mr Mo Mentum had just changed uniforms.

16

WHY DO BARCELONA ALWAYS WIN?

Barcelona got antsy after the *Copa del Rey* defeat. They were hurting, mentally as well as physically. Andrés Iniesta, their star midfielder, was in the sickbay for the upcoming first-leg Champions League semi-final in Madrid. They were goosed at left full back too – their three squad options were injured. Pep Guardiola, normally reserved in his media exchanges, made a surly remark about the possible choice of referee, saying that Pedro Proenca, if chosen, would play well for his fellow Portuguese José Mourinho. This was a new departure, replied Mourinho – criticising the origin of a referee. As it turned out, Wolfgang Stark, an experienced German referee, got the job.

Everyone in Spanish football seems to have an opinion about refs. Unlike most countries, its match officials are listed in advance of – rather than after – fixtures, which opens them to scrutiny. 'The real show is the players,' says Rafa Guerrero, a former linesman in La Liga, 'but if a journalist starts a week before to examine the referee and says, "This is the guy who damaged Barça last year" or this kind of information, it's terrible because fans read this and go to the stadium influenced by what they read. This generates violence. I have experienced it; I have had to get protection at my house. My boy came home from school one day because the other children said that his father was a robber.'

Guerrero is possibly Spain's best-known match official. He retired in 2008, after 14 seasons of service in the *Primera División*. Born in 1963, he still has the bubble perm, flecked with grey, which distinguished him during his career. He's also bubbly by nature, but unsentimental about business. He once had to send off his father, who was a team coach, during a local match in León. His co-authored memoir, *¡Rafa, No Me Jodas!* is a bestseller, the proceeds of which he has given to charity. When I asked him about its risqué title, *Rafa, Don't Fuck With Me!*, he said he couldn't call it anything else. It's his moniker.

In September 1996, he was running the line for a Barcelona match at Zaragoza. During the match, Luís Figo floated a free kick towards Zaragoza's goalmouth, which was gathered by the goalkeeper. As both sets of players were jogging back out of the box, Barcelona's Fernando Couto took a tumble and clutched his head as he hit the ground. Guerrero shot up his flag to draw the ref's attention to the incident. The ref ran over to Guerrero. His advice, which was caught on camera, was brief: 'Penalty and red card.' The ref was shocked. 'Fuck, Rafa! I shit on my mother! Red card for who? What number?' Pep Guardiola, Barça's captain, leaned in to eavesdrop as Guerrero said: 'No. 6.' The ref had a weary look as he walked back towards the penalty spot surrounded by irate players. He got halfway and turned back to consult again with Guerrero. He was unconvinced: '*¡Rafa, no me jodas!*' he said. Guerrero was adamant. The ref awarded a penalty and sent off No. 6, Xavi Aguado. They got the wrong man – Zaragoza's Jesús Solana was the culprit. Guerrero received death threats after the match for his error. In Spain, referees and their assistants are a maligned species. Spanish football supporters are very provincial. They don't like refs. Michael Robinson told me they take it personally when a referee makes a dubious call, as if he has brought 'local dishonour'.

'It's different in other countries,' says Guerrero. 'For example, I was a linesman in a Champions League semi-final between Manchester United and Juventus in 1999. The referee was Manuel Díaz Vega, a Spanish guy. It was in Manchester at the Theatre of Dreams. Manchester United were losing 1–0 until the 88th minute, when they scored a goal, from Teddy Sheringham, but he was a little offside. I disallowed the goal and nothing happened. There was no problem. I didn't hear anything, only a low groan. If this happened here in Spain, for me, it would have been impossible to get out of the stadium without a police escort. I would have had to leave by helicopter,' he says, with a laugh.

The jibes continued in the run-up to the match at the Bernabéu. Mourinho mocked Guardiola for a comment he made about one of Guerrero's old colleagues. Guardiola made the point that but for 'the linesman's good eyesight' in the *Copa del Rey* final, in which he flagged offside for a goal by Pedro, which was disallowed, Barcelona would have won. Mourinho pounced. 'Up to now we have had two types of coaches,' he said at his press conference on the eve of the match. 'A very small group of coaches who never speak about referees. After that, there is a bigger group, of whom I am one, who criticise the referees when they make big mistakes. People like me who don't control their frustration. But it is also a group who are happy to highlight the good work of the referee. And now, with the declaration of Pep the other day, we are entering a new era with a third group, which for the moment includes only him, who criticises referees when they get decisions right!'

He went on speaking for several minutes. He dropped a couple of other slurs, including one about 'the scandal of Stamford Bridge' when Barcelona got a few lucky refereeing decisions in the semi-final of the competition two years earlier, but mostly he was in good spirits. Marcelo was by his side. Earlier, he had been telling the assembled journalists how he quotes aphorisms to Marcelo and his other players from 'Alberto, a certain Albert Einstein'. He concluded by wishing the ref good luck for the match. 'I don't want the referee to help my team. I only want the teams to be happy with his work,' he said. 'For Pep, it seems impossible to be happy – for him to be happy, the referee must be wrong.'

The *rauxa*, the madness, was coming out in Guardiola when he arrived shortly afterwards for his press conference. He'd always been civil in his institutional dealings with Real Madrid. He's good mates with Raúl and Fernando Hierro, Real Madrid's greatest heroes from his time as a player. But this *clásico* series was taking its toll. He didn't much like it, says Ramón Besa, when he heard that Florentino Pérez greeted his arrival in the dugout at the Camp Nou with the disparaging comment, 'Guardiola is the López Caro of Barça,' a reference to the former reserve team coach at Real Madrid who briefly managed the first team for Pérez. Now, after nine months of provocation, Mourinho had finally tipped him over the edge. He reacted, according to one of his confidantes, because he felt the team needed it. Their honour had been violated. They were jaded and dejected after the defeat at the Mestalla. Doubt, that gnawing worm, had entered their heads. Mourinho, of all people, was threatening to derail their season again, as he had done with Inter a year beforehand.

'Because Mr Mourinho permitted himself the luxury of calling me Pep,' he said, rocking from side to side on his seat, 'so I will call him José. Tomorrow at 8.45 we will face each other on the pitch. He has already won the battle off the pitch. He has been winning all season, and in the future. If he wants a personal Champions League, I'll let him have his own off-field Champions trophy. I hope he takes it home and enjoys it as much as the other trophies. But this is a game. When it comes to sport, we will play and sometimes we will win; sometimes we will lose. I can also talk about a comparative list of grievances, which would go on forever. We could remember Stamford Bridge and another thousand things but I do not have that many people working for me – secretaries and referees and general managers pointing things out. So tomorrow, we will try to play football as best as possible. In this room, he is the fucking chief, *el puto amo* – the fucking man. He's the most knowledgeable man in the world. I do not want to compete for a moment. Just remember we were four years together [at Barça]. He knows me and I know him.'

He raged for 45 minutes. He's a cool cat so his fury was calibrated. His composure didn't extend, however, to answering foreign reporters' questions in English, as he normally does, and he took an unusual turn or two. By queasily referring to Barça as a small team that represents 'a small country, from where one church steeple can be seen from another church steeple', he alluded to a song by the Catalan separatist songwriter,

Lluís Llach. Born in 1948, Llach is a tenacious political activist, a kind of Pete Seeger of the Catalan music world. Mourinho could continue reading Alberto, Guardiola added, and the *Central Lechera*, an expression coined by a Catalan journalist for the media acolytes of Pérez. (In Spanish, *mala leche*, bad milk, refers to malicious propaganda.) He clarified that his reference to the good-sighted linesman in the *Copa del Rey* was merely to point out that results come down to small things. And when asked if his spiel was a motivational ploy, he replied: 'What? You think my players will run around more because I tried to steal some limelight from Mourinho? It's a semi-final!'

His players gave him a standing ovation when he returned to the team hotel.

Real Madrid had a couple of enforced changes for the match. Ricardo Carvalho, their wily centre half, was suspended and Sami Khedira, one of their central midfielders, was injured. Lassana Diarra, or Lass as he's known, slotted into midfield in the latter's place. Lass is a fine physical specimen with a big engine. He would excel, one imagines, at several other sports like squash and long-distance running. He wore No. 10 for Real Madrid. Barcelona's No. 10 is Lionel Messi. Real Madrid also had Kaká, who had scored two goals against Valencia the previous weekend, in their squad, but decided to keep him on the bench. Lass scored two goals in eight seasons as a professional.

The match settled into a familiar pattern early on – Barcelona held onto the ball; Real Madrid stood off them until they got towards the halfway line, where play got very cluttered. Cristiano Ronaldo, the world's most gratuitously entertaining footballer, played as a lone striker for Real Madrid. He cut a forlorn figure. His task was to press Barcelona's defence. He ran and ran like a sheepdog after the ball, but was always a fraction behind where it came to rest. At one stage, about 16 minutes into the game, having got caught again in one of Barcelona's Bermuda Triangles, he gave up running and threw a hissy fit. Nobody in football does upset like Ronaldo. He flailed his arms like he was trying to unhinge them from his body. He looked achingly towards Mourinho on the line for redress to a cruel world. Mourinho looked away.

The game got increasingly ugly, with rare flashes of skill. The only enterprise was used in trying to con the ref. Just before half-time, Álvaro Arbeloa picked up a yellow card for blocking Barcelona's Pedro off the ball. It was a harsh sanction. He barely touched Pedro's chest with his shoulder. Pedro collapsed onto the ground after the collision and lay on his back, for what seemed an age, gently swaying from side to side holding his face with both hands. Three minutes later, Barcelona's Sergio Busquets tried to mount Marcelo from behind in an attempt to get to the ball. Without looking behind, Marcelo repelled him by pushing his hand into his chest. Busquets fell to the ground, covering his face with both hands as if he was in agony.

'Diving is the thing I most dislike about Spanish football,' Michael Robinson said to me, echoing a sentiment of many football fans. 'Unfortunately, it's almost like a national tick. I remember when my kiddie, Liam, was small I saw him playing in our garden with his mates and I saw him dive and I said, "What are you doing, you tart? That wasn't a foul." And he said, "Well, Stoichkov does it." I remember my manager at Osasuna saying to me, "Why don't you go down more in the area?" I had a long debate with him and wouldn't do it. I wasn't brought up that way. When Spanish players do it today it's not premeditated; it's already in there. It forms a part of their football kit.'

The black art of feigning injury has been added to the diver's repertoire over the last few years. Busquets is a serial offender. He's a *teatrero*, an actor. In the previous year's semi-final of the Champions League against Inter he was handed off by Thiago Motta in an almost identical take on Marcelo's innocuous flick. Having been pushed in the neck, he fell to the ground and grabbed his face with his hands. Notoriously, while writhing on the floor, he was caught on camera opening his hands, peek-a-boo style, to check on how the referee's inquiries were proceeding.

'In Spain, a lot of players are more *pícaro*, cunning,' said Rafa Guerrero. 'They play with their hands or fall down on purpose. In other

European countries, they would be punished, but here it is more toler-
ated. Players act. They try to deceive the referee. It's to do with their
football education.' The *pícaro*, a rogue, is a subversive figure from
Spanish literature of the Renaissance period who navigates a corrupt
world through skulduggery. He is celebrated for his wiles. When the ref
produced a red card for Thiago Motta, Barcelona's bench sprung onto
their feet, as noted by Mourinho, Inter's manager at the time, as if they'd
scored a goal. Marcelo's brush with Busquets, however, went unpun-
ished. As play resumed, Busquets walked past him and was caught on
camera twice, it is alleged, calling him a monkey, a *mono*.

At half-time, as the teams made their way to their dressing rooms, a
rumpus broke out. There was an exchange between Arbeloa and Barcelona's midfielder Seydou Keita as they converged on the tunnel. Arbeloa
pushed him away. Pinto, Barcelona's hip hop producer-cum-reserve goalkeeper challenged Arbeloa. He pushed Pinto. Chendo, Real Madrid's
match day delegate, the middle-aged guy Mourinho had tasked with whis-
pering sweet nothings to fourth officials during match-time, grabbed Pinto
by the neck. Pinto swung at Chendo. Chendo took a spill but was stopped
from hitting the canvas because so many people had congregated; including players, subs, suited officials, heads in yellow bibs and security guards
in military fatigues and sunglasses, who stood gormlessly in the middle of
what was an unexpected brouhaha. Real Madrid's Sergio Ramos, while
making sure that he was well restrained, gestured to Pinto to come over to
where he was so that they could settle it. Pinto duly got a red card.

Play plodded on in the second half. It looked as if neither team
would ever score. Fifteen minutes in, Pepe lunged for a fifty-fifty ball
with Dani Alves, Barça's marauding full back who has the name of his
son, Daniel, tattooed on his chest. Pepe's studs were up, but it appeared
that both players connected with the ball. Alves rolled around holding
his shinbone with both hands until a pair of stretcher bearers arrived
to take him off the field. Alves used to *fuck* with Rafa Guerrero. He
and Sergio Ramos were the two players that Guerrero singled out from
Barcelona and Real Madrid's ranks for being deceitful. 'It's complicated,'

said the former linesman. 'Alves is an amazing player. He's physically incredible, but he is abusive. He doesn't play fair. He is a player that doesn't need to fall down on purpose. In England, his own fans would whistle at him. He is an actor and Barcelona don't need actors. Sergio Ramos is like him, he always says, "he did it, ref"'.

In this instance, it seemed, once again, Alves deceived the ref. Pepe, who probably deserved a caution for his recklessness, got a red card. Alves, full of vigour, returned to the action. A bewildered Mourinho approached the fourth official to sarcastically praise the decision. He also got sent off. Real Madrid's fans, as Michael Robinson would say, had been dishonoured. They were livid. Because the Bernabéu is a tighter, more enclosed stadium than the Camp Nou, the berating from fans is louder, shriller. It would be unbearable if it weren't for unintentional moments of comedy – a guy on the same row of seats as me jumped onto his feet when he saw that a red card was given to Pepe and screamed: 'Stand up, this is a robbery!'

Barcelona found more space. Fifteen minutes later, Ibrahim Afellay, who had just come on as a sub, skinned Marcelo on the right flank and crossed as he entered the box. Messi was on hand to guide the ball home from a few yards out. With a few minutes to go, Messi redeemed what had been a dour match with his famous sashay through Real Madrid's defence for his second goal of the evening. After the final whistle, the match officials were shepherded off the pitch under a hail of missiles.

Mourinho's press conference performance after the match was embarrassing. We heard the unborn chicken voices in his head. He was paranoid. Or at least his alter ego was. He said if he told us his real thoughts, he'd never work in football again. The second leg was going to be mission impossible for Real Madrid, he added: 'If, somehow, we go there and score and perhaps open this tie just a little bit, they'll kill us all over again. We have no chance no matter what we do.'

He wondered out loud about who they might be. And why they favoured Barcelona. Maybe it was because Barcelona were nicer people, *más simpáticos,* or that they donated money to UNICEF and put its logo on their jerseys, or because of their man Ángel María Villar. *Villarato* is a conspiracy theory named after the chief of the Spanish Football Federation. It had been running for several years and was propagated by Madrid-based journalists with the zeal of religious fundamentalists. The theory is that referees help Barcelona because Barça's former president Joan Laporta supported Villar's election while Florentino Pérez backed the man he defeated. 'If referees make mistakes which help Barça,' Tomás Roncero informed me, 'they get promoted, and if they make mistakes which help Madrid, they are *machacados,* smashed. The referees know all this and so they apply self-censorship. They realise that if they make a mistake, it is better if it favours Barça or if it damages Madrid.'

Mourinho majored on referees. He gave us names and the details of matches. '*¿Por Qué?*' he asked. 'Why? Why? Why Øvrebø? Why Busacca? Why De Bleeckere? Why Stark? Why? Because every semi-final the same things happen... Why? Why does a team as good as they are need something that is so obvious that everyone sees it?'

If he won the Champions League the way that Pep Guardiola had won his in 2009, he said he'd be ashamed, and that if Guardiola won again this year, after 'the scandal of Bernabéu' that title would also be 'tainted'. 'I hope,' he said, 'that maybe one year he will win a Champions League that will have been totally deserved. I thought that I could address him as "*tú*"... Well, now I see that I'm not allowed to. OK then. I will call him "*Señor* Josep". "Well *Señor* Josep, I hope that one day you too will win a clean Champions League, not yet another one sullied by scandals."'

It was a bizarre, slanderous outburst. Historically, Barcelona cornered the market in self-pity when it came to *clásico* misfortune. They had been overrun. With his latest sermon, Mourinho had become the high priest of *victimismo.* Amongst his outpourings, he went on at length about how the game – without referee interference – could have gone on for three hours and remained at 0–0, as if this was a desirable loop to be caught in. His pre-season pledge to honour Real Madrid's tradition of attacking football had evaporated. Spooked by the early season 5–0 thrashing at the Camp Nou, he was afraid to come out and play. He left Kaká, Karim Benzema and Gonzalo Higuaín, who had scored six goals against Valencia four days earlier, unused. To be so craven at home was disheartening. Roberto Palomar, writing for *Marca*, said that Real Madrid used to play at the Bernabéu in great European Cup matches with 12 men, now they had to make do with ten. Mourinho had got his comeuppance for his defensive, bullyboy tactics. Pepe's sending off had been harsh, but he, along with Xabi Alonso and Arbeloa, had been lucky not to get red cards in the *Copa del Rey* final. 'If you play with fire, sometimes you get burnt,' said Barcelona's centre half Gerard Piqué. Barcelona had, of course, contributed to a woeful spectacle. Alex Ferguson reckoned their theatrics had short-changed us of 30 minutes of action. 'It's a man's game and every time you play against Barça, every time you touch them, they throw themselves to the ground like cry babies,' cried Emmanuel Adebayor, who came on as a sub for Real Madrid in the second half.

The shrieking – from both sides – had hardly begun.

Both clubs mobilised their lawyers. Barcelona petitioned UEFA first. They objected to Mourinho's slander. They complained that the pitch hadn't been watered an hour beforehand, as had been agreed. In the bedlam that ensued after the final whistle, the Catalan announcer was also prevented from making security announcements over the PA system. It is customary for opposition fans in European competitions to be given instructions in their own language. Real Madrid officials claimed that the disembodied voice of a Catalan echoing around the Bernabéu stadium at such a fraught moment could have triggered violence. Real Madrid's fans had been unhinged. An angry mob hit upon Andy Townsend, ITV's commentator, in a restaurant later that night. He was at a table with Adrian Chiles and executives from the television station when he noticed people were looking at him strangely.

'Some of them started taking pictures,' said Townsend, the former Aston Villa midfielder, 'and then someone came and gave me a pot plant, saying, "This is for you" with a funny look on his face. There were ten of us around the table thinking, "What is going on here?" When I stood up I got booed and when I went to the loo I got followed there and back. A waiter escorted me to my seat. I didn't know why. Then people came up to me, talking aggressively in Spanish and there was a man shouting at me from the other side of the restaurant. It was all getting out of control. Then it dawned on me. Because I still had my UEFA accreditation around my neck they thought I was the referee. To them I was Wolfgang Stark, so I had to turn around and tell them I was from English television.'

Townsend blamed Mourinho for incensing the plebeians of Madrid. 'The crowd were baying for the referee's blood. They totally saw the referee as the villain of the piece. As ITV were going off air there was actually a fight going on in front of me in the stadium – two men were exchanging blows. And these were the decent seats. I witnessed first-hand the effect Mourinho has on fans.'

Real Madrid's complaints followed four hours after Barcelona's. They cited six Barça players for their 'premeditated anti-sporting behaviour', and did some legwork for UEFA regarding the penalties that ought to be doled out. Dani Alves, Pedro and Sergio Busquets should get two-match bans while one-game suspensions would suffice for Seydou Keita, Víctor Valdés and Javier Mascherano. They left it to the discretion of the football governing body as to what the appropriate sanction should be for the ringleader of their theatrics, Pep Guardiola. The complaints – from both clubs – were rejected by UEFA, while it pressed ahead with its own charges, which included a probe into the 'inappropriate state-ment' made by Mourinho after the match and the unruly behaviour of Real Madrid's fans.

Shells continued exploding in the propaganda war in the days running up to the second leg. Undeterred by UEFA's dismissal of their complaint, Real Madrid loaded a highlights reel on their television station and website of Barcelona's finest playacting moments, drawing particular attention to the versatility of Pedro and Busquets. Ironically,

Frank de Bleeckere, one of the refs name-checked in Mourinho's '*¿Por Qué?*' litany, was appointed for the match at the Camp Nou. He had sent off Thiago Motta, following Busquets' feigned facial injury, in the Inter v. Barcelona semi-final a year earlier.

Busquets was a maligned man. On the eve of the match, Real Madrid also posted a video of his alleged racist taunting of Marcelo, which included subtitles. The footage showed Busquets cupping his mouth with his hand to avoid detection. Barcelona insisted Busquets hadn't called Marcelo a monkey. He wasn't mouthing the words, '*mono, mono*,' the club explained. He was just saying, '*mucho morro*' – 'what a cheek'.

17

ENDGAME

Eidur Gudjohnsen is cool like the other side of the pillow. His people come from Iceland going way back. His grandfather was a fisherman who, they say, used to get sick every time he went out to sea. They breed hardy, languid men on that island, men not given easily to skittishness. You can see it in Gudjohnsen's eyes when he considers a question. He delays for a fraction of a second in replying while his eyes lazily tell you in advance: relax, an answer is on its way. He's in the autumn of a long, itinerant football career and is currently playing in Belgium. He's had his ups and downs. Not much would rattle him, although he got a jolt when he left José Mourinho's Chelsea to play for Barcelona in 2006.

'I always remember one thing when I signed for Barcelona,' he says. 'Coming from Chelsea, we'd just won the league, we'd gone close in the Champions League, it was the Abramovich era, there was a lot of pressure to win things, I thought, "Yeah, can't get much bigger than this," and then I arrived in Barcelona and I thought, "Wow, what's going on here?" It was the biggest thing. It's difficult to explain. It was the expectations, the people, the press. It was a bit of a shock. I don't know what it is. Maybe in London you have so many big teams in the city. You have certain areas – you've got your Arsenal, your Spurs, your West Ham. Here, in Barcelona, obviously you've got Espanyol, who are like its little brother, but everything really just revolves around this club.'

Born in September 1978, Gudjohnsen has the unique distinction of having played in the same international match as his father. Iceland played Estonia in Tallinn in April 1996. He came on as a sub for his dad, Arnór, who was also a striker, in the second half. Unfortunately, they never got to play together. Eidur fractured his ankle a month later, which threatened to end his career just as it was starting. The doctor at his club PSV Eindhoven – where he was a teammate of a young kid from Brazil called Ronaldo – said he would never play top-class football again. By the time he'd revived his career with Bolton Wanderers, his dad, who once scored four goals in a game against Turkey, had retired from international football.

Eidur passed the first 12 years of his life in Belgium, where his father spent the prime of his career, but he used to head to Iceland for holidays in the summer and at Christmas. The family spoke Icelandic indoors. Arnór left Iceland in the early 1980s to play for Anderlecht, where he won three league medals and got to play on grass for the first time. Eidur says that when he was growing up, it was 'a treat' to train on grass in Iceland. Most of the time himself and his mates played on gravel or an Astroturf pitch that was basically 'concrete with a carpet on top'. Their legs were scorched with burns. 'When you had a warm shower afterwards, the big thing was to get through the first minute of stinging,' he says. How different it is for his three sons. Although he left Barça a few years ago, his family lives in Barcelona, close to the airport. Meanwhile, his two eldest sons are learning about business at La Masia, Barça's youth academy. Their training is similar to his own when he was at the club. Everything is copied, he says. 'You can already see the little Xavis and Iniestas running around. They all have the little Barcelona stamp.' They play in a league against boys who are a year older. Andri, for example, is playing as a central midfielder these days. He brings home a school report card every month. It has 50 categories, like control – right foot; control – left foot; vision; punctuality; respect towards coaches. He's graded on each attribute. Andri, Gudjohnsen tells me, will be ten at his next birthday.

Gudjohnsen played alongside Lionel Messi, La Masia's most famous graduate. People don't realise, he suggests, how strong Messi is. He's 'physically an animal' with a low centre of gravity, which helps him ride tackles so effectively. Gudjohnsen was on the field the day Messi scored all of Barcelona's goals in a 3–3 thriller against Real Madrid at the Camp Nou in 2007. 'A nineteen-year-old gets a hat-trick in the *clásico* and it was the most natural thing for him,' he says.

Gudjohnsen has vivid memories of his first *clásico*, which was in Madrid. 'The week before was like leading up to the World Cup final. I think we played a game midweek in the Champions League against Chelsea and four days before it everybody was talking about Real Madrid. It was a case of, "Let's get the Chelsea game out of the way and then we've got *El Clásico*." I was thinking, "Wow." Then you're watching television – which is continually replaying highlights from old matches – and you realise you go to the Bernabéu and get a big result and you're a hero forever in Barcelona.' Pause. 'But we lost,' he says, letting out a laugh from the gallows. 'And I missed a big chance. I felt how bad… bad is not the word… how much it hurt the people in Barcelona that we lost. How difficult it was for them to forgive someone missing a chance in Madrid. The miss wasn't the worst miss in the world, but it did feel like it. It felt like it for weeks after. It actually took me a good few performances, and a good few goals, to get the people back onside. This is what you perceive from the press. I think we went to Mallorca and I scored two goals; after that I started to think, "I'm winning people over again."'

Gudjohnsen arrived in Barcelona just after they had won the Champions League. Their hunger had been sated. Decay set in. 'Everyone slacked off – players, training,' he says. When Pep Guardiola was appointed in the summer of 2008 to replace Frank Rijkaard, he didn't know what to think initially, but that quickly changed. 'After my first meeting with him, after the first couple of training sessions,' he says, 'I realised, "OK, there'll be no problems with this guy." He's got a big personality. He stamps his own authority and that's what was needed at the time in Barcelona. In Spain, you always worry about the politics within the club. You always worry about the interference of football directors and presidents. And I'm not saying so much here, in Barcelona, but Guardiola, from an outsider's point of view, would be perfect for a president or somebody higher up to control a little bit, but there was none of that. He was the boss and that was it. In his first meeting he had with the team, he said, "We're going to work and we're going to do this and we're going to finish our season in Rome [at the Champions League final].'"

Which they did – beating Manchester United 2–0 to win the club's third European Cup. Gudjohnsen describes Guardiola as a thinking man's coach, a boffin who is constantly rolling ideas around in his head. 'He can get frustrated and upset,' he says, 'but not in the typical hairdryer, screaming-and-shouting way. It's more that he shows his disappointment if things are not going right rather than having a go or getting crazy with someone.' Gudjohnsen won two English league titles under Mourinho at Chelsea. He says both coaches are almost identical in their training methods and their eye for detail.

In the press room, Mourinho is, of course, more expansive than Guardiola. The Portuguese man's baiting of the opposition can work both ways, says Gudjohnsen. 'On the opposition side, as I was playing for Barcelona in my first season against Chelsea, you realise he can get under your skin with his mind games. In my first game against him, funnily enough, he had a go at me. He had always called Barcelona a theatre. Theatre as in Spanish league players dive too much compared to the English game; and theatre as in Barcelona hasn't got a real hardcore of support. He came here and one of the first questions from the journalists was, "So, Mourinho, how do you like the theatre of Barcelona?" And his reply was, "Ask Eidur." Because in the previous game, I got a penalty and he'd thought I'd gone down a little too easily for his liking. He said, "I had the guy for two years and he never got me one penalty and he comes to Spain and all of a sudden he starts getting them. It's impossible." He was wrong because I did get a couple of penalties for him. I found it spurred me on. I scored in that game and it was more me wanting to score against him than against Chelsea.'

The effect was different when Gudjohnsen was a Chelsea player. He says Mourinho told him and his teammates not to take any notice when he started his media mischief. 'I think what he does very well,' he says, 'is transfer the pressure from his team onto different things. He gets people thinking about things other than just the football match. Because if you look at it now, he's gone out talking about Barcelona and their connection with UNICEF and how it's all a big conspiracy and referees and blah, blah, blah. All of a sudden, half of Spain is going, "Well, he's got a point there."'

Ferran Adrià, the world's greatest chef, is from the half of Spain which is riled by Mourinho's scheming. 'I don't understand him,' he says. 'It's as if someone from Mars has arrived. The current situation is very strange. You could understand that something would happen during these 18 days – it's normal that there is a lot of pressure – but the problem is not the four Barça–Madrid matches. I don't know very much about Mourinho's evolution, but it seems that in England he did the same. His purpose is to manipulate. I'm not interested in controversies. In my field I've won more prizes than Mourinho and I don't say that everybody is bad. I don't understand why he does it and I don't think it's good for football. Football players are an image for millions of children. I don't think the best image is polemics. I'm 49 and I don't need anybody to tell me things, neither Mourinho nor anybody. Last year, with Manuel Pellegrini as Real Madrid manager, this didn't happen. Or something like it didn't happen in the previous 50 years. I think it's surreal.'

There is a lot of jumping around in a conversation with Adrià. He's a passionate, rambling man. His thoughts can be ambiguous; often he doesn't finish sentences. He has a funny way of pronouncing *fútbol*. It comes out more as fumbol. And he has the slightly distracted look of a man whose mind is always racing. He is an original. His El Bulli restaurant, which closed in July 2011 to reconstitute itself as a food research foundation, used to field 2 million requests a year for 8,000 sittings. Dinner consisted of 44 helpings of his whimsical, thimble-sized experiments in food, like frozen chocolate air. In satirical shows, he is often depicted fashioning dishes out of string or old boots. He grew up in L'Hospitalet, one of the satellite cities that have been absorbed by

Barcelona. Like Gordon Ramsay, he was a keen footballer, 'a Xavi, an organiser,' he says, but packed it in after a chat with his coach. He was told at best he would only ever be a second-rate player. 'I only play in the kitchen now,' he says.

He was at the Camp Nou on the day Johan Cruyff played his first match for Barcelona in 1973. They are fast friends today. 'He is very nice,' he says of the Dutchman. 'People don't think so, but he is. He's a genius. He's very absent-minded. He can go from zero to a hundred. He can be talking about trivial things and immediately after makes a thought that impresses you. The axiom he said to Barcelona's players before the European Cup final at Wembley in 1992: "Let's enjoy. This is Barça." This is the most important thing about him – his philosophy.'

Adrià describes himself as apolitical when it comes to football. 'To think that Barça is the only team in the world that represents a city or a country is stupid,' he says. 'Milan is important in Milan. Barça is the feeling; it's the emotion of a country, but not the political feeling of a country. For me, football has never been a political subject. Mixing politics and sport is not good. It's the sport in my country, in my city, and I like it. And when we play against Real Madrid, I want to win 10–0. But football *es de locos* – it's a matter of mad people. It's the most fanatical religion. When a match finishes, I've friends, close friends, from Real Madrid, and they say to me, "This is unacceptable – what Messi has done in kicking the ball petulantly against fans," as he did in the first of the quartet of *clásico* matches. "He should be banned for ten matches." And I say, "Poor Messi! He never does anything bad!" If there is a controversial player, it is Cristiano Ronaldo.'

Cristiano Ronaldo broke ranks after the first-leg Champions League defeat to Barcelona. When asked by a journalist after the match what he thought about Mourinho's tactical approach, which left him chasing shadows for most of the game as a lone striker, he responded tetchily: 'I don't like playing like this but I have to adapt.' As insubordination goes, it was a mild indiscretion, but enough to earn him a correction from his manager. He wasn't picked for Real Madrid's league game against Zaragoza, which fell between the two Champions League matches. It was interpreted as a penance for 'The Anxious One', who was desperately chasing Messi for top spot in Spain's goal-scoring charts. He was, however, restored for the second-leg tie in a new-look, attacking Real Madrid line-up. Gonzalo Higuaín, an out-and-out striker, came into the side, as did Kaká in midfield for the suspended Pepe. Barcelona welcomed back Andrés Iniesta, who had recovered from a calf strain. Mourinho had given up the ghost, maintains Diego Torres of *El País*. Apparantly, during a team speech that stretched to almost an hour a couple of days before the match, he said the tie was beyond them. UEFA and what Mourinho called 'the pretty boys of world football' had done a number on them in the first leg. The players were 'stunned' by his defeatist attitude, Torres has written. Serving a touchline ban, Mourinho chose to watch proceedings in a hotel room rather than endure the ranting of Barcelona's fans from the club's presidential box. UEFA, in response to Real Madrid's badgering, flew in the fearsome Pierluigi Collina to oversee Frank De Bleeckere's refereeing job.

The skies rumbled overhead on the evening of the match. Three hours before it kicked off, the heavens opened. Lightning crackled in the sky above. Unseasonable, early May rain came down in heavy sheets. The 200-metre incline from the cross-street Diagonal down to the Camp Nou, which acts as a funnel towards the ground for people on match day, was turned into a sea of bobbing umbrellas. Still, it was felt, there wasn't enough water on hand to nurse Barça's passing game. Barcelona, who have the jitters about playing Real Madrid on hard, dry surfaces, comically launched their sprinkler system half an hour before kick-off. The away section of the Camp Nou, which is high up in the south end of the stadium, was sparsely populated. Little over a hundred *Ultras Sur* made the journey from Madrid to support their side, in contrast to the thousands of Barça fans who showed up at the Bernabéu the week before. The odds on Real Madrid prevailing were almost insurmountable. In over 50 years of the European Cup, no side had ever come back from a 2–0 loss at home.

Real Madrid's players took no notice of history. From the kick-off, there was a restlessness about them; they charged around in search of the ball. In the opening minute, Marcelo conceded a free-kick around the halfway line for trying to straddle Pedro. Grown men around me started shouting, '*Mono, mono*'; others grunted, 'Ugh, ugh,' like monkeys, beginning a trend whenever Marcelo or Emmanuel Adebayor, who came on as a sub later, did something conspicuous during the match. A minute later, Kaká gave away another free-kick, this time on Barcelona's goalline, for an over-enthusiastic challenge. Rather than sitting back, Real Madrid, it quickly appeared, were intent on trying to snaffle Barcelona high up the pitch. The ploy unsettled Barça. Ronaldo found room to make a couple of darting runs through their defence. The play was more open than at any other stage during the preceding matches, with both sides trading swift counterattacks. Real Madrid were standing toe to toe with Barça. The Camp Nou turned into a bowl of petulant screeching at one stage in response to a prolonged period of possession by the opposition. Real Madrid's tackling was relentless. Ricardo Carvalho, who had been sent off in a league match at the weekend, picked up a yellow card early on for a late tackle on Messi. Twice more in the half he re-offended, but was lucky to escape further censure.

As half-time approached, Barcelona hit a few high notes. Xavi passed to Messi on the edge of the box. Like he has done a million times, he ran across the outside of it, inviting challenges before unleashing a curling shot which drew a diving save from Iker Casillas. A minute later, he collected a deep, floating cross from Dani Alves on the exact same spot where he had just shot. Real Madrid's defence, which expected him to volley, were caught off-guard when he chested the ball down, dummied a shot and skipped into the heart of the box, but his low shot hooked wide of Casillas' goal. The salvos continued. Casillas was forced to make two more saves in quick succession from Messi, again, and Pedro. In the middle of the flurry of goalmouth action, bullfighting cries of '*Olé*' accompanied Barça's passing in midfield. Real Madrid almost stole a goal before the half-time whistle. Kaká, in probably his only notable contribution in the game, dodged two tackles at the edge of the centre circle and sent a long, scorching pass in behind Barcelona's defence, which Ronaldo picked up and crossed, but Víctor Valdés came quickly off his line to snatch the ball off Ángel di María's feet.

Two minutes into the second half, Real Madrid were given the lines for the key address of their post-match script. Ronaldo went racing down the middle of the pitch with the ball. As he came towards the box, he moved left to avoid a static Gerard Piqué, but was hurtling at such speed that Piqué's shoulder block knocked him off balance. He tripped and landed on the heel of Javier Mascherano, Barcelona's other central defender, who was side-peddling furiously, causing him also to fall, theatrically. The ball, which paid no heed to the falling dominos in its wake, carried on into the box where Higuaín arrived to curl it first time into the corner of the net. The goal was disallowed.

Undaunted, Higuaín seized on a slip-up by Carles Puyol moments later, but his shot from 20 yards out was deflected wide for a corner. A goal was on its way, but it came from Barcelona. An Iniesta pass cut open Real Madrid's defence. It reached Pedro who controlled the ball with a touch before finishing low into the corner. Real Madrid fought on. Shortly after, Xabi Alonso gatecrashed a Barça rondo and with a single interception put Di María flying through on goal. The Argentine neatly skipped around a despairing tackle by Mascherano and cannoned a shot off the post. When the rebound came back to him, he trapped the ball and passed square to Marcelo who only had to knock on the door. The sides were level again.

Real Madrid weren't done. They were infuriated by Barça's attempt to hold onto the ball and wear them out. Their players hared after it. Marcelo and Adebayor picked up yellow cards for their rambunctiousness in the tackle. Their teammate Lassana Diarra was lucky not to get a second yellow for cleaving Mascherano near one of the corners. When Real Madrid got possession, they showed flashes of ingenuity. Both defences held firm, though. Breakaways by Ronaldo and Di María were swiftly aborted while a long-range shot from Messi was comfortably saved by Casillas.

Sensing the final whistle wasn't far away, the Camp Nou became convulsed in people singing the refrain, '*¿Por qué? Because we're the best – so fuck you.*' The jingle has become a popular Catalan folk song since Mourinho, in his infamous press conference, took to wondering why Barça always wins. With a couple of minutes to go, Eric Abidal, who had surgery to remove a cancerous growth on his liver six weeks earlier, came on as a sub for Barça to thunderous acclaim. The clock wound down. Barcelona went through to the final 3–1 on aggregate. Their players, substitutes and backroom staff convened in the centre circle to celebrate. Abidal was given the bumps. The players did a lap of honour. Chants of '*¡Ese portugués, hijo puta es!*' rang around. Mourinho's absence was noticeable, a black mark in the Corinthian's ledger. He had, after all, been so quick to provoke with his own frenzied lap of honour in the same stadium a year earlier. Now, in defeat, he wasn't even around to congratulate his opponents.

The ground was slow to empty. Despite being cold and wet, Barça's fans were keen to dwell on this one, even if it hadn't been a classic conclusion to *El Clásico*'s greatest saga. Over four games, the football, sadly, had only rarely reached any grace notes. In the press conference afterwards, Pep Guardiola had one final twist of the knife to administer. 'I want to congratulate Madrid,' he said, 'for being so daring, playing face to face.' *¿Por qué?*, Real Madrid's fans were left to ponder, had their team not played with such ambition in the first leg?

There had been giddy talk on the streets in Barcelona that Mourinho might get six months from UEFA for his press conference rant. He got a five-match ban, with the last two suspended. Shortly afterwards, he also picked up a two-match ban in the *Supercopa de España*, the pre-season tournament between league and cup champions. In August 2011, there was an ugly postscript to the four-match series. Barcelona led Real Madrid 3–2 in the second leg of the playoff. The teams had drawn 2–2 in the first leg. Both games were thrillers. In the third minute of stoppage time, Real Madrid's Marcelo hacked down Cesc Fàbregas, who was making his debut for Barcelona, on the touchline by the two dugouts. The ref immediately drew a red card. Monkey chants echoed around the Camp Nou. A mêlée followed Marcelo's ugly tackle. Both benches leapt at each other. Mourinho rambled into the middle of the fray and gouged Tito Vilanova, Barcelona's assistant manager, in the eye. Vilanova responded by giving Mourinho a shove in the back. Mourinho turned around and smirked. When asked about it by the press, Mourinho said he didn't know who 'Pito' Vilanova was. *Pito* in Spanish is slang for penis.

Barcelona's fans are obsessed with Mourinho. Ramón Besa says they fear him more than Real Madrid itself; that he evokes Chelsea or Inter more than Real Madrid. He is undoubtedly a formidable political operator. As Barça marched towards their domestic league title in May 2011, Jorge Valdano crossed Mourinho, saying he should 'lower the decibels' in his war of words with Barcelona. It was the last kick of a dying horse. Three days before the Champions League final at Wembley, Real Madrid announced that Valdano was sacked, drawing to an end an association with the club that went back to 1984. 'Florentino has clearly decided the winner of the fight,' he acknowledged wearily, as Pérez explained his plans to align the club's organisational structure with an 'English model'. It would be one voice from now on.

In London, on the day of the Champions League final, it was impossible to escape Mourinho's presence. At midday, during a lull in a Barça singsong at Trafalgar Square, a lone Manchester United fan clambered on top of one of the lions at the foot of Nelson's Column and started chanting, 'José Mour-INHO, José Mour-INHO, Jooooosé Mourinho'. In the underground on their way to the stadium, disorientated Barça fans sang, 'Mourinho, where is Wembley?' *¿Por Qué?* got a regular airing from the hymn sheet of *antimadridista* songs sung during the match.

There was a prominent 'God supports United' banner draped along one of the railings in the stadium. There must be no god. Manchester

United, champions of England, looked ordinary on the same field as Barcelona, who swept to a 3–1 victory. The English side were bamboozled. They were left cockeyed from 90 minutes spinning around on Barcelona's carousel, to borrow Alex Ferguson's phrase for Barça's mesmerising passing game. Given the stage, it was one of Barcelona's greatest symphonies, and a reprisal at the home of football of its first European Cup win in 1992. With two minutes to go, their fans launched into a medley of an old terrace favourite: 'Madrid, bastards, salute the champions!'

EPILOGUE

Sergio Busquets played in the 2011 Champions League final. UEFA held an investigation into his alleged racist taunting of Marcelo, but declared 12 days before the final that the evidence to convict him was inconclusive. Pep Guardiola, who was obviously nervous about losing him for the match, fudged in his defence of Busquets before the verdict was announced. He said he had spoken to Busquets. He suggested that his player had made a 'mistake' and that it was up to UEFA to decide. What is in the past is in the past, he said: 'It won't happen again.'

'Perhaps Guardiola didn't denounce racism in favour of the club,' concedes Ramón Besa. 'It's possible, but Barça also has videos about similar things that Real Madrid have done in the past but it hasn't reported them to UEFA. There is a "law" in Spanish football – not in the English game – that says that what happens on the pitch stays on the pitch. According to this code, the Busquets affair shouldn't have been reported by Real Madrid. Spanish culture thinks that rivalry justifies doing certain things, even above respect for human beings.'

Besa cites a couple of other racist incidents. In 2004, the Spanish football coach Luis Aragonés was caught referring to Thierry Henry in training as a 'black shit'. A global media storm ensued. 'Spanish newspapers said there was no need to make such a fuss,' says Besa. In 2008, the Formula One driver Fernando Alonso fell out with his former teammate Lewis Hamilton. The pair did some pre-season testing at the Circuit de Catalunya. A group of spectators, kitted out in wigs, dark make-up and

T-shirts bearing the words, 'Hamilton's Family', turned up to racially abuse the English driver.

'They did that,' says Besa, 'not out of racism, but just to unsettle Hamilton. It's a problem of Spanish culture, of the brain, of lack of education. Yes, perhaps people like Guardiola must say, "¡*Ojo!* Hey, watch out! This can't ever happen again." But I think he didn't do it because Real Madrid would have used it in its favour, because Madrid doesn't do it with its players. All this rivalry means we haven't faced up to problems like racism.

'Mourinho started this because he's very *puñetero*, bloody-minded. He says that Barça plays theatre and is racist. Barça isn't racist, but some of its supporters use racist signs [and make monkey noises] to fuck with the opposition, but they are not racist or so they think. They don't insult Arabic people, for instance, only black people. In the Camp Nou, for example, the first Real Madrid player who was acclaimed was Laurie Cunningham in 1980. He played an extraordinary match and was applauded by the people in the Camp Nou, and he was from Real Madrid, and he was black.'

That *El Clásico* has provided a playground for racists is appalling, and particularly ironic in Barcelona's case given its vaunted affiliation with UNICEF. After three years immersed in the rivalry, it's one of the most jarring things I've noticed; that and the partisan media industry it sustains, which busies itself daily in manufacturing suspicion and enmity. There are other, odd things, like the fact the matches – which are often the highlight of the football calendar – only tempt a couple of hundred away fans. It boggles the mind.

To the clubs' credit, their supporters, though easily riled, rarely get violent, unlike bloodier football rivalries elsewhere on the globe. During the volatile spring 2011 series, things never got completely out of hand. With the exception of the odd punch thrown, both sets of fans largely kept the peace. They didn't throw lumps of human excrement at each other, as happened at Anfield during an FA Cup tie between Liverpool and Manchester United in 2006; nor were they prompted to riot amidst all the heckling over the four games. Tanks didn't roll, as they did during the Soccer War along the El Salvador-Honduras border in 1969. It was a very bourgeoisie dispute. There was lots of cattiness. Two huge institutions came crashing into each other. The bickering was bitchy and calculated. Their fallout had a similar temper to the hubbub between Republicans and Democrats that followed George W. Bush's dubious presidential election win in 2000. For arbitration, the clubs ran along to UEFA's headquarters in a small town in Switzerland called Nyon.

Mourinho left Real Madrid in June 2013. To use his own parlance, he added pepper to the fun. He will forever be remembered in the annals of *El Clásico* as one of the saga's great hate figures. That he has been an agent provocateur isn't surprising, but the response to his antics is illuminating. For taking the fight to Barcelona, he became a poster boy for Spain's political right; serenaded by the *Ultras Sur*, even in defeat, and applauded by some of the country's figureheads. It is not uncommon for footballers to get lassoed into the political bullring, willingly or otherwise. Real Madrid's majestic team of the 1950s is the obvious case in point. Sometimes, as in the Maradonian Church, they can even spawn mock religions. Mourinho is noteworthy because he's not an athlete. He was adored – and was egged on by his president, Florentino Pérez – because of his polemics.

The Portuguese despised the holier-than-thou attitude of Guardiola and the Barça project, a collection he refers to as 'the beautiful children of football'. The insinuations in his press exchanges about Guardiola, implying that he's deceitful, continued into the 2011–2012 season. 'The interesting thing,' he bemoaned in a press conference in March 2012, 'is that there are people much smarter than me that sell an image and get to have a completely different picture than mine.' All the while, he remained oblivious, of course, to the ridiculous contortions required to transform Real Madrid, the ultimate team of the establishment, into some kind of victim at the mercy of a bizarre cabal, incorporating bent refs, the media and UEFA.

Mourinho's last year at Real Madrid was a soap opera of infighting with his players, most notably a spat with Iker Casillas, and nasty quarreling with the Spanish press. When it comes to a reckoning, his adventure in Madrid was a failure. He departed with a paltry haul for three seasons, the highlights a league title in 2012 and a *Copy del Rey* in 2011, a cup that has little value at the club. He failed to deliver *la décima*, the club's great obsession, its tenth European Cup. Ironically, he did, however, finally get a number on Barça, beating them three times in his final season in charge.

Guardiola left Barcelona a year earlier than Mourinho's exit from Madrid. The Catalan cited exhaustion as the reason for his departure. It seemed extraordinary that he would walk away from the finest collection of players he is ever likely to manage, with the best days yet to come for many of them, but the stresses at FC Barcelona are not normal. Only two men served longer management terms at the club since the Second World War. Both of them were broken by the experience. Johan Cruyff, Guardiola's mentor, suffered a heart attack during his reign and never managed a football team again after being sacked. Frank Rijkaard, Guardiola's predecessor, became so unhinged at one stage during his last, rudderless season that he moved out of his family home and into a hotel near the Camp Nou. His nerves, by his own admission, were shot.

Guardiola, who was reduced to taking sleeping pills, had reached his threshold. 'I don't have good memories of the Madrid–Barça games – neither the victories nor the defeats. There were always other things that took away from the football,' he said before his final *clásico* match as coach, a 2–1 loss at the Camp Nou in April 2012. He spoke with a dejected air. The rope-a-dope tactics favoured by him in the press room had taken their toll. 'Many things have been hidden by our silence,' he said as his time drew to a close. In Mourinho he encountered a foe whose modus operandi – like Alex Ferguson's – is one of siege mentality. In Spain, Mourinho had found the most fertile ground yet for instilling an Us v. Them mindset in his charges.

The effect of the Spanish Civil War still lingers. It is impossible to escape the politics of that conflict when sizing up today's Madrid–Barça rivalry. The Spanish and Catalan flags that billow in their stands during games testify to this. It was notable that the most high-profile incidence of sledging between the players during the historic 2011 four-game series was politically tinged. After the 1–1 draw in the league, Gerard Piqué had a cut at some Real Madrid players in the tunnel, allegedly calling them *'españolitos'*, cocky little Spaniards. He denies he made the taunt, but Iker Casillas, Real Madrid's captain, disputed his denial, saying: 'Piqué knows what he said.' So long as Barça promotes itself as a vessel for *Catalanismo*, so long as Catalonia dissents and its separatist parties continue to push for greater freedom – *la gota malaya*, the Malaysian water drop, as *madrileños* call it – the rivalry will continue to crackle with political tension. Touchiness will go on pervading their relations.

There is a paradox, however, to this political hostility. How many *españolitos* actually play for Real Madrid? Three Spaniards started in that 1–1 league game, one of whom, Xabi Alonso, is Basque. His dad played for Barcelona. Their squad is populated with Argentinians, Brazilians, Germans and Portuguese. Barça, too, has its share of international, jobbing pros. Modern footballers, in the main, are mercenaries, not fans. Barcelona and Real Madrid employ the game's most expensive ones.

There are hallmarks to the great, visceral rivalries. Individuals have perennial traits, like Ali and Frazier in boxing or Borg and McEnroe in tennis. Teams of individuals from a particular place, like the All Blacks and the Springboks in rugby union, draw from a store of shared folk memory, which has a resonance for each of their players when they pull on a jersey before their battles.

This disappears, somewhat, in the mercenary nature of club football and, in particular, with Madrid–Barça encounters. There is a gulf separating the two 'traditions', between the political and cultural drivers that animate their fans watching on from the sidelines, and the reality of the sporting action on the field. This was evident when Barça's players lined up to hug Luís Figo after his torrid first night back at the Camp Nou in 2000 as a Real Madrid player. Perhaps something is being lost here. Some day the distance between the *clásico* teams' aficionados and players will undermine – or certainly alter – the nature of their emotional attachments, a situation that is exacerbated by the increasingly global composition of their fanbase.

The aggrandisement of major club football has also changed their rivalry over the last decade. It is a trend that looks as if it will accelerate. It is sickening the way they gobble up the largesse from La Liga's TV rights, a greed that is crippling the Spanish league as a competition. They are formidable financial enterprises. It is remarkable how they both prosper in perilous financial times. Deloitte, who love to tot up the monies of football clubs ever year, 'expect a battle between Spain's two superclubs for top spot in the Money League for the next few years at least'.

They've got the marketing chops. There is a lustre to their brands which is the envy of peers. They are objects of desire. When Edward Freedman took over the newly minted role of head of merchandising at Manchester United two decades ago, he was struck by an interesting realisation. Sportswear companies scrapped with each other to sponsor his club's kit. Yet these were giant corporations with brand recognition of their own. Nike's revenue, for instance, is 40 times that of Barça's, one of the football teams it sponsors, and it's a company, in the author of *No Logo* Naomi Klein's words, 'that swallows cultural space in giant gulps'. Why don't football teams, like Barça or Brazil, pay to have their logo on Nike gear instead of the other way around? Freedman reckoned it must be because their brands, those intangible entities, are more potent.

Barça and Real Madrid have the most powerful brands of all in football at the moment. It underpins their corporate might, the sharp edge of which, we, as punters, get to see realised in the incredible skill and goalscoring feats of their stars, Lionel Messi and Cristiano Ronaldo, the two giants of contemporary football. It makes for titanic struggles between the two clubs, full of energy and *élan*. They drive each other on. Each summer they replenish their squads with football's most coveted players. Whenever the two sides meet again, it may well be the match of the century. Until the next one comes.

APPENDIX: HEAD-TO-HEAD STATISTICS

BARCELONA
Founded: 1899
Number of members: approx. 173,000
Stadium: Camp Nou (opened 1957; capacity: 99,354)

Spanish League (22): 1929, 1945, 1948, 1949, 1952, 1953, 1959, 1960, 1974, 1985, 1991, 1992, 1993, 1994, 1998, 1999, 2005, 2006, 2009, 2010, 2011, 2013
*Copa del Rey** (26): 1910, 1912, 1913, 1920, 1922, 1925, 1926, 1928, 1942, 1951, 1952, 1953, 1957, 1959, 1963, 1968, 1971, 1978, 1981, 1983, 1988, 1990, 1997, 1998, 2009, 2012
Spanish League Cup (2): 1983, 1986
Spanish Super Cup (10): 1983, 1991, 1992, 1994, 1996, 2005, 2006, 2009, 2010, 2011
Champions League (European Cup) (4): 1992, 2006, 2009, 2011
European Cup-Winners' Cup (4): 1979, 1982, 1989, 1997
Fairs Cup** (3): 1958, 1960, 1966
European Super Cup (4): 1992, 1997, 2009, 2011

FIFA Club World Cup (2): 2009, 2011

*The *Copa del Rey*, or King's Cup, has had different names since its inauguration in 1902, including a spell during General Franco's regime when it was called *Copa de su Excelencia El Generalísimo.*

**Precursor to UEFA Cup.

REAL MADRID
Founded: 1902
Number of members: approx. 95,000
Stadium: Santiago Bernabéu (opened 1947; capacity: 85,454)
Spanish League (32): 1932, 1933, 1954, 1955, 1957, 1958, 1961, 1962, 1963, 1964, 1965, 1967, 1968, 1969, 1972, 1975, 1976, 1978, 1979, 1980, 1986, 1987, 1988, 1989, 1990, 1995, 1997, 2001, 2003, 2007, 2008, 2012

Copa del Rey (18): 1905, 1906, 1907, 1908, 1917, 1934, 1936, 1946, 1947, 1962,
    1970, 1974, 1975, 1980, 1982, 1989, 1993, 2011
Spanish League Cup (1): 1985
Spanish Super Cup (9): 1988, 1989, 1990, 1993, 1997, 2001, 2003, 2008, 2012
Champions League (European Cup) (9): 1956, 1957, 1958, 1959, 1960, 1966,
    1998, 2000, 2002
UEFA Cup (2): 1985, 1986
European Super Cup (1): 2002
Intercontinental Cup* (3): 1960, 1998, 2002

* Precursor to FIFA Club World Cup.

LIST OF MANAGERS – BARCELONA

Name	Nationality	Tenure	Honours
John Barrow*	English	1917	None
Jack Greenwell	English	1917–24	King's Cup (2)
Jesza Poszony	Hungarian	1924–25	King's Cup (1)
Ralph Kirby	English	1925–26	King's Cup (1)
Richard Kohn	Austrian	1926–27	None
Romá Forns	Spanish	1927–29	League (1), King's Cup (1)
Jim Bellamy	English	1929–31	None
Jack Greenwell	English	1931–33	None
Richard Kohn	Austrian	1933–34	None
Franz Platko	Hungarian	1934–35	None
Patrick O'Connell	Irish	1935–37	None
Josep Planas	Spanish	1939–41	None
Ramón Guzmán	Spanish	1941–42	None
Joan Josep Nogués	Spanish	1942–44	King's Cup (1)
Josep Samitier	Spanish	1944–47	League (1)
Enrique Fernández**	Uruguayan	1947–50	League (2)
Ramón Llorens	Spanish	1950	None
Ferdinand Daučík	Czechoslovakian	1950–54	League (2), King's Cup (3)
Sandro Puppo	Italian	1954–55	None
Franz Platko	Hungarian	1955–56	None
Domingo Balmanya	Spainish	1956–58	King's Cup (1), Fairs Cup (1)
Helenio Herrera	French	1958–60	League (2), King's Cup (1), Fairs Cup (1)
Enric Rabassa	Spanish	1960	None
Ljubiša Broćić	Yugoslavian	1960–61	None

Enrique Orizaola	Spanish	1961	None
Lluís Miró	Spanish	1961–62	None
Ladislao Kubala	Hungarian	1962–63	None
Josep Gonzalvo	Spanish	1963	King's Cup (1)
César Rodríguez	Spanish	1963–64	None
Vicenç Sasot	Spanish	1964–65	None
Roque Olsen	Argentinian	1965–67	Fairs Cup (1)
Salvador Artigas	Spanish	1967–69	King's Cup (1)
Josep Seguer	Spanish	1969	None
Vic Buckingham	English	1969–71	King's Cup (1)
Rinus Michels	Dutch	1971–75	League (1)
Hennes Weisweiler	German	1975–76	None
Laureano Ruiz	Spanish	1976	None
Rinus Michels	Dutch	1976–78	King's Cup (1)
Lucien Muller	French	1978–79	None
Joaquim Rifé	Spanish	1979–80	Cup-Winners' Cup (1)
Helenio Herrera	French	1980	None
Ladislao Kubala	Hungarian	1980	None
Helenio Herrera	French	1980–81	King's Cup (1)
Udo Lattek	German	1981–83	King's Cup (1), League Cup (1), Cup-Winners' Cup (1)
José Luis Romero	Spanish	1983	None
César Luis Menotti	Argentinian	1983–84	King's Cup (1), Spanish Super Cup (1)
Terry Venables	English	1984–87	League (1), League Cup (1)
Luis Aragonés	Spanish	1987–88	King's Cup (1)
Johan Cruyff	Dutch	1988–96	League (4), Spanish Super Cup (3), European Cup (1), European Super Cup (1), King's Cup (1), Cup-Winners' Cup (1)
Bobby Robson	English	1996–97	King's Cup (1), Spanish Super Cup (1), Cup-Winners' Cup (1)
Louis van Gaal	Dutch	1997–2000	League (2), King's Cup (1), European Super Cup (1)
Llorenç Serra Ferrer	Spanish	2000–01	None
Charly Rexach***	Spanish	2001–02	None
Louis van Gaal	Dutch	2002–03	None

Antonio de la Cruz	Spanish	2003	None
Radomir Antić	Serbian	2003	None
Frank Rijkaard	Dutch	2003–08	League (2), Spanish Super Cups (2), Champions League (1)
Pep Guardiola	Spanish	2008–2012	League (3), King's Cup (2), Spanish Super Cup (3), Champions League (2), European Super Cup (2), FIFA World Club Cup (2)
Tito Vilanova	Spanish	2012–present	League (1)

*Barrow is officially recognised by Barcelona as the club's first coach. He was sacked after four months in the job.

**Fernández is one of two men to have managed both Barcelona and Real Madrid, having delivered league titles for both *clásico* rivals. The other is Radomir Antić.

***Rexach served as caretaker manager on three occasions – 1988, 1991 (deputising for Johan Cruyff while he underwent heart surgery) and 1996.

LIST OF MANAGERS – REAL MADRID

Name	Nationality	Tenure	Honours
Arthur Johnson	English	1910–20	King's Cup (5)
Jua de Cárcer	Spanish	1920–26	None
Pedro Llorente	Spanish	1926	None
Santiago Bernabéu	Spanish	1926–27	None
José Berraondo	Spanish	1927–29	None
José Quirante	Spanish	1929–30	None
Lippo Hertzka	Hungarian	1030–32	League (1)
Robert Firth	English	1932–34	League (1)
Francisco Bru*	Spanish	1934–41	King's Cup (2)
Juan Armet	Spanish	1941–43	None
Ramón Encinas	Spanish	1943–45	None
Jacinto Quincoces	Spanish	1945–46	King's Cup (1)
Baltasar Albéniz	Spanish	1946–47	None
Jacinto Quincoses	Spanish	1947–48	None
Michael Keeping	English	1948–50	None
Baltasar Albéniz	Spanish	1950–51	King's Cup (1)
Héctor Scarone	Uruguayan	1951–52	None
Juan Antonio Ipiña	Spanish	1952–53	None
Enrique Fernández	Uruguayan	1953–54	League (1)
José Villalonga	Spanish	1954–57	League (2), European Cup (2)

Luis Carniglia	Argentinian	1957–59	League (1), European Cup (1)
Miguel Muñoz	Spanish	1959	None
Luis Carniglia	Argentinian	1959	European Cup (1)
Manuel Fleitas	Paraguayan	1959–60	None
Miguel Muñoz	Spanish	1960–74	League (9), King's Cup (2), European Cup (2), Intercontinental Cup (1)
Luis Molowny	Spanish	1974	King's Cup (1)
Miljan Miljanić	Yugoslavian	1974–77	League (2), King's Cup (1)
Luis Molowny	Spanish	1977–79	League (2)
Vujadin Boškov	Yugoslavian	1979–82	League (1), King's Cup (1)
Luis Molowny	Spanish	1982	King's Cup (1)
Alfredo di Stéfano	Argentinian	1982–84	None
Amancio Amaro	Spanish	1984–85	None
Luis Molowny	Spanish	1985–86	League (1), UEFA Cup (2), League Cup (1)
Leo Beenhakker	Dutch	1986–89	League (3), King's Cup (1), Spanish Super Cup (1)
John Toshack	Welsh	1989–90	League (1), Spanish Super Cup (1)
Alfredo di Stéfano	Argentinian	1990–91	Spanish Super Cup (1)
Radomir Antić	Yugoslavian	1991–92	None
Leo Beenhakker	Dutch	1992	None
Benito Floro	Spanish	1992–94	King's Cup (1), Spanish Super Cup (1)
Vicente del Bosque	Spanish	1994	Spanish Super Cup (1)
Jorge Valdano	Argentinian	1994–96	League (1)
Vicente del Bosque	Spanish	1996	None
Arsenio Iglesias	Spanish	1996	None
Fabio Capello	Italian	1996–97	League (1)
Jupp Heynckes	German	1997–98	Spanish Super Cup (1), Champions League (1)
Guus Hiddink	Dutch	1998–99	Intercontinental Cup (1)
John Toshack	Welsh	1999	None
Vicente del Bosque	Spanish	1999–2003	League (2), Champions League (2), Spanish Super Cup (2), European Super Cup (1), Intercontintal Cup (1)

Carlos Queiroz	Portuguese	2003–04	Spanish Super Cup (1)
José Antonio Camacho	Spanish	2004	None
Mariano García Remón	Spanish	2004	None
Venderlei Luxemburgo	Brazilian	2004–05	None
Juan Ramón López Caro	Spanish	2005–06	None
Fabio Capello	Italian	2006–07	League (1)
Bernd Schuster	German	2007–08	League (1), Spanish Super Cup (1)
Juande Ramos	Spanish	2008–09	None
Manuel Pellegrini	Chilean	2009–10	None
José Mourinho	Portuguese	2010–13	King's Cup (1), League (1), Spanish Super Cup (1)

* Bru left Real Madrid once the Spanish Civil War took hold of the country, returning to manage the club after the conflict ended.

HEAD-TO-HEAD RESULTS

Total matches: 224
Real Madrid wins: 90
Barcelona wins: 86
Draws: 48
Real Madrid goals: 378
Barcelona goals: 361

TOP 10 HIGHEST-SCORING LEAGUE MATCH VICTORIES

Date	Home	Away	Score	Goals (home)	Goals (away)
3 Feb 1935	Real Madrid	Barcelona	8–2	Lazcano (15, 42, 73), Sañudo (21, 35, 47, 81), Regueiro (29)	Escolà (17), Guzmán (68)
24 Sept 1950	Barcelona	Real Madrid	7–2	Nicolau (9, 56), César (14), Marcos Aurelio (39, 88), Marià Gonzalvo III (62), Basora (82)	Molowny (15), García González (66)

18 Sept 1949	Real Madrid	Barcelona	6–1	Olmedo (2), Gonzalvo II (85) Cabrera (4), Pahiño (40, 68), Macala (62, 69)
21 Apr 1935	Barcelona	Real Madrid	5–0	Ventolrà (43, 62, 68, 82), Escolà (48)
25 Mar 1945	Barcelona	Real Madrid	5–0	César (41, 46), Bravo (52), Escolà (77) Marià Gonzalvo III (86)
25 Oct 1953	Real Madrid	Barcelona	5–0	di Stéfano (10, 85), Roque Olsen (34, 35), Molowny (39)
17 Feb 1974	Real Madrid	Barcelona	0–5	Asensi (30, 54), Cruyff (39), Juan Carlos (65), Sotil (69)
8 Jan 1994	Barcelona	Real Madrid	5–0	Romário (24, 56, 81), Koeman (47), Iván Iglesias (86)
7 Jan 1995	Real Madrid	Barcelona	5–0	Zamorano (5, 21, 39), Luis Enrique (68), Amavisca (70)
29 Nov 2010	Barcelona	Real Madrid	5–0	Xavi (10), Pedro (18), Villa (55, 58), Jeffrén (90)

TOP 10 SCORERS IN CLÁSICO MATCHES

Lionel Messi (Barcelona, 2004–present): 18
Alfredo di Stéfano (Real Madrid, 1953–64*): 18
Raúl (Real Madrid, 1994–2010): 15
César (Barcelona, 1942–55): 14
Francisco Gento (Real Madrid, 1953–71): 14
Ferenc Puskás (Real Madrid, 1958–64): 14
Cristiano Ronaldo (Real Madrid 2009–present): 13
Carlos Santillana (Real Madrid, 1971–88): 12
Hugo Sánchez (Real Madrid, 1985–92): 10
Juanito (Real Madrid, 1977–87): 10

*Years spent at Barcelona or Real Madrid

RECORDS

Most consecutive league match wins: Barcelona, 16 (2010–11)
Longest time undefeated at home: Real Madrid, 8 years, 121 games (1957–65)
Highest league scorer in a season: Lionel Messi, Barcelona, 50 (2011–12)
Most individual Spanish league medals: Francisco Gento, Real Madrid, 12
Most individual European Cup medals: Francisco Gento, Real Madrid, 6
Most league goals in a season: Real Madrid (2011–12), 121
Most individual league appearances for one club: Raúl, Real Madrid, 550
Most league points in a season: Real Madrid (2011–12), Barcelona (2012–13), 100
Only clásico *team to play an entire league season undefeated:* Real Madrid (1931–32)
Most individual goals in a league match: 7, Ladislao Kubala, Barcelona (v. Sporting de
  Gijon, 10 February 1952)

BALLON D'OR*

1957: Alfredo di Stéfano (Real Madrid)
1958: Raymond Kopa (Real Madrid)
1959: Alfredo di Stéfano (Real Madrid)
1960: Luis Suárez (Barcelona)
1973: Johan Cruyff (Barcelona)
1974: Johan Cruyff (Barcelona)
1994: Hristo Stoichkov (Barcelona)
1999: Rivaldo (Barcelona)
2000: Luís Figo (Barcelona/Real Madrid)
2002: Ronaldo (Real Madrid)
2005: Ronaldinho (Barcelona)
2009: Lionel Messi (Barcelona)
2010**: Lionel Messi (Barcelona)
2011: Lionel Messi (Barcelona)
2012: Lionel Messi (Barcelona)

* won while playing with either Barcelona or Real Madrid

** merged in 2010 with FIFA World Player of the Year award to become FIFA *Ballon d'Or*

FIFA WORLD PLAYER OF THE YEAR*

1994 Romário (Barcelona)
1996 Ronaldo (Barcelona)
1997 Ronaldo (Barcelona)
1999 Rivaldo (Barcelona)
2001 Luís Figo (Real Madrid)
2002 Ronaldo (Real Madrid)
2003 Zinedine Zidane (Real Madrid)

2004 Ronaldinho (Barcelona)
2005 Ronaldinho (Barcelona)
2009 Lionel Messi (Barcelona)

* won while playing with either Barcelona or Real Madrid

PLAYERS WHO PLAYED FOR BOTH CLUBS

1905*: Luciano Lizarraga (Real Madrid to Barcelona)
1906: Charles Wallace (Barcelona to Real Madrid)
1906: José Quirante (Barcelona to Real Madrid)
1911: Alfonso Albéniz (Barcelona to Real Madrid)
1911: Arsenio Comamala (Barcelona to Real Madrid)
1913: Walter Rozitsky (Barcelona to Real Madrid)
1930: Ricardo Zamora (Barcelona via Espanyol to Real Madrid)
1932: Josep Samitier (Barcelona to Real Madrid)
1939: Hilario Juan Marrero Pérez (Real Madrid via Valencia to Barcelona)
1950: Alfonso Navarro (Barcelona to Real Madrid)
1961: Justo Tejada (Barcelona to Real Madrid)
1961: Jesús María Pereda (Real Madrid via Real Valladolid and Sevilla to Barcelona)
1962: Evaristo Macedo Filho (Barcelona to Real Madrid)
1965: Fernand Goyvaerts Deyrdey (Barcelona to Real Madrid)
1965: Lucien Muller (Real Madrid to Barcelona)
1980: Lorenzo Amador (Real Madrid via Hércules to Barcelona)
1988: Bernd Schuster (Barcelona to Real Madrid)
1990: Luis Milla (Barcelona to Real Madrid)
1992: Fernando Muñoz García (Barcelona to Real Madrid)
1994: Gheorghe Hagi (Real Madrid via Brescia to Barcelona)
1994: Julen Lopetegui (Real Madrid via CD Logroñés to Barcelona)
1994: Michael Laudrup (Barcelona to Real Madrid)
1995: Robert Prosinečki (Real Madrid via Real Oviedo to Barcelona)
1995: Miquel Soler (Barcelona via Atlético de Madrid and Sevilla to Real Madrid)
1996: Luis Enrique (Real Madrid to Barcelona)
1999: Daniel García Lara (Real Madrid via Real Mallorca to Barcelona)
2000: Luís Figo (Barcelona to Real Madrid)
2000: Albert Celades (Barcelona via Celta Vigo to Real Madrid)
2000: Alfonso Pérez (Real Madrid vía Real Betis to Barcelona)
2002: Ronaldo (Barcelona via Inter to Real Madrid)
2004: Samuel Eto'o (Real Madrid via Real Mallorca to Barcelona)
2007: Javier Saviola (Barcelona to Real Madrid)

* Year player joined *clásico* rival.

ACKNOWLEDGEMENTS

The most fortunate thing to happen me in writing this book was to hook up with Charlie Brotherstone, my agent at A. M. Heath. We were on the same wavelength from the kick-off. He's got a cool head. He gave me the confidence to take the book in particular directions, and as well as giving me invaluable tips he was the perfect sounding board for ideas. *¡Gracias señor!* A shout-out, too, to Charlie's colleagues at A. M. Heath – Vickie Dillon and Hélène Ferey, and to Kate Rizzo Munson, who has since moved on.

It was a joy to work with the folk at Bloomsbury. I hope the finished product does their professionalism justice, especially Emily Sweet and Nick Humphrey, who saw the project through so smoothly. Charlotte Atyeo was my chief. I found her enthusiasm for the project inspiring, and her dry sense of humour made working with her a breeze.

Lee Greenberg, an authority on every sport from hockey to hurling, and Eoin Kirwan (not widely known as an *aficionado* of Association Football) helped knock my early jottings into presentable shape, which must have been the worst of all jobs. Matthias Krug selflessly took a break from writing his hilarious novel *Selfishness* to proofread the manuscript for errors. I was lucky to have someone of the calibre of Julian Flanders to edit the manuscript. He brought a keen football brain and literary nous to the table. Any remaining mistakes in the text rest with the author.

Nobody helped me more with this book than María José Martin Iranzo. She proofread the manuscript, helped with translation work and as an interpreter, but most importantly her tutorials on Spanish culture and Catalan politics were invaluable. We've had endless interesting conversations. I can't thank her enough.

Jordi Donadeu was my first and best tutor on Spanish football. He's a *culé*. Once you get past his hopelessly biased perspective, he has interesting things to say about the game. I'm indebted to him also for help with sourcing tickets and for translation and interpreting work. He and Claudette, his wife – who also helped in arranging an interview with Periko – are about to have a boy. I look forward to seeing him kick a ball at La Masia one day.

There are dozens of people who helped me along the way. They include Colm Tóibín, Cliona Lewis, Michael McLoughlin, Declan Heeney and Margaret Daly for counsel in the early days; Cormac Kinsella and Ellen Williams for their marketing and PR cunning; Colm O'Connor and Carol Kirwan for help in getting match accreditations; the ever cheerful Xavier Guarte Serrano and Francesc Orenes at FC Barcelona's press office and their counterparts at Real Madrid, in particular Marta Santisteban López and Raquel Baena Pulido; and all of my editors. I owe a special debt of gratitude to Siobhan Cronin and Marc O'Sullivan for putting regular bread on the table.

Of the books and newspaper articles I pored over during the last two years, I have to single out those of the *Guardian*'s Sid Lowe, who also kindly agreed to be interviewed for this book, and Diego Torres of *El País*, for their insight into the day-to-day machinations of Spanish football. Others who helped on the research trail include Rafa Arias; Don Fergal Kenny, who laid the groundwork for an abortive field trip to the Basque Country; Derry Nalty, with reminiscences about her days working as an *au pair* for Alfredo di Stéfano; Rafael (if you ever need to root out someone on a witness protection programme) Logedo; and Carles Viñas, master chronicler of the world of *ultras*.

Word up to Tommy Flynn and Nikki for putting me up in their caddyshack for four memorable days in London; to Neil Coffey for marshalling a crack French translation team; to José, Antonio, Pedro and all the lads at Juanito; to Donal Whelan for more biased *culé* commentary but useful research and marketing advice; to the mighty Barry Molony for looking after business while I drafted the manuscript; to Brian Connellan for help sourcing a *clásico* ticket (from Dublin!); to Brendan Ginnelly for taking a break from drinking absinthe in Barcelona one weekend to proofread the index; to Nobby and the Buzzmen for lessons in life (Gaffer, when stood beside José Mourinho, the Portu-geezer is only a little man); and to John O'Malley, Jimo, Mannix, Martin Nugent, Fonzo and Avenue United: what can I say? Thanks for twenty years of kicks.

I want to thank my mom, who is the great athlete in our family, for the love and support she gives me, and my dad, who probably believes that Raich Carter didn't mature as a player until he started playing in the Mardyke with Cork Athletic. Going to Liverpool and Irish soccer matches with him as a soccer-mad kid was heaven on earth. I still get a tingle from thinking about the time we floated into a packed Dalymount Park in 1985 for a match against Italy.

Lastly, thanks to Michelita, my beautiful wife, to whom this book is dedicated, for her help with translation, as an interpreter and for tapping her Venezuelan mafia contacts. They include Daniel Paz, who put me up in his Madrid apartment on too many occasions to count, Ariana Basciani Fernández, Pablo López Hurtado, Javier Torres, Ernesto Lotitto and Sebastian Encina. Michelle made untold sacrifices while I worked. If I wasn't hunched over a book, notes or a laptop, I was jumping on a bus to traipse around Spain and beyond for interviews and matches. I hope I can make it up to her. Until the next one comes.

INDEX